IN THE
BLOODY FOOTSTEPS
OF
GHENGIS KHAN

Books by Jeffrey Tayler

Siberian Dawn

Facing the Congo

Glory in a Camel's Eye

Angry Wind

River of No Reprieve

IN THE
BLOODY FOOTSTEPS

 OF

GHENGIS KHAN

AN EPIC JOURNEY ACROSS THE STEPPES,
MOUNTAINS AND DESERTS
FROM RED SQUARE
TO TIANANMEN SQUARE

Jeffrey Tayler

BOOKS

First published in Great Britain in 2009 by
JR Books, 10 Greenland Street, London NW1 0ND
www.jrbooks.com

ISBN 978-1-906779-00-9

1 3 5 7 9 10 8 6 4 2

Printed by MPG Books, Bodmin, Cornwall

NOTE Certain names and minor identifying characteristics have been changed to protect the privacy of people described in this book. Specifically, the following names are pseudonyms: Ahmad in chapter 4; Nadia in chapter 8; Victor in chapter 16; and Güzel in chapter 20.

In Memory of My Mother

A Note on Transliteration

When transliterating Russian place names and nouns without accepted English spellings, I have used an apostrophe to indicate the Russian letter *myagkiy znak* (soft sign), which palatizes the preceding consonant and for which there is no English equivalent.

Most famous Russian historical personae have established anglicized names, and I have preferred these to the Russian. Hence, when referring to tsars, I write Basil III for Vasily III and Michael for Mikhail. However, for lesser-known or more contemporary Russian figures, I have retained the Russian, as is now customary in the press. By this convention, the first name of former president Gorbachev is Mikhail, not Michael.

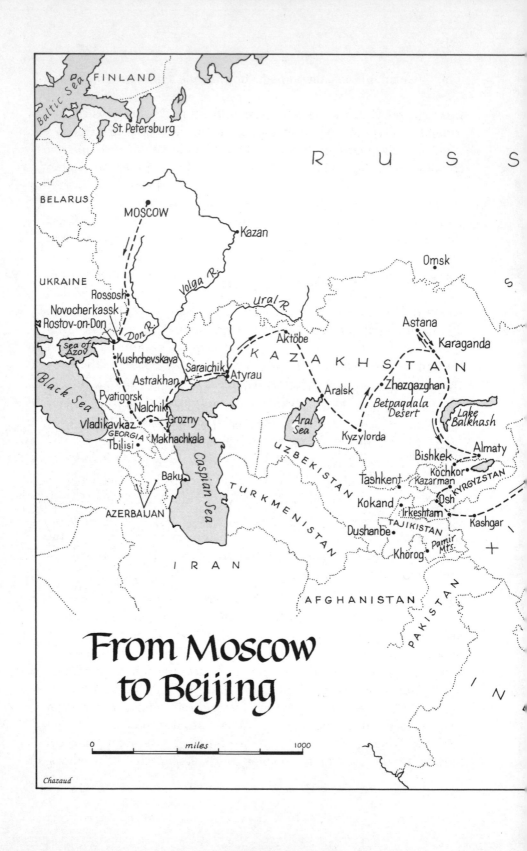

From Moscow to Beijing

0   *miles*   1000

Chazaud

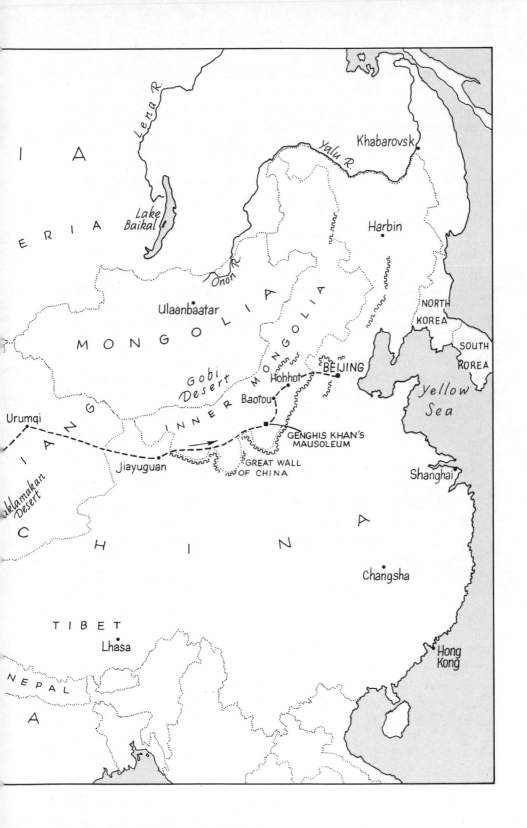

IN THE
BLOODY FOOTSTEPS
OF
GHENGIS KHAN

Prologue: *The Scourge from Hell,*
the Retreat of the West, Great Games
Past and Present

BORN INTO THE ROYAL Borjigin family in 1162, Temüjin, heir apparent to the Mongol clan's chieftaincy, found himself, at age nine, scorned by his people, cast out of the communal fold, and reduced to hunting for rodents and roots to survive. A tribe of Tatars had poisoned his father, erstwhile ruler of the Borjigin, and his subjects, refusing to invest a scion so young, usurped power and consigned Temüjin to debasing destitution. The usurpers would have done well to note one circumstance, whether as augury or omen: Temüjin was born clutching a clot of blood.

Seven years later the Merkit, a rival Mongol tribe, kidnapped Temüjin's wife and triggered a series of apparently local events that would result in the downcast youth's ascension to power not only over all the Mongols but, eventually, over half the known world. Supported by the leader of the allied Kereit tribe, Temüjin, who by then had matured into a giant more than six feet tall, endowed with charisma, cunning, and formidable intelligence, raised an army of twenty thousand mounted archers, with whom he routed the Merkit and recovered his wife. Astonishingly, he then turned on and trounced his benefactors, the Kereit nobility. Impressing commoner Kereit into his cavalry, he proceeded to decimate the Tatars, imposing vassalage on those he spared; after this, the Tatars would fight alongside Temüjin's troops. In 1206, on the wind-swept grasslands by the river Onon, Temüjin's moment of triumph had arrived: the twenty-seven Mongol tribes, whose elites he had either slaughtered or subjugated, invested him with the title of Supreme Ruler—or, in Mongolian, Genghis Khan.

Genghis Khan was a complex figure, at once paranoiac, fearless in combat yet afraid of dogs, and fascinated by sorcery and shamanism. Believing himself divinely charged with establishing justice on earth, he set about his mission. The Mongols' martial prowess, discipline, and military tactics were unmatched, even before he came to power, and constituted his most fateful asset.

Trained in archery as tots and reared as equestrian warriors, Mongol males amassed battle experience early on by raiding neighboring peoples for cattle, women, and livestock. Ever flexible in war, they advanced as they could and retreated when necessary. Their horses were small, hardy, and agile, capable of covering immense distances with lightning speed. Each Mongol warrior campaigned with four spares, which allowed fresh mounts as needed and dawn-to-dusk travel. Living off their livestock, hunting, or the food stocks of the people they plundered, the Mongols campaigned without provisions. They fed on the run, drinking their mares' milk or piercing their mares' jugulars with sharpened straws to sip their blood, or sustaining themselves with dried meat heated under their saddles. They wielded bows fashioned from bone, wood, and gut that fired bone-tipped arrows with a range of eight hundred feet (twice that of European bows) that could pierce armor. In their innovative siege techniques they employed powerful catapults called mangonels to reduce immured cities.

The Mongols lived only to fight. A Chinese chronicler of the time wrote, "They possess neither towns, nor walls, neither writing, nor books . . . legal institutions they know not. . . . They all feed on the meat of the animals which they kill . . . and they dress in their hides and furs. The strongest among them grab the fattest pieces; the old men, on the other hand, eat and drink what is left. They respect only the bravest; old age and feebleness are held in contempt." However fearsome they were, they were also notoriously fractious. To counter this, Genghis Khan created an elite personal guard unit of 10,000 men and reorganized his 100,000-strong army into divisions of 10,000, incorporating Tatars and mixing clan origins to hinder potential lineage-based conspiracies against him.

Thus arrayed, Genghis Khan and his men were ready to conquer the world. They began with China, to Mongolia's south. They had long coveted China's civilized riches and raided Han farmers in the borderlands. Before invading in 1213, Genghis Khan issued the Chinese an ultimatum he was to repeat across Eurasia: Accept Mongol suzerainty and become allies, or resist and perish. They declined. The Mongols then exploded across the north of the country, razing ninety cities and villages and slaughtering their populations, at times sparing people for use as human shields in the next assault. In two years Genghis Khan's army reached Beijing, which it plundered and set afire, leaving it to burn for a month, and sallied on into Tibet and even Korea (from which, decades later, his descendants would launch an ill-starred invasion of Japan).

Then Genghis Khan turned his eyes west. Within five years he would conquer a hundred million people and ravage Central Asia, including Persia, Armenia, and Georgia. Finally, between his hordes and Europe lay only one state: Russia.

THIRTEENTH-CENTURY RUSSIA little resembled the country we know now. It was, comparatively, of middling size, stretching from Kiev in the south to Novgorod in the north, and was not at all unified; rather, it was a confederation of princedoms known as *Kiyevskaya Rus'* (Kievan Russia). Kievan Russians were mostly peaceable traders and farmers. Though they owned slaves, they practiced an incipient form of democracy, assembling in town councils called *veche* to decide their affairs and, at times, dethrone their princes. In 988 Prince Vladimir of Kiev adopted Christianity from the Byzantine Greeks and made it the state religion — a move that would later impede alliances with the Rome-affiliated Christians of western Europe (whom Russians would disdain as heretics, especially after the Eastern and Western Churches split in 1254) and isolate Russia from the Renaissance, Reformation, and Industrial Revolution, with fatefully damaging consequences for its national development.

Since time immemorial Kievan Russia's southern reaches had endured harrying raids from steppe nomads, which were driving some Russians north into the forest, to then obscure wilderness towns with names like Rostov, Vladimir, and Moscow. But suddenly in 1223, on those steppes, the Russians found themselves facing an unprecedented peril: Genghis Khan and his army, which had just crossed the Caucasus Mountains. The fierce battle that ensued on the river Kalka ended in victory for the Mongols. But the invaders mysteriously turned back and vanished. In 1227 Genghis Khan died of natural causes in Mongolia.

Leadership of the Mongols passed to Genghis Khan's third son, Ögödei, who, a decade later, tasked his nephew, Batu, with a renewed Russian-European campaign. The violence Batu unleashed on the Volga town of Ryazan in 1237 was exemplary, and was repeated across the land. As recorded by Riasanovsky in his seminal *A History of Russia,* a chronicle of the time reads:

> The churches of God they devastated, and in the holy altars they shed much blood. And no one in the town remained alive; all died equally and drank the single cup of death. There was no one to moan, or cry—neither father and mother over children, nor children over father and mother, neither brother over brother, nor relatives over relatives—but all lay together dead. And all this occurred to us for our sins.

The Mongols rampaged on across Russia, exterminating much of its population, leaving town squares stacked with skulls, enslaving those they spared. They then ripped through Hungary, Poland, and Germany, and their advance guard reached the Adriatic. The rampage would have doubtless burned on into western Europe, but in 1241, back in the Mongolian capital of Karakorum, Khan Ögödei succumbed unexpectedly, possibly during an orgy. Batu decided to retreat, and he set up his own capital on the lower Volga. But he had established the maximal bounds of the Mongol Empire, which would eventually fracture into autonomous khanates. The peoples of Europe, ascribing elements of theodicy to the barbarians' invincibility, confounded the name of Genghis Khan's Tatars with *Tartaros,* a Greek word for the underworld (specifically, that part of the underworld in which sinners are punished), and came to call the Mongols the "Scourge from Hell."

Territorially the Mongol Empire was the largest in history, covering between eleven and twelve million square miles and comprising half the known world in the Middle Ages. It united Eurasia, including Russia, China, and the states of Central Asia, for the first and only time under a sort of Pax Mongolica characterized, in part, by religious tolerance and free trade. The Venetian Marco Polo availed himself of this unity and traveled the empire's safe roads to China, where he spent seventeen years as the guest of Kublai Khan (Genghis Khan's grandson and founder of the Yuan dynasty, the one who, Coleridge wrote, "In

Xanadu did . . . A stately pleasure-dome decree"); his memoirs, *The Travels of Marco Polo,* written in 1298, introduced Asia, or an exotic, half-mythologized version of it, to Europe.

Yet this stability hardly compensated for the lasting damage the Mongols inflicted on their victims, even apart from the initial slaughter. The Yuan dynasty unified China, to be sure, but the Mongols taxed the Chinese onerously, expropriated their land, took them as slaves, and favored Tibetans and the Turkic people of the west, the Uygur, over the Han. Authoritarianism, state-sponsored violence, and corruption have, since the Yuan, characterized Chinese governance. In Russia the Tatar-Mongolian yoke (as it would be called) proved even more baleful, locking the Slavs in prison lands with their Mongol masters, who subjected them to rapine, isolation, and terror, and this just as the Renaissance was dawning in Europe, with which they forbade contact. Kievan Russia disappeared from history for two hundred years. The Mongols appointed Russian vassal-princes, who mimicked Mongol despotism, demanded of their subjects the same cringing submission the Mongols exacted from them, and plundered them as the Mongols' tax collectors.

In the fourteenth century the Mongol Empire fragmented and began embracing Islam, and the Turkic language, influenced by Arabic, came to replace Mongolian (outside Mongolia, at least). The Yuan dynasty sinicized and fell to a renegade Han general who established the Ming in 1368. In Russia, Khan Batu ruled as khan of the Golden Horde. Russian Muscovite princes, however, while still officially vassals, embarked on the "gathering of Russia" through raids of conquest against their overlords and against fellow princes desiring to maintain the autonomy granted them by the Mongols. Moscow's strategic location in relation to major rivers gave it the upper hand in the fight for sovereignty. In 1480 Ivan III, tsar of Moscow, prevailed, freeing the last Russians from Mongol rule. He also carted away Moscow's symbol of democracy, the *veche* bell. From then on, and especially after the savage reign of Ivan IV (alias the Terrible, or, to translate his epithet, *Grozny,* more accurately, the Dread), Russia would know autocracy and dictatorship, with few interludes to the present day.

Genghis Khan's hordes do not deserve all the blame for the misrule and despotism that followed their conquests, of course, but the fact remains that the peoples of Eurasia, from Manchuria to the edges of eastern Europe, share a bloody historical patrimony: a long, often dark period of Mongol rule marked by the subversion of the state to criminal ends of plunder.

THE RUSSIAN ANNEXATION of Central Asia started in the mid-eighteenth century. The tsars, facing no geographic barriers, obeyed the logic of their country's own manifest destiny and dispatched Cossack explorers and settlers across the Eurasian steppes into the flatlands through which Mongol armies had ridden their agile horses west, until Russia's borders touched China's. Then began the Great Game—the century-long contest between Britain and Russia, conducted by stealth, diplomacy, and espionage—for influence in Central Asia, with Britain scheming to thwart what it perceived to be tsarist moves toward its prize colony, India. The British succeeded in penetrating what is now Xinjiang, in western China, but most of Central Asia went to Russia.

To the outside world, Central Asia remained terra incognita, a vast, daunting mosaic of steppe and desert inhabited mostly by backward, Turkic-speaking nomads, gifted (apparently) with few notable natural resources. After the Russian Empire collapsed in 1917, Central Asia fell to the Red Army, which consigned its peoples to another spell in limbo under Soviet rule. The Soviets, however, would discover huge deposits of oil, natural gas, and minerals and exploit them far from Western eyes.

The demise of the Soviet Union in 1991 and the emergence of independent states across its domain drew some Western media attention to the region. Yeltsin's Russia, laid low by economic depression, crime, corruption, and the war in Chechnya, renounced conflict with the West, even in its Near Abroad, which let several Central Asian leaders welcome Western investors and the political overtures of their governments. By all appearances the West (especially the United States) was on the path to ascendancy in Central Asia, stamping out vestiges of Russian influence and securing the region as a pliant supplier of energy for Western markets.

No longer. In ways that would have been unimaginable five or ten years ago, change has convulsed many countries of the former Soviet Union, and China's star is rising. Across Eurasia alliances are forming that may soon threaten Western security.

This has everything to do with the Russian president Vladimir Vladimirovich Putin, in office since 2000, and his adroitly executed scheme to restore authoritarian rule and his country's great-power status. Soon after Yeltsin's departure, the Kremlin launched a legalistic assault on the media; today the Kremlin exerts control over all national television stations, as well as most radio stations and key newspapers. After the 2004 terrorist attack in Beslan, Putin canceled elections for regional governors and arrogated the right to appoint them. Pro-presidential parties now prevail in sixty-three of eighty-eight local parliaments, often with two-thirds majorities. Occasional opposition marches draw heavy-handed suppression from security forces but few crowds. Russia's nascent civil society has been eviscerated.

Putin has effectively renationalized the energy sector, which the Yeltsin government had sold off to oligarchs in rigged auctions. Kremlin-backed companies now wield majority stakes across the spectrum of oil and gas companies. Gazprom, the state-dominated natural gas monopoly, continues to expand, recently acquiring, for example, a 63-percent stake in the development of the east Siberian gas field of Kovykta, the reserves of which equal those of Canada, the world's third-largest gas producer. (Russia on the whole holds one-quarter of the planet's natural gas reserves.) Rosneft, now battened on assets seized from the Kremlin-dismantled oil giant Yukos, has in the past three years gone from being a minor player on the Russian petroleum market to being the country's largest oil company. Putin has deployed Russia's energy resources as weapons against former Soviet republics that won't toe his line, cutting off supplies to Ukraine and Georgia (with less dramatic, yet still alarming, reductions following downstream in Europe, itself increasingly dependent on Russia for gas).

The oil and gas industry, with its profits filling state coffers, has financed Russia's return to international prominence. Russia is the second-largest exporter of crude after Saudi Arabia and the largest gas-producing country on earth. Per day ten million barrels of oil now flow from its reserves (mostly in Siberia and the far north), plus 354 million cubic meters of natural gas (increasingly acquired from Central Asia) to Europe alone. Energy sales account for a third of state budgetary receipts and 63 percent of exports, and drive an annual economic growth rate of 6.5 percent, buttressing Russia's trillion-dollar economy, the world's tenth largest.

Yet since Putin began his first term, prosperity for the Russian people has not come as easily as the oil and gas have flowed. Deepening corruption, concentration of revenues among the urban, often hydrocarbon-affiliated elite, and capital flight are to blame. Epidemics of HIV and tuberculosis are the worst in Europe. The suicide rate has increased by 50 percent. Drugs and drink afflict more Russians than ever, contributing to the lowest average life span (fifty-eight years) for men in the developed world. The birthrate continues to fall, with Russia's population decreasing by 700,000 a year, leading demographers to predict a drop from 143 million to 100 million by 2050. Although Putin came to power pledging to establish a "dictatorship of the law," spectacular terrorist attacks and episodes of untimely death have still occurred: the Kursk submarine disaster (111 dead), and hostage-takings at the Dubrovka Theater in Moscow (121 dead) and in Beslan (331 dead), to name a few. Even outside Chechnya, conditions at times approximating civil war convulse parts of the Northern Caucasus.

Nevertheless, Putin's restoration of Russia's authoritarian state has won the support of his people; his popularity rating has rarely dipped beneath 70 percent. The popularity of the West, however, and in particular of the United States, has plummeted. Anti-Western sentiments now saturate the state-controlled media and the state-monitored press, as well as casual conversations everywhere—an astonishing reversal of pro-Western passions so widespread at the time of the Soviet collapse. Angered by, among many things, the two-step expansion of NATO into former Soviet domains and its 1999 war against Yugoslavia (an Orthodox Christian people and Russian ally), as well as the Bush administration's abrogation of the Anti-Ballistic Missile Treaty and its plans to base a missile-defense shield in the Czech Republic and Poland, the majority of Russians reject alliance with the West and favor their president's policy of Machtpolitik over submission and diplomacy. In a way no one could have foreseen, dour Putin has turned a Russia brought to its knees by Yeltsin-era chaos into a power capable of, and now clearly determined to, challenge the United States.

A new Great Game between Russia and the West is on; and Russia, flush with energy profits, is returning to its old Soviet fiefdoms and expanding its presence mightily to win it. Backed by American NGOs, popular upheavals have ousted corrupt governments in Georgia, Ukraine, and Kyrgyzstan, but democracy and prosperity have failed to ensue. Georgia's Western-leaning president, who came to power after a pro-democracy street revolt in 2003, hopes to enroll his country in NATO, but he finds Russia supporting separatist movements in South Ossetia and Abkhazia; Russia has banned Georgian products from its markets, cut off flights from Moscow to Tbilisi, and denied Georgians visas. Kyrgyzstan has given notice that American troops will not be welcome once Afghanistan settles, and Uzbekistan has evicted the United States from bases it opened there in 2001. Turkmenistan's dictator has died, but his country's course has veered not toward the West but back to Moscow. The Iraq debacle has done much to strengthen Putin's hand, affording him both high oil revenues and cogent proof of America's ultimate weakness in projecting military power abroad (to say nothing of its hypocritical stance on human rights, as evidenced by Guantanamo, "renditions," and Abu Ghraib).

Mired in Baghdad, the United States has discredited itself as a wielder of force in the formerly Soviet sphere, where force means so much to national prestige and may be the only tool corrupt Central Asian regimes can deploy against threats. Russia, however, in razing Chechnya over the course of two decades, has shown its willingness to use force long-term; it could, if need be, put tens of thousands of conscript boots on Central Asian ground in defense of its allies. Distant America, bogged down in Iraq, cannot do this; and even if it could, it would no doubt attach troublesome conditions to its military aid (respect for human rights, the holding of free elections, and so forth) that Moscow wouldn't dream of imposing.

As they do in Russia, energy resources and their conveyance to market dominate the new Great Game unfolding in Central Asia. Russia, Kazakhstan, and Turkmenistan recently announced plans to build a gas pipeline connecting with Russia's network, for subsequent re-export to Europe, thwarting a U.S. project for a pipeline that would bypass Russia; in fact, Russia now controls all of Central Asia's westward-flowing gas exports. Gazprom will soon be able to exert powerful political pressure over countries such as Ukraine, which NATO hopes to embrace, and Turkey, a traditional Western ally, using Central Asian reserves in addition to its own. Central Asian oil will also strengthen Russia's hand. Kazakhstan, for example, exports 1.25 million barrels a day, an amount that will double in ten years, partly owing to Kashagan, the world's largest oil field discovered in the past thirty years, which will come on line in 2010. Kazakhstan's GDP growth rate of 8.5 percent gives the former steppe-and-desert basket case the wherewithal to chart its own course, which, for now at least, leads toward a partnership with Russia. Four out of ten people in Kazakhstan are, after all, Slavic, and mostly Russian.

If Russia is one of the new Eurasia's "poles," China is the other—and the stronger of the two. In the thirty years since Deng Xiaoping launched market reforms, China, with 1.3 billion people, has become the world's fourth-biggest economy and the third-largest trading nation; it has increased its GDP by 90 percent and brought two hundred million people out of poverty. Its foreign currency reserves exceed one trillion dollars—the largest on earth. Within another thirty years, assuming growth rates remain the same, China will outstrip the United States economically altogether. The White House's National Security Strategy of 2006 describes the Chinese economy as the key threat to U.S. global hegemony.

This is not to say that China is prospering uniformly, any more than Russia is. Its coastal areas may be thriving, but in outback towns, workers from the countryside find themselves abused and indentured in monstrous factories, and riots—tens of thousands a year—erupt over corruption and other injustices. China estimates its "floating" jobless, or sporadically employed, migrants to number 140 million—almost equivalent to the entire population of Russia. If China's per capita income was $200 at the start of reforms, it is still only $1,700—twenty-five times less than that of the United States. Three-quarters of China's surface water supplies are too contaminated to drink or fish in. A scarcity of energy resources has caused worsening brownouts in two-thirds of its cities; and its ravenous appetite for oil is compelling China to search abroad for reliable suppliers.

China, thus, needs energy, land, and water—all of which Russia has in surplus. Might the two countries form an alliance? Western capitals dismissed the creation, in 2001, of the Shanghai Cooperation Organization (SCO), comprising China and Russia (plus Kyrgyzstan, Kazakhstan, Tajikistan, and Uzbekistan), as a talk shop, or as an attempt to coordinate the suppression of Islamic radicals and nothing more. After all, had not the United States outwitted the Soviet Union by opening relations with China in the 1970s and thereby deepened the already troublesome Sino-Soviet split? To be sure, relations between the two giants will always be fraught with suspicion.

Now alarm is spreading in Washington, D.C. India, Pakistan, Iran, and Mongolia have acquired observer status in the SCO, and SCO member states conducted their first joint military exercises in Russia in 2007. Russia is supplying China with advanced arms; and China is engaging in a military buildup that includes space and anti-submarine weaponry. Moscow and Beijing have announced the construction, due to start in 2008, of an oil pipeline that would transport Siberian oil to China. SCO countries sit on one-fifth of the world's crude supplies. In 2007 an official at the U.S. Department of Energy stated, "The SCO has the potential to develop into an anti-American energy giant in competition with our hopes of making Central Asia a reliable energy source, bypassing Russia"—an ominous possibility, since according to the International Energy Agency world demand for oil will rise from 86 million barrels (in 2007) to 116 million barrels a day by 2030.

Indeed, the SCO may well devolve into an alliance capable of challenging the United States from Alaska to western Europe. A member of the U.S. National Security Council declared that such a threat "strengthens the argument to constrain Russian power." The same official added, "Unless we act now to constrain Russian power, we risk long-term damage to our international interests." Just what action can be taken is unclear. The SCO is even attracting positive notice from countries beyond its membership. At a conference in Tehran in 2006, representatives from Russia, China, Iran, Venezuela, and Georgia gathered to discuss a regional pipeline system that could reach from China to Egypt—a major American ally in the Middle East.

One has to ask, Why *shouldn't* Russia, China, and the countries in between form an anti-American alliance? What has the West offered them, besides criticism of their (obviously deficient) human rights records, the expansion of a military alliance around their borders, and the prospect of facing ever-more-sophisticated weapons systems? Why *shouldn't* Russia sell its fuel to China or use it to intimidate its rivals? What else *does* it have?

IN THE POPLAR-SHADED COURTYARD of my apartment building in central Moscow, where I've lived since July of 1993, labors an ever-increasing contingent of *dvorniki*, or yard cleaners in Russian. Distant progeny of the invasions of Genghis Khan and his grandsons (and of ancient Turkic migrations within Central Asia), the *dvorniki* are mostly male Uzbeks and Kazakhs (though their wives and children are arriving to join them), and all dress in the Day-Glo orange jumpsuits of municipal employees; some speak only their native Turkic languages. The *dvorniki* sweep sidewalks and swab down entranceways, trim trees and paint railings, haul trash, and do other odd jobs for minimal wages, something around six to seven hundred dollars a month. (Annual per capita GDP in Russia is now $12,100.) Living five or ten to a rented room, they remit much of their income to relatives back in their Central Asian homelands, where their salaries count as big money. Six or seven years ago, they replaced Russians, who are now loath to do this kind of menial work.

These *dvorniki* are but the most visible and prosperous members of an immigrant population in Russia that began heading north with the fall of the USSR—a pervasive, mostly illegal underclass that Russians do not want to see yet without which no yard stays clean, few food markets can function, and little trade would be accomplished. Fourteen years ago, when I asked Russians how they felt about the then distant Turkic peoples, I would hear, *"Oy, kakoy russky ne tatarin!"* (Oh, what Russian isn't a Tatar!)—an adage reflecting a benign acceptance of the mixing of bloods fostered by the Tatar-Mongolian yoke. These days public opinion is no longer tolerant. Central Asians are viewed as uncivilized Muslims, beggars, melon vendors, petty crooks, and *mafiozy* who keep on coming. Facing daily threats of extortion and even assault from the police during spot document checks, they understandably keep low, making the news only when attacked by multiplying skinhead gangs whose slogan is *Rossiya dlya Russkikh* (Russia for the Russians). Most other migrants, including large numbers of Muslim males from the Caucasus, also find themselves in similar straits.

Moscow has devolved into a hub of illegal immigration from across Eurasia, and this exodus of the economically hapless is changing Russia's ethnic composition. During the years 1989 to 2002, Slavic Russians in Russia diminished by 2 percent to just short of 80 percent; by the middle of this century, some demographers predict that migrants and Caucasian minority peoples will form a majority and turn Russia into a predominantly Muslim country.

With ever-more-valuable supplies of oil and gas coming from their lands, why are these folk living poor and downtrodden in Russia? We hear almost nothing from the people *between* Moscow and Beijing. Yet the only country that can menace the United States militarily (with its nuclear arsenal) is Russia; the only economic power that could sink the United States is China. We ignore their impoverished, mostly Muslim hinterlands at our peril, for even under the current autocratic regimes, on their peoples' submission to state authority hinges the stability of Russia, China, and the states in between—members of the SCO alliance that now constitute the most potent threat to American (and, by extension, Western) global dominance. How are people once repressed by Moscow and Beijing reacting to the resurgence of Russia, the rise of China? What does the middle class—the potential motor for political change—feel about the strengthening of the state? In lands once part of the largest empire on earth, and in the world's most populous country, life for a billion and a half people is changing, but into what remains unclear.

To see for myself how people are getting by in the villages and rust belt towns and ignored metropolises between Moscow and Beijing, and therefore to arrive at some conclusions about the future of Eurasia, I decided to quit the Russian capital and head south to the Caucasus, and then wander east across the steppes and deserts of Kazakhstan, over the mountains of Kyrgyzstan, and into the deserts and grasslands of northern China until I reached Beijing. During the Yeltsin years, while the Moscow-based Western press corps reported on Russia's "democratic reforms" and "free-market transformation," those of us who ventured into the hinterland saw scenes of poverty and anger and mounting nationalism that presaged Putin's rise—indeed, made it inevitable—and preordained Russia's present rejection of the West. Is the West, across the strategically vital expanses of Russia and Central Asia, set to lose the new Great Game? The mood among Eurasia's "masses" should provide clues: how they feel now about the West, and in particular the United States, could presage the actions of their governments, which, though authoritarian, depend more than in the past on their peoples' approbation, given the spread of information technology and its potential use in mobilizing resistance. We should listen to what they have to say.

So, in the summer of 2006 I embarked on a 7,200-mile overland journey from Red Square to Tiananmen Square, following a winding route through the least-visited corners of southern Russia, Central Asia, and northern China. I decided to eschew pundits and talk with whomever came my way. I spoke Russian and Turkish, and possessed a fair knowledge of spoken Mandarin, which I set about sharpening. I had already traversed Russia from east to west, rafted through its Arctic north and trundled across its Caucasian south; I had twice sojourned in outback China, and for a while, before moving to Moscow, had even worked in Central Asia. I hoped this experience would stand me in good stead and help me understand what I saw.

I bore in mind a well-known yet portentous fact. In Red Square and Tiananmen Square, in stately mausoleums, lie the embalmed corpses of the two most transformative and controversial leaders of Eurasia, Vladimir Lenin and Mao Zedong, men who steered their countries out of chaos and collapse, and yet in doing so murdered tens of millions of their own citizens. (Stalin also lay beside Lenin, until his successor denounced his crimes and had him removed.) Why are Lenin and Mao still there, with the Soviet Union having fallen and China now de facto capitalist? What does their formaldehyded presence say about their peoples? In the grasslands of northern China, on my route, also stands the mausoleum of Genghis Khan. Was it true, as I had read, that one of the most ruthless killers of all time enjoyed a cult following in a country he had destroyed?

I didn't know, but I hoped to find out.

1

Thunderclouds fissured with streaks of brilliant blue sky were advancing on Red Square, their dark underbellies presenting an ominous backdrop for the candy-striped cupolas and gilt spires of Saint Basil's Cathedral. Ivan the Terrible commissioned this outlandishly baroque shrine to celebrate his capture, in 1552, of the Muslim town of Kazan, on the Volga—a victory heralding the demise of Russia's once mighty eastern rival, the Kazan Khanate of the Golden Horde, and clearing the way for Muscovy's annexation of Siberia. My wife, Tatyana, and I stood at the square's edge, looking out over its expanses, 800,000 square feet of charcoal-gray granite as grimly grand as the events that have taken place there: the beheadings of traitors, revolutionary addresses, theophanies of tsars and emperors and Communist Party general secretaries, military parades and May Day celebrations and commemorations of World Wars. Across the square, above Lenin's mausoleum, deserted save for a pair of honor guard soldiers, rose the Kremlin's crenellated ramparts.

Soldiers had patrolled those ramparts during the reactionary rebellion of October 1993. I had stood beneath them then, watching pro-Yeltsin demonstrators toss together barricades of junk metal on Nikol'skaya Street, as they prepared to defend the Kremlin. Red Square seemed to be the center of the universe in those days, when the fate of humanity hinged, or so we in Moscow thought, on whether Yeltsin would suppress the revolt and lead Russia toward democracy or the

Communists would return and embroil the country in more violence and another cold war.

President Yeltsin ended the uprising by shelling mutinous deputies holed up in the Supreme Soviet—an astonishing move for the leader of a supposedly democratic nation, and one with a portentousness that eluded its Western apologists, including President Clinton. Now, in mid-July 2006, there was no hint of moment, not a trace of crisis. A breeze ruffled the spruces beneath the Kremlin walls and broke into gusts, blowing into disarray Tatyana's long black hair. Tourists on the square, mostly Russians from the provinces, shuddered in the blustery cool as they positioned their digital cameras and posed for pictures, and women in raincoats holding megaphones hawked in ever more urgent tones the last places left on buses about to leave for excursions around town. Just as the din grew insufferable, the bells of Saint Basil's rang out, sounding five o'clock, followed by the lyrical chimes of Russia's Big Ben, on the Tower of the Savior, atop the main Kremlin gate. The chimes, relayed by the radio station Mayak, reach every corner of Russia, from Kaliningrad on the Polish border to villages seven thousand miles west on the Bering Strait, just fifty-two miles from Alaska. Vast as this territory is, Red Square has always been the spiritual heart of Russia, even during the two hundred years when Saint Petersburg served as the capital. On the Kremlin grounds, in Archangel Cathedral, the divinely ordained tsars were crowned and buried; and the Russian Orthodox Church was long headquartered.

It was getting late and I had a train to catch, an all-nighter to Novocherkassk, the Cossack capital six hundred miles to the south, near the Sea of Azov, on the Don River. We turned and walked briskly along Nikol'skaya Street and ducked into the covered staircase leading down to the ten-laned Okhotny Ryad and our taxi. Rush hour was starting, and our driver, with Muscovite brashness, sped, dodged, and barreled around Mercedes and SUVs and decrepit Volgas, braking for a police-escorted convoy of shiny black Volvos topped with blue flashing lights (government officials, to be sure), and honking to scare off Soviet-era trucks, steel brontosauruses that refuse to die and still carry much of the country's freight. We shot by the Bolshoi Ballet and swerved up Bol'shaya Lubyanka Street, past the yellow brick leviathan, squat and sooty, that was once the KGB and now houses its successor, the FSB. All around us Moscow was simultaneously undergoing demolition and reconstruction. Office buildings as glitzy as any in Manhattan were rising above rows of two-story nineteenth-century stucco homes and tin-plated kiosks selling buns, nuts, vodka, and porn, all begrimed by exhaust. At corners *gaishniki* (traffic cops) stood sullen, waving over vehicles with black and white batons, preparing to demand payment of "fines"; near metro stations police officers, also surely hoping to exact bribes, halted passersby for document checks.

We passed under a railway bridge and pulled up in front of Kazansky Station. Our mood sank on walking into its main hall, a puke green, fluorescent-lit chamber crowded with travelers who had the haggard aspect of refugees from some unnamed conflict, sweaty folk dragging taped-up suitcases and ratty bundles. For a hundred rubles, however, we bought tickets to the "Hall of Heightened Comfort." There, vaulted ceiling murals displayed a mélange of scenes from Russia's medieval past and the Great Patriotic War, *Pirates of the Caribbean* played at full volume on a plasma-screen television, and windows banged open and shut with the wind.

I felt sad about saying goodbye to Tatyana, and not just because I would be away for months. More and more before long, uncertain journeys, I tend to sense what Gide called *"l'avant-goût de la mort"*—the "foretaste of death" inherent in all leave-takings. No place on earth seemed farther away than Beijing.

The PA system announced that the "Platov Express Number 100" was departing and all passengers had to board. Half an hour later I was looking out at Tatyana through the train compartment window, talking to her on my cell phone, feeling vaguely ridiculous in front of the auburn-haired young woman across from me sitting, in a most un-Russian way, with her bare feet pulled up beneath her.

Tatyana said, "She looks like an *intelligentnaya* [cultured] girl. I feel good leaving you with her."

At that the train started pulling away, and we signed off.

I put down the phone. The young woman had been watching me talk, and she averted her eyes bashfully, smiling. I took in the compartment. It was orderly and clean, especially compared to those I had ridden in during the Yeltsin years. White-laced pink curtains hung on washed windows. A menu offered Russian dishes redolent of the southern steppes: *zharkoye* (fried chunks of pork) and mushrooms cooked *po-kazach'i* (Cossack-style), salads of cucumber and mayonnaise, sausage *po-kazach'i*, and tea fresh from a samovar bubbling at the corridor's end.

"Let's get acquainted," my compartment mate said in Russian that was fluent but lilting with a melodious, if slightly nasal, accent. "My name is Marina." She extended her hand for a shake—something Russian women rarely do. Buxom but thin, she had a roundish face and sensitive brown eyes. She wore a beige pants and jacket ensemble and a black designer T-shirt.

We started chatting. Marina was born in Kiev in the early 1980s but had emigrated to Israel at age ten. She was on her way to Rossosh, a town north of Novocherkassk, where she worked in a joint venture with her husband, who was also an Israeli of Soviet descent. Her Russian was native but Yiddish-accented. It reminded me of my graduate school days, of long-lost friends who were also Soviet Jewish émigrés and who had welcomed me into the university's Russian-speaking community. During my first trip around the Soviet Union, in 1985, I had met many of their relatives. They turned out to be the only Soviets with whom I felt no cultural barriers whatsoever. All this disposed me to feel at ease with Marina and enjoy the rhythms of her Russian.

Two militia officers rapped on our door and asked to see our passports. Trains to the Northern Caucasus received special scrutiny from the security services, owing to the fighting in Chechnya.

"So your country is at war," one said to Marina, handing back her passport, in reference to the Israel-Lebanon conflict of that summer.

"Yes, you could say that," replied Marina.

"Hmm. Interesting, an American and an Israeli in one compartment," he added. "Well, good travels."

They shut the door and walked off.

"Oh," she said, turning to me. "We just want to live in peace. Israel is thriving and rich. Why would we want to invade Lebanon? We just need security."

"This must be a frightening time for Israelis, what with Iran getting stronger and the United States mired down in . . ." Discussing the Middle East had to involve mention of the Iraq war, and fearing she would be for it, I didn't want to say anything weighty on the subject or risk spoiling the mood.

"Arabs and Israelis lived in peace not long ago," she said. "But now Arabs brainwash their kids with suicide dogma and talk of heaven and all those seventy virgins."

"Well, I think—"

"The U.S. for Israelis is a great country, truly a *great* country."

"Well, we ended up with Bush as president, twice. And the Iraq war will create just as many problems, or more, for Israel. Don't you agree?"

She pulled back from me, her face darkening. I told her I was an Arabist, and this seemed to arouse her suspicion even more. She said she had studied Arabic but disliked it, and had "no illusions" about Arabs.

To change the subject, I told her of my interest in Buddhism and the *Tao Te Ching* and how happy I was to be on my way to China.

"Oh, you know what? I don't really practice Judaism," she said, leaning forward again, "even if I believe in one god, the God of all three religions. But I won't offend Orthodox Jews in Israel by driving on the Sabbath. There's no need to spit in people's faces, you know? By the way, in Hebrew we don't have *vy*"—the formal "you" form we were using to address each other. "We just have one way of saying 'you' to all," she said. "Can we just switch to *ty*?"

"I would like that."

Poems have been written in Russian about the warmth and intimacy of using *ty* instead of *vy*. With *ty*, we again became new friends sharing a train compartment.

Outside, the clouds had dispersed and the late-evening sun was pouring glorious gold over gray-brown *izbas* and mud roads, over lucent groves of birch and pines, the mixed forest of north-central Russia that would turn deciduous as the train progressed south, toward the *chernozem* (black earth zones). An hour out of Moscow and we were already slipping into a timeless rural land.

"Oh, how I miss this forest, all the green!" said Marina. "It's *so* beautiful to see, for an Israeli from the land of palms and sand, you know?"

From then on, our conversation ranged lazily over the Soviet films she had loved as a child, Kiev and its flowering chestnut groves, her pity for Russian women, who "start off so beautiful" but end up as "stocky, mannish broads lugging around plastic bags of potatoes, doing all the work while their husbands drink," and, finally, to her (naive, to my ears) admiration for Putin and her shock at Russia's corruption ("It'll take Russians two hundred years to root it out").

We talked until long past the late nightfall.

Shortly after dawn Marina got up, scribbled out her e-mail, and debarked in Rossosh. The train rocked on through tunnels of green, passing scarved peasant women leading cows on ropes along the pebbly banks of brooks, skirting hedges and blooming trellises of roses that at times engulfed lopsided *izbas* in riotous growths of yellows and reds and blues. In through the open window came the loamy scent of black earth and aspens and honeysuckle, of scalloped fields of sunflowers and daisies—the languid, intoxicating aroma of the deep Russian south in summer.

JUST PAST NOON the Platov Express slowed as it penetrated neighborhoods of wooded lanes and log cabins and cement apartment blocks, then eased to a stop in Novocherkassk, the capital of the Cossacks, Russia's holy warriors, the fervid Orthodox Christian nationalists to whom the tsars entrusted the expansion and protection of Russia's borders. On the sunny platform waited tanned militia officers, ready to check documents. Chechnya lies 375 miles to the southeast, and during the past fifteen years Muslim rebels have taken to crossing from the Caucasus into the southern provinces of Russia to blow up buses, trains, and markets. Most of these attacks get little publicity in the West, but they represent a reversion to what was the norm for centuries in the region before the 1917 revolution: violence between Christians and Muslims (who number some twenty million), Russia's two dominant religious groups. For many Cossacks, the war in Chechnya is only the latest manifestation of an age-old Islamic campaign to dismember Russia, the territorial integrity of which it was historically the Cossacks' sacred duty to defend.

My friend Yana, a Cossack folk singer, was there to meet me on the platform. She strolled up in a loose white pantsuit, her thick dark hair and fleshy curves embodying the Cossacks' concept of beauty, which is decidedly non-Russian and almost Middle Eastern. She was proud of her heritage. "You have to be *born* a Cossack," she had told me during a vodka-soaked dinner in 2004. "No matter what I do, I can never become a Chechen. Being a Cossack is a matter of *blood*."

We kissed three times on the cheeks, as is the Russian Orthodox custom, and she told me her father the ataman (Cossack commander) would come to see me at the café by my hotel. I was eager to meet him. He had helped defend the Gorbachev government in Moscow during the reactionary coup attempt of 1991. How would he view the ascendancy of Putin, a former KGB colonel? After all, the Soviet security services had hounded the Cossacks to near extinction, dispossessing, exiling, and murdering large numbers of them.

"My father's an encyclopedia of knowledge about the Cossacks," Yana said, "a national treasure."

I put up at the concrete-block Hotel Novocherkassk, which, if nothing else, had a pleasant veranda café out front. At the reception desk a stout brunette with a beehive hairdo bristled when she saw me.

"Tell your friend," she said wearily to Yana, "to read this sign." GUESTS MAY ENJOY HOT WATER BETWEEN THE HOURS OF 17:00 AND 22:00.

"Excuse me," I said. "You can talk to me."

"Have your friend fill out this form, and *neatly*—it goes to the police and they're *very* picky." She slid the form to Yana, and I took it.

Yana whispered, "I *hate* this town. We've got a Communist mayor and he's setting up his own totalitarian regime. Prices are rising and salaries are falling. You see it in little ways, like how everyone is becoming so rude again. Anyway, Dad will be at the café in twenty minutes."

"Okay, then let me take a quick shower"—I checked the hot water times on the sign—"a cold shower, that is, and I'll be right down."

But there was no water at all. I returned to the front desk to confront the beehive. "I have no water in my room."

Intimating infinite fatigue, she slowly raised her hairdo and fixed her eyes on me. "Have you read the sign?"

"Yes. It's about hot water, not cold."

"Exactly. We know when we have *hot* water, because the city gives it to us according to schedule. Cold is *obviously* another story. It's not mentioned because we have no schedule for it."

"That's ridiculous. That sounds like something straight out of the old Soviet Union."

"So write a complaint. I don't care."

Yana stepped in. "Shame! You're totalitarians here, all of you! I'll write that complaint and send it to the city administration!" She grabbed my arm. "Come on, Dad is waiting for you."

Out front the ataman was standing by a table under an umbrella. Bulbous-nosed, meaty-shouldered, potbellied, and half bald, a hard-eyed sixty-year-old, he crunched my hand in a ferocious shake, and we all sat down.

"So you want to know about Cossacks?" he asked me in a hoarse, accusatory bass. "Well, since the days of the battle on Kulikovo Field"—when, in 1380, on the nearby Don River, Cossack forces helped

Prince Dmitry of Muscovy rout the Tatar-Mongolians—"the Cossacks have never had to be *asked* to save Russia. We've done it of our *own free will.* Our role has always been to protect Russia's borders and *extend* them, all the way to Khabarovsk, in the Far East!" He raised his eyebrows. "You know what Napoleon said about us? 'Give me a division of Cossacks and I'll conquer the *world!*' We are the *born warriors* Russia needs *now!*"

He growled out his words, his sinewy fists clenched on the table. Nothing in the Cossacks' past, either as slaughterers or slaughtered, has disposed them to subtlety. Legendary for both their equestrian skills and martial talents, the Cossacks galloped into Russian history in the fourteenth century. The homeland of the first Cossacks, the Don Cossacks, was the sea of billowing, feather-grass steppe beyond Novocherkassk that surrounds the lower meanderings of the Don and Volga rivers. Military organization and discipline allowed the Cossacks to survive unrelenting assaults from an array of fearsome nomads now long vanished, and from raiders based in the Crimean and Astrakhan Tatar khanates (two of the Muslim successor states to the Golden Horde) that eventually fell to expanding Muscovy.

The Cossacks defined themselves and their homeland in military terms. They called their country *Oblast' Voiska Donskogo* (the "Province of the Don Host"), and all men served as irregulars (though with rank) who were called to battle when the need arose. They ruled themselves democratically, electing atamans in rowdy informal village assemblies known as *krugi* (circles). In the fifteenth and sixteenth centuries, the Cossacks' golden era, the *Oblast',* the borders of which encompassed what now are the Volgograd and Rostov regions, enjoyed diplomatic recognition from Russia as well as Persia.

Early on, the Cossacks earned a reputation as anti-Semitic, Catholic-hating fanatics with a penchant for pogroms, in addition to being, of course, implacable foes of the region's Muslims. Bound as much by fervent Orthodox Christian faith as by a spirited animus against Islam, Cossacks frequently pillaged their non-Orthodox neighbors, killing men, carrying off women, and seizing whatever loot they could toss in their saddlebags. In pre-Soviet Russia—the history of which from the rise of Muscovy on was marked by tyranny, serfdom, and oppression, to say nothing of timid, even groveling deference toward despotic rulers—Cossacks held themselves above others as *vol'nyye,* a word meaning "free," but in a defiant sense that approaches "willful" or "domineering." A love of *vol'nost'*, or unbridled liberty, seemed to define their identity—even if that liberty often amounted to bloody plunder for those around them.

Mostly hostile to Communism, the Cossacks suffered widespread repression during Soviet days. Numbering around five million at the time of the Soviet Union's collapse, they launched a revival under Yeltsin. Since 1991 sixty Cossack academies have opened across Russia to educate the young. Cossack units have been formed in the Russian army. Cossack troops have guarded Orthodox churches and monasteries, patrolled "border" towns like Novocherkassk, and helped police conduct searches during terrorist alerts. Some were even calling for the reestablishment of the *Oblast' Voiska Donskogo*, which the Bolsheviks abolished after coming to power.

As was the ataman. "After the Soviet Union fell apart, we had a chance to reestablish the *Oblast' Voiska Donskogo*. Our *Oblast'* used to include eastern Ukraine and Kalmykia and Ingushetia"—the latter two being republics in the Caucasus region. He gritted his teeth. "I *lived* for this dream."

It sounded more like he was ready to die, or to kill, for it. "Why can't you realize it?" I asked, leery of his rage.

"Being a Cossack is not about folk costumes; it's about having an ataman as commander and living the Cossack way of life, the *free* way of life. The essence of being a Cossack is *vol'nost'*—*vol'nost'* and spirit. All the Cossacks you see here in town today are just clowns, they're mercenaries, and they don't understand or care about *vol'nost'*. I can't even say *I'm vol'ny* these days."

"You mean you can't be free because you have the Russian government here now, and so atamans are no longer the rulers."

"It's more than that. When I was born in this town there were three—*three*—Caucasians"—meaning the mostly Muslim indigenes of the Caucasus. "Now they've *all* migrated here, and they're everywhere, everywhere! We can't live our Cossack way of life surrounded by them, *swamped* by them.

"But I haven't sat idly by. I've offered the Cossacks here concrete plans, guns and ammo included, to seize power. For this the authorities have labeled me an extremist. The local government has tried to buy me off with offers of a big new apartment, as they've done with other atamans. But I refuse to accept. In the coup attempt of 1991, I offered my help personally to Yeltsin and [vice-president] Alexandr Rutskoi, but they turned me down."

"You're talking about a revolt, aren't you?"

He sneered. "What we need now are atamans like Bulavin, Razin, and Pugachev!"—Cossack leaders of cataclysmic peasant rebellions against autocracy and serfdom that shook the Russian state in centuries past, took thousands of lives, and ended in defeat. To hear their blood-soaked names now sent a chill down my spine.

Still, the ataman's anger has solid grounds in Cossack history, a history first of sovereignty and freedom and then of massacre and humiliation. The Cossacks' golden era began slipping away with a job offer, in 1570, from Ivan the Terrible, who hired them to defend Russia's southern frontier, paying them in lead, gunpowder, and bread. But as Muscovy grew more powerful, it enserfed ever-greater numbers of peasants, entrenching misery throughout its population. In 1670 a Cossack named Stepan Razin raised the banner of revolt from the Caspian Sea to Kazan, far beyond the *Oblast'*, decrying tsarist serfdom as worse than the slavery practiced by "Turks or heathens." The revolt was crushed, and Razin executed. In 1707 another Cossack uprising broke out, and Peter the Great issued what may have been the first genocidal order in history: "Burn [the Cossacks], leaving nothing behind; slaughter the people; strap the ringleaders to the wheel and impale them, for this mob cannot be pacified save by cruelty." His army razed forty-eight Cossack settlements and killed seven thousand people, but later, fearing Ottoman expansionism, he allowed a revival—on the condition that the Cossacks accept an ataman appointed by the tsar to rule their oblast. They agreed. Later, sensing that they couldn't resist the embrace of a newly powerful Russia, the Cossacks found a role as the tsar's most effective shock troops and bodyguards.

For this the Bolsheviks despised them. In 1919 the advancing Red Army drove abroad tens of thousands of White Army Cossacks and captured most of the rest. A widely circulated editorial in a Bolshevik paper published that year read, "One has to notice the similarity between Cossack psychology and certain representatives of the animal kingdom. The Cossacks must be burned up in the flame of social revolutions."

Many were. On December 30, 1919, Lenin issued the second order for mass murder in Cossack history, demanding that 765,000 Cossack prisoners be "executed to the last man"—that is, men, women, children, and elders all. At least two million Cossacks were shot or, soon after, exiled to Siberia, stripped of their land and livestock in Stalin's campaign for the collectivization of agriculture, and reduced to Soviet serf status like the rest of the country's peasants. From then on, in Russian, "Cossack" became a byword among non-Cossacks for extremism, the reactionary, and the retrograde.

I asked the ataman what he thought of the Cossack revival under Putin.

"All we've got now are collaborators," he replied. "They say they serve Russia, but what Russia do we have to serve? A KGB-led regime, a thieves' regime! I hate all the bastards. I refuse to submit." He sat back. "I just want a country run by normal people." He rubbed his face, then pulled away his hands to reveal hardening eyes. "What did you say your profession is?"

"I'm a writer."

"For all I know, you're a spy. But anyway, I'll have my say. I'm *vol'ny*, just as a writer is. I use my freedom to work on overthrowing the Putin regime."

I ignored his spy remark. "What would you do if you did come to power?"

"We need to return to the Cossack way of life. We need to establish self-rule down here and have a *voluntary* union with Moscow, just as we once did. We need to elect our atamans. We need to enforce a draft for the Don Cossack Army." He halted abruptly. "May I invite you home?" he asked, saying "invite" in a weirdly aggressive way.

"Oh, I was actually about to order us something to eat here."

"Here? *Here?*" He heaved an exasperated sigh. "Look, the city tells us this complex, this café and all, is the new 'center' of town. I refuse to recognize it. It was built by bandits. I'd prefer to invite you to my *home*. You shouldn't spend your money here. You'd just be giving it to bandits."

I ended up accepting his invitation. Yana and I agreed to meet later, and she left us to run errands.

The ataman and I set off down a long lane umbrageous with poplars and ash and bisected by a paved walkway. He resumed his diatribe against the regime and the Caucasians we encountered on every corner. I found him as wearying as he was provocative. We turned down a side street and entered a neighborhood of weathered hovels sunk to their windowsills in dark earth, surrounded by rotting fences and overhung by a profusion of willows and firs. His house was, he said, like all the rest here, a *kuren'* (from the verb *kurit'*, "to smoke," from the smoke emitted by the wood-burning stoves used in the old days). It was cellar-like, filled with Soviet-era furniture and dusty knickknacks, and gloomily wallpapered in ochre, but still, all in all, homey.

We sat down in the kitchen, which was illuminated by weak light filtering in through the ground-level window. His eighty-year-old mother, spry and smiling, offered us tea. He took out sheaves of black-and-white photos that looked quite old but nevertheless were shot in the eighties. Many showed Yana speaking at a demonstration against Chernobyl in 1986. She was, he said, a gifted child, a wunderkind who always cared about society.

"So," I asked, suspecting I knew the answer, "what would you do if you came to power in Moscow?"

"You know *Lobnoye Mesto* [the Forehead Place] on Red Square?"

"Yes."

"It's called *Lobnoye* because the cut-off head of the decapitated struck the stone *forehead* first!" He pounded the table. "Ha! I'd gather all the thieving former Soviet bastard leaders on Red Square and hold a nationally televised vote. By raised hands, just like in Cossack times, the people would vote for sparing them or executing them! And not with any sissy French guillotine! I'd use an *ax,* whish-whop, off go their heads, bouncing onto *Lobnoye Mesto,* right on Red Square! Mass executions, mass beheadings, that's what I'm for!"

I sat back. Whatever Russia needed, it wasn't this. Yet a great many Russians might agree with him.

"He doesn't like the way I talk, Mama!" he declared. Mama hobbled over from the stove and regarded me with warm eyes; the gory words hadn't fazed her. The ataman continued. "You don't like all this talk of killing, eh? I'm for killing thieves and crooks, not the common man."

"And how would you determine guilt?"

"Easy! I'd say to them, 'Where'd you get the cash to buy that Mercedes? Prove you earned it legally, or off with your head!'" Again he slammed down his fist. My face must have registered displeasure. "Oh, don't be so squeamish. What we need here is *order.* My aim is *order.*"

So often talk of politics among poor Russians—one might just as well call them "the masses"—turns to killing. Since the rise of Moscow revenge has been a recurrent theme in Russian history, with serfs slitting their masters' throats in rebellions, tsars staging mass executions of insurgents, revolutionaries plotting to assassinate (and once succeeding) the tsars. Finally the Bolsheviks came to power and eliminated entire strata of society—vengeance dictated by ideological agenda. Somehow, in post-Soviet Russia (Chechnya excepted) less blood has been shed than one might have expected. These days more educated Russians are generally thankful for this, believing, as the folk adage says, that *khudoy mir luchshe dobroy voiny* (a bad peace is better than a good war). But I wondered if an incendiary leader such as this ataman might still be able to incite the "masses," people in outback towns like Novocherkassk, to revert to old ways.

He furrowed his brow and leaned over the table. "What's your nationality?"

"American."

"But what's your *blood?*"

"I was born in America and have an American passport. So I'm American."

"Don't say you're American. It's the same as saying you're a *mutt,* a *nobody.* Don't say you're a nobody."

"I don't agree at all. What counts, or what should count, is not blood but upbringing, education, and shared ideals. We've passed out of the tribal age, at least I hope, haven't we?"

"Oh, come on! What is your *blood?* Where does your *blood* call for you to be buried?"

"Well, I'm of Italian and Anglo-Canadian 'blood.'"

"And your *blood,* your burial?"

"My 'blood' doesn't call for me to be buried anywhere, and it doesn't determine who I am. Blood and race—"

"Thinking like that leads to racial impurity. It takes four generations for white genes to be reestablished after mixing blood, you know. *Four* generations."

"That's absurd. At least ideally, being American means we can become what we want through education. Reality is another thing, but race and blood *should* have nothing to do with it."

"I've told you: being an American means nothing at all. What counts is your *blood.* If you don't understand that, you don't understand anything."

Mama spoke up, apparently hoping to change the subject. "Oh, people say no one loves us Russians. In fact, in the Baltics and Eastern Europe, I hear they hate us. I wonder why."

"Because we're the most principled people on earth!" the ataman thundered. "That's why!"

After this exchange there was little left to say. He had expressed the most backward Cossack views imaginable, views harsher than anything the Bolsheviks espoused. We drank the rest of our tea in silence.

THE NEXT EVENING Yana and I took a tram out to see the Firsovs, an educated (and moderate) Cossack family she had introduced me to the last time I was in Novocherkassk. Irina Firsov was the genial director of the five-member Cossack musical ensemble called Rodnik ("the Source") in which Yana sang. On a snowy evening in 2004, in the sepia glow of low-wattage bulbs, I had sat with Irina, her husband, Vladimir (a lecturer in engineering at a local college), and four other Rodnik cohorts around a kitchen table covered with sausage, cheese, salted cucumbers, mushrooms, and, of course, bottles of vodka. Then as now, I sought from them answers about what it meant to be Cossack.

Vladimir, a large man in his fifties with a defiant high shock of white hair, poured us all hundred-gram shots of vodka and asked everyone to stand. We did, and raised our glasses. The ensemble welcomed me with a song as deafening as it was spirited—and to which one could imagine men coiffed in dark sheepskin *papakhi* hurling aside tables and performing the famous, tendon-tearing Cossack squat-and-kick dance called the Kazachok. After finishing they shouted, *"Na zdorov'ye! Na slavu!"* (To health! To glory!), and we gulped down our vodka.

Seated again, I mentioned that I had read much about the Cossacks' prowess as the tsar's military caste. During my years as a graduate student in Russian history, in the mid-1980s, I had learned the conventional theory of the Cossacks' origins: that they were serfs who escaped bondage in Russia during the Middle Ages, fled south, and established themselves in a remote frontier zone that the Kremlin allowed them to occupy as long as they functioned as a sort of military caste that kept the Turks and other Muslim peoples at bay. This is a view still widely held in Russia. Today Cossack academies, funded by the state, teach cadets not to work for the rebirth of the *Oblast' Voiska Donskogo* but to serve Russia with honor as members of this military caste.

My remark sparked a voluble reaction from my hosts. "We are *not* a caste," said Yana.

"We accepted the runaway-serf theory to please Russia, the imperial power," Vladimir added. "Look, you don't call a Chukchi 'reindeer herder' because that's his occupation; he's a Chukchi first. The same with us and soldiering. We're a *people*, not a profession." He produced a photocopied page from a tsarist-era encyclopedia that showed Cossacks listed as second (after Russians) among the Slavic peoples of Russia, and then another copied document showing that Cossacks wrote *"Kazak"* (*Cossack* in Russian) under the heading "ethnic group" on government forms in the first years after the 1917 revolution. "Democracy was the law of our land," Vladimir said. "This was *real* democracy, unlike in America, where your electoral college chooses the leader. The Cossack *krug* had legislative power: we voted by raising our hands and shouting *lyubo!* [it pleases us] or *nelyubo!* [it does not please us] for our three officials: the ataman, the scribe, and the treasurer. The greatest disgrace in our eyes was to be a *kholop*"—a serf or slave.

Irina said, "Cossacks *never* bowed or curtsied when greeting others; they only nodded their head. We *never* knew slavery."

They stood up and raised their glasses, which Vladimir had just refilled, and belted out another song. The rousing opening lyrics went, "Cossacks, a military people, who couldn't help loving you!" More songs of defiant pride followed. A few hours and bottles of vodka later, Yana proposed a valedictory toast ("To a *vol'ny* Don and a free Russia!"), and we drank our umpteenth vodka to the dregs.

Now it was summer, and all was awash in the lambent light of endless evening. We jumped off the tram and took a battered *marshrutka* (a minivan outfitted with benches and used as a shared taxi) down potholed roads, through slanting columns of amber sun falling on umber houses, *izbas* on which elaborately carved bright blue wooden frames encased glinting panes of glass, and red gutters ran along the edges of bare steel roofs. The aspens and maples and rosebushes and honeysuckle and peonies overgrew the walkways and yards. Here in Novocherkassk reigned the sleepy spirit of Goncharov's fainéant hero, Oblomov, the dreamy ambience of a Turgenev novel.

The *marshrutka* bounced on and on, and we started dozing off. Just before the Church of Saint Michael, the green union domes and gold crosses of which peeked above densely packed poplars, we got out. The

Firsovs' yard around the edges abounded with blossoms violet and pink; plots of cucumbers and tomatoes occupied the middle. Vladimir and Irina welcomed us in, looking as fit as ever, wearing homey jeans and T-shirts—no pretense here.

In the kitchen, streaked with beams of sunlight angling through the overhanging trees, they had set a table with mushrooms, eggplant fried in garlic, cucumbers, and vodka and cognac. We drank a toast to our meeting, exchanged a few pleasantries, and talked about how much the mood in Russia had worsened since 2004. Extremist nationalists, including skinheads and fascists, now outnumbered Cossacks. I asked Vladimir why.

"Lenin called [tsarist] Russia 'the prison of nations.' He taught us that Russians were oppressing the minority peoples in the tsarist empire. Stalin continued the same line, setting up 'ethnic republics' and favoring the minorities at the Russians' expense. As a result, all the minority peoples now have their own republics and autonomous regions; Tatarstan, for example, doesn't pay taxes to Moscow to this day. We had no ethnic conflicts during the Soviet era and we all felt like brothers. But think of it. The Tatars get a republic, the Yakuts get a republic, the Ingush and the Chechens get a republic, and the Russians? Russians are stuck with the label 'subject' of the Russian Federation. *Subjects!* They find this humiliating. A genocide is happening to us Russians. We're dying out, losing a million a year. Now Russians are coming to understand that they need to assert their identity. We're undergoing a national revival. I admit, to speak of 'Russian nationalism' sounds dangerous and chauvinistic, even jingoistic, to our ears, nowadays. But let's not confuse nationalism with extremism or chauvinism. It's natural that there should be a few excesses, at least in the beginning, especially among the young."

"So what do you think of the slogan that's so popular now among nationalist groups, 'Russia for the Russians'?"

"It's a dead-end slogan. 'Russian' is just an adjective meaning 'Russian speaker,' the adjective of *Rus*. It just means a Russian speaker living here in Russia. There were once *Velikorussy, Malorussy, Belorussy*"—historical names for Great Russians, Lesser Russians (present-day Ukrainians), and White (or Belo-) Russians, the three peoples who emerged from speakers of Old Russian in the thirteenth century. "The point is, we Russians aren't a separate nation. Russian encompasses all the Russian speakers in our historic domain, the domain of the Russian Empire. But all the minorities feel strongly that they aren't Russian. That by exclusion helps define us."

Today Russians account for 79 percent of the country's population. He might have added that, generally, Russians profess Russian Orthodoxy and consider religion a pillar of their national identity—another element that sets them apart from the growing numbers of Muslim migrants.

"So," he said, "nationalism doesn't really have a blood basis. It's a reaction. Who nowadays, by the way, are the biggest racists? The western Ukrainians. When we hear their slogan, 'We will drown the Jews in Russian blood,' what are we supposed to think? The militancy of the minorities provokes a reaction among once passive Russians. But we have to *save* our people, not kill anyone."

We drank to that. Vladimir then summed up his thoughts in a Russocentric way that, if it ignored the conflicts in the Northern Caucasus, would probably suit most of his compatriots.

"The very minorities who are so militant now once served the tsars. Chechens were in the army. Tsar Boris Gudonov was a Tatar. Levitan, our great 'Russian' landscape painter, was Jewish. In contrast to all other empires, the Russian Empire was a voluntary one. All its peoples united to serve the tsar, and then Soviet power. After the Soviet collapse, well, then the ethnic battles erupted. But we Russians have not been able to express an identity because we've needed to unite all the other minorities."

Through the years I've come to hold my own ideas about what being Russian means, apart from language and religion. "Russian" means *shirota dushi* ("breadth of soul," magnanimity); loyalty among friends; fortitude and courage. It means gimlet-eyed cynicism and a distrust, even hatred, of the authorities that often verges on anarchism. It means carpe diem, the liberating, glass-smashing Kazachok. It also signifies a civilizational legacy embracing writers as diverse as Tolstoy and Nabokov, Pushkin and Mayakovsky, Chekhov and Pelevin, and many more musicians and artists than I could name here. "Russian," in short, is in part a state of mind, a matter of cultural patrimony that is neither East nor West but blends both and is unique. Russia belongs not to Europe, not to Asia, but to itself. It is a separate world, with worldly dimensions as well as pretenses—most notably, the messianic Russian "mission" deriving from Moscow's medieval-era vision of itself as the Third Rome (and a fourth there shall never be), with Russians as God's final Chosen

Nation. This vision outlasted the fall of the Russian Empire and found embodiment in Communism, with its universal aspirations, but now has slipped quietly into the history books.

We ate and drank, and night drew on. Vladimir wrapped up our talk by telling me, "President Bush has become a laughingstock, and he's discredited the American message of free markets and democracy, telling us that Russia needs the same sort of democracy the United States gave to Iraq. In fact, as you know, America stole democracy from the Cossacks. Americans may not know this, but we never forget it."

ON SATURDAY NIGHT Yana and I went to Café Isador, her favorite nightspot, a smoky, dim rathskeller with a dance floor. We took seats in a wooden booth and ordered champagne to celebrate our evening out. We had not had a chance to talk since my arrival. She began opening up, telling me about her wunderkind years as a chess master. But when she decided not to go to college, her father, disappointed, kicked her out. She then spent a few years studying at an astrology institute, and did odd jobs. She moved to Sochi but found nothing for herself there, and soon ended up back in Novocherkassk, singing Cossack folk songs.

As we drank our champagne, she lowered her head and grew morose. "Nothing has gone right in my life. I recently lost twenty thousand rubles, and then fifty thousand, all my savings, in the slot machines. All doors ahead in this town are closed. I can't see a future for myself here or anywhere. Just the other day, I was partying with people I thought I could trust, and they stole my cell phone! Now I have no more money for a phone."

Around us the drinking went on fast and furious, with much toasting and shouting and smoking. We downed glass after glass of champagne. The dark wood booths made us feel intimate, and we poured our hearts out to each other.

The MC announced a contest: a small prize would go to the girl who gathered the most men's clothing from members of the audience. Three girls volunteered and raced from table to table, pulling sleeves and trousers off laughing male patrons. One giddy young woman got to me and, huffing vodka fumes in my face and giggling, furiously unbuttoned my shirt, stripped it from my back, and tossed it on her pile.

But our talk went on. I told Yana about my mother's recent death. We toasted, without clinking, honoring the passing away of loved ones in our families. Her own mother had left her family for another man, and now Yana had nothing more to do with her. All at once, in that smoky, hot rathskeller, life seemed hopeless and drink the only escape.

The contest ended and I retrieved my shirt. Men and women, drunken and swearing, one step away from a bar-wide brawl, rushed lurching out onto the floor and danced to Russian *popsa* (pop music).

"You know," Yana said, "I've been to Germany. I've seen that it *is* possible to live differently. But I've decided there's no way to get ahead in my country; all doors are closed before me. So this year I won't waste time: I'm going to kill myself."

I pulled Yana to her feet, hugged her, and led her out to join the dancers.

2

The following morning broke torrid and sunny. Yana came to my hotel to see me off, dressed in loose beige shorts and a gauze top, looking summery and carefree, as though our soulful talk of the night before had never happened. This didn't surprise me. In Russia, alcohol-induced confessions rarely lead to prolonged melodrama, for life is tough and life is grief, all have to do their share, and one gets on with things. (Still, I remembered her words about suicide and resolved to check up on her later in the year.) We said our goodbyes and she hailed me a gypsy cab—a white Devyatka in surprisingly fine repair—and instructed the young female driver to take me to Rostov-on-Don, my next stop, some fifty miles to the southwest, by the Sea of Azov.

The driver turned out to be, despite the 90-plus-degree heat, fresh and svelte. In her twenties, she wore sleek black wraparound sunglasses, electric blue shorts, and a white halter top that hugged the muscles on her tanned torso; her dark hair was bobbed in a bouncy pageboy. Her nose was pointed and her cheekbones high—vestiges of Tatar ancestry. Her polished look befitted the bravura she displayed in piloting her Devyatka down streets on which women drivers usually evoke disdainful stares from men. We picked up the road leading out of town. Soon we were jolting through glaring dust clouds on a two-lane highway under construction, competing for the hemmed-in tarmac with trucks rumbling along belching fumes and sometimes stalling, with steam seeping out from under their hoods.

The Don River slid by beneath a bridge, meandering green, wide, and reedy; Novocherkassk was behind us. But the traffic didn't let up. My driver maneuvered between vehicles and shot down the shoulder; when others did the same and the shoulder grew crowded, she swung the wheel to the right and we crashed through fields of sunflowers, at times tipping precariously on the uneven embankment as huge yellow blossoms broke free and bounced off our windshield.

"You're a gutsy driver," I said, dusting off the petals showering me through the open side window. She smiled. "What's your name?"

"Inna. Yours?"

I told her, and explained who I was.

"You moved from the States to *Russia?*" she replied. "We do the *opposite.*"

I told her about my passion for Russia, my marriage to a Russian, and whatever other exonerating aspects of my biography I could muster in my defense.

She shook her head incredulously. "Well, anyway, I'd like to visit your country to make some money, but that's about it. I wouldn't emigrate. I have my family in Rostov, and I wouldn't leave them, even though I'm a doctor by profession and could use some extra training at a good American medical school."

"So why not work as a doctor instead of driving a cab?"

"Because you have to pay a bribe to get a decent job, and even that would only pay me two hundred and fifty a month. I make more driving this car, and I'm my own boss."

"You're not married, I take it?"

"Marriage is tough here now. So many men just want to leech off their wives. The first question they ask a girl is how much she makes. They just want to sit around and drink and live off her. That's not for me."

Even deep in the provinces the allure of emigration to the West had faded, at least compared to what it had been in the past. In recent years I had met so many young women who had mastered their piece of Russia, once so brutally a man's land, found a way to make a decent living, and chosen to stay single. With their looks, grooming, acumen, and education, they almost seemed like members of a different race, and one far superior to that of the often slack-bellied boozing men they lived among. If Russia's perennial straits were their lot, depression and complaints were foreign to them; they were often as shrewd—even cunning—as they were alluring. From this brief drive I sensed that Inna belonged to their number.

An hour later we were passing by nine-story cement apartment blocks and overgrown courtyards, stark and still in the midday sun. Rostov-on-Don. I opened the window; the breezeless air hung hot and humid, imbued with marshy scents from the Don. Bottlenecks began straight away. Again Inna displayed her prowess at the wheel, forcing her way through truckers and *marshrutki,* showing no mercy until she screeched to a stop by my hotel.

She leaned back and smiled, as if to say, "How did you like *that!*"

I gave her my cell phone number and asked her to call if she had a free evening. But she never did.

> *Vskolykhnulsya, vzvolnovalsya*
> *Pravoslavny tikhi Don*
> *I poslushno otozvalsya*
> *Na prizyv svobody on*

> The Don rippled and stirred,
> Quiet-flowing and Russian Orthodox,
> Obediently answering
> Freedom's call—Hymn of the Rostov Oblast

Ancient Greeks from Miletus, in Asia Minor, first settled the area north of the Sea of Azov, wary of the marauding Scythian nomads inhabiting the steppes beyond. Genghis Khan's troops conquered the region in the thirteenth century; and the Mongols, after converting to Islam, introduced Arabic as the official language. As their empire broke up into khanates, the coasts of the Black Sea and the Azov fell under the sway of the Ottoman Turks, who raised a great fortress here. But the Cossacks, eager to help Russia expand southward, daringly seized the fortress in 1637 from the khanate of Crimea (an ally of the Ottomans) and presented it to Tsar Michael as a gift. The tsar declined to accept, and returned the fortress to the sultan, fearing that Russia was ill prepared to take on the still considerable military might of the Sublime Port. So, the Turks proceeded with settlement, founding the town of Temernika, Rostov's predecessor, a port and trading center. But a century later, Russia was strengthening, the Ottoman Empire past its apogee. In the 1770s, Catherine the Great launched a successful invasion of the northern shores of the Black Sea. Temernika's Russian conquerors christened it "Rostov-na-Donu" (Rostov-on-Don) in honor of its hallowed Orthodox namesake city in the north. From then on, Rostov-on-Don served as a staging post for Russian advances east into the Caucasus, and so flourished during the empire's final hundred years. Stalin's construction of the Volga-Don Canal assured it of a vital economy in the Soviet decades.

Living on the fringe of the Muslim world in a town once Islamic but now Christian, a good number of Rostovans, understandably, wear their Orthodox faith on their sleeves. Soon after my arrival, Dmitry Rubanov, who handles Don Cossack relations with the municipal government, told me, "We Cossacks are the sand in a kettle of gunpowder, meaning we stabilize the volatile ethnic situation in the Rostov Oblast. But we're 'controversial' and can't be deployed too much." Controversial? I asked. "Let's just say that the Muslims here call us the White Wahhabis."

He added that a few weeks before, he had helped lead busloads of Cossacks into Ukraine to the Crimea (which is predominantly ethnic Russian), where they staged protests and thwarted the Ukrainian government's plans to welcome NATO troops for joint military exercises. (Ukraine's aspirations to join NATO accord perfectly with Russian fears of encirclement and the unfolding of a new Great Game against them.) The Cossacks are often as hostile to "infidel Catholic Westerners" (and especially Americans) as they are to Muslims.

Cossack currents of dissent have always flowed strong here, if, at times, underground. Alexander Solzhenitsyn, the dissident nationalist writer, fervent Orthodox Christian, and Nobel Prize winner, was born to Cossack parents in nearby Kislovodsk and studied at Rostov's university. Other local dissidents have received much less publicity in the West, probably because their cause, the reestablishment of the *Oblast' Voiska Donskogo*, has failed to resonate with Western reporters favoring stories about market reforms, natural resources, and the struggles of minority peoples such as the Chechens.

One of the most prominent Cossack firebrands in Rostov-on-Don today is Mikhail Bespalov. We had met back in 2004. Balding, stocky, and in his thirties, Bespalov is a filmmaker and writer who had risked his life in performing his Cossack duty to Russia, first as a commander defending the Supreme Soviet from the Communist coup attempt in 1991, and later as an officer in the Trans-Dniester and Abkhazia conflicts, fighting in support of Russian minorities in those regions that were under assault by ethnic majorities eager to establish sovereignty in their homelands. (The Russians, partly thanks to Cossack intervention, prevailed in both cases, at least unofficially.) Bespalov traces his roots to a seventeenth-century ataman from the Zaparozhian Cossacks immortalized by Gogol in the novel *Taras Bulba*.

Bespalov has a steely smile, literally: he lost his front teeth in the Trans-Dniester war and replaced them with a metallic bridge. "If you don't recognize the Cossacks as a people, then we have nothing to discuss," he told me in lieu of more polite greetings when we met for a talk at the lobby bar of my hotel in 2004. Dressed in a camouflage jacket and heavy boots, he explained what is generally considered the most radical theory about the Cossacks' origin: they were a warrior people of Scythian stock, referred to in ancient Greek inscriptions as the Kossaraka; runaway Russian serfs came later, bringing Christianity and the Old Russian language. By this account, Cossacks are only incidentally Russophone and Orthodox Christian, a postulate that would jibe with demands for a free *Oblast' Voiska Donskogo* and run counter to President Putin's authoritarian reforms, the key mission of which is strengthening the unitary Russian state.

"The Cossacks were never serfs," Bespalov said, "so we couldn't be driven back into slavery the way the Russians were"—an allusion to the abolition of serfdom in 1861 and the "reenslavement" following the 1917 revolution. "The Bolsheviks knew they could only give the Cossacks their independence or destroy us to the last man." They of course chose to do the latter, with Lenin's issuance of the 1919 genocidal order.

In 1991 Bespalov had organized the Cossacks' storming of the Communist Party headquarters in Rostov-on-Don, with the aim of seizing documents that would incriminate the outgoing regime in the slaughter of his people. "The civil war [of 1918–21, which pitted Reds against Whites] has never ended here. In 1991 we put tremendous pressure on the authorities"—those in Moscow, that is, who viewed then as now the issue of Cossack statehood as long since resolved in the Kremlin's favor. "The One hundred and first Don Division came over to our side. The deputies of our Rostov Oblast soviet voted to reestablish the Cossack Republic, but it was never implemented."

During our talk then, Bespalov never dwelled on his own role in these conflicts; always, he was just doing his duty, both to Russia and to his Cossack brethren. He lamented the machinations of the Russian secret services, which, he said, had hounded the Cossack movement "out of the sphere of the visible," but he spoke like a disciplined and capable dissident who, working within the system rather than galloping off wildly like his ancestors in pursuit of unbounded liberty, had ambitions for the future, not complaints about the past. "There could have been another Chechnya here, so maybe [the Cossack movement's] faltering saved people from . . . from major disruptions. If the *Oblast'* is restored, it will be because people here want it." This seemed reasonable, and I felt no discomfort in believing him when he told me, smiling steel, "One day we'll have our republic here."

But these days, Bespalov's views, guts, and filmmaking talent make him a threat to the regime; and with the crackdown on dissent of the past few years I wondered how he was getting along. After settling into my hotel room, I invited him for a talk in the lobby bar. He showed up in a crisp white shirt and dark trousers, the attire of a businessman, but he looked so thin that at first I didn't recognize him.

As ever, he wasted little time with greetings. We took seats in the back so that no one could overhear us.

Outside the window, Caucasians, mostly men, were streaming by on the street, recognizable by their swarthy pigmentation and bristly black hair.

"We Russians are their golden goose," Bespalov remarked, glancing at them. "They come here and engage in prostitution, pimping, gambling, and *mafiya* extortion, and drain us of cash. Thirty percent of teachers in the eastern part of our oblast don't even speak Russian." I had no way of verifying this statistic, but documents tell us that at the beginning of the twentieth century, 95 percent of the *Oblast' Voiska Donskogo*'s population of 3.5 million was Slavic, of which Cossacks numbered 1,508,170. For the past decade and a half, the war in Chechnya and worsening poverty have been fueling the mass displacement of Caucasians, which has destabilized the entire Northern Caucasus (with its population of 23 million) and sharpened Muslim-Christian animosity in the areas to which they move.

His thinness looked more haggard than hale, and his skin was strangely smooth. He had an uneasy, even tormented look in his eyes.

"How's your health?" I asked.

"I've got allergies brought on by stress," he said, scratching his forearms.

"What kind of stress?"

"The authorities. They've fenced in the Cossacks more and more. They're driving us to survival level, so we think only about how to put food on the table. They're trying to force us to assimilate and disappear as a people. Our atamans do little more than serve the state and their own private interests."

"What have they done to you, specifically?"

"They've forbidden my film"—*Otechestvo Donskoye Sokhranyaya,* or "Preserving the Don Fatherland," about Cossack history—"from being shown on television. And they canceled funding for the second part."

"Could you find another sponsor?"

"How? No one *dares* defy the state now, with Putin in charge. Our system, our country, is corrupt and lawless. So many Cossacks are either embittered and angry or totally despairing; even the small amounts the state allots them for dances and folk shows are pilfered. Nothing good can come from anything organized through the government. We need simple accountability, for people to be punished for stealing, but we don't have it. It's impossible to predict anything here. There's no stability. People are getting angrier and angrier. One spark and Russia will explode and disintegrate along ethnic lines. There will be chaos here."

The growing strength of extreme Russian nationalist movements seemed to support his assertion.

"This corruption," he went on to say, "stems directly from our system and the ruler at the top. A system of total corruption can be broken only from the top down. People here are afraid, but they would unite around a force, if there were one. Organization is everything. But how can you organize a movement if your every step is watched and you fear starvation? A financially independent person is a *free* person. People here are not financially free. Nothing is thriving in production and construction. Our rich steal and send their money abroad, knowing that it could be seized here at any moment. We have no law here except thieves' law."

"That sounds as bad as it was during Soviet days."

"Listen, things were *better* for dissidents then. Yes, they could arrest you and throw you in jail. But they'd never cut off your means of livelihood. Now the state uses the most terrifying weapon of all—the power to get you fired and cut off your income—to control you. How can we resist? We have wives and families to support! And they can get your wife fired as well. One phone call to a company director saying they 'recommend' you be fired, and he fires you. He'd never risk the tax raids and the unofficial harassment that could result from refusing. In Soviet days, or at least after Stalin died, the state would arrest you but leave your family alone. Anyone who refuses to live by *blat*"—connections to people in power—"who won't bribe and connive, can't get by now. My brother (God rest his soul!) just drank himself to death, and he was only in his early thirties. He was a qualified engineer who refused to play the game. Drink was his only escape." He paused. "Our women no longer bear children. We live in anxiety, in fear of losing our jobs, hounded."

By "we" I understood he was talking about himself mostly, and other Cossacks. Things now, however, were manifestly *not* worse than during Soviet times: arrest and forced labor were hardly preferable to dismissal from one's job. But then, espousing a more nuanced perspective on repression would hardly help him attain his goal of a Cossack republic. The Yeltsin era of liberties, flawed as they were, had clearly come to a close.

"Why aren't people resisting?" I asked.

"Where would we get the means? You can speak your mind and some people do, providing there're no *Chekisty* [secret service agents] around. But who else cares? No one reads the newspapers or believes anyone these days."

"So what is to be done?"

"We need a force to come from the outside, to help us."

"What sort of force?"

"My only hope is that the United States might step in on our behalf, on the basis of Public Law Eighty-six Ninety, 'Concerning Captive Nations.'"

Eisenhower signed this legislation in 1959. Public Law 86-90 requires the U.S. president to declare solidarity, every third week in July, with the peoples "imprisoned" in the Soviet Bloc, and states, "Those submerged nations look to the United States, as the citadel of human freedom, for leadership in bringing about their liberation and independence and in restoring to them the enjoyment of their Christian, Jewish, Moslem, Buddhist, or other religious freedoms, and of their individual liberties." It is a ceremonial cold war relic of no practical import, especially given that the Soviet Union no longer exists, Communism is dead, and many of the "captive nations" now belong to NATO or the EU or both. Moreover, aiding a secessionist group in Russia in its struggle against a nuclear-armed, resurgent Kremlin is the last thing the United States, bogged down in Iraq, would consider doing.

"But that's a cold war law. What makes you think any American president today, in his right mind, would—"

"Look, we need help from the *outside*. Sooner or later, otherwise, a huge crisis will erupt here: violence, chaos, you name it. Right now, I'm a smalltime trader, doing business just to pay expenses and stay alive. But if I could, I'd start a newspaper and a radio station, and in a year I'd have built an organization. For that I need help from the outside. Always in Russia revolts have been organized from the *outside*. Think of it: Razin and Bulavin were Cossacks who stirred up the Russian peasantry. On their own, the peasants, who depended on their landowners, would never have done anything to help themselves." *Razin and Bulavin again!* I thought. *Mutiny and bloodshed!* "Razin got his funds from robbing Persia, for instance. At the moment, our people out in the countryside live untouched by the state. But not for long. A census was carried out recently—it must be for tax purposes. If the state starts taxing them, they'll rise up."

Will they? If there was a whiff of revolt in the air, I had not sensed it. Not yet.

We pledged to keep in touch and said goodbye. I sympathized with Bespalov. I admired his devotion to his people, and I did not doubt that the prevailing winds now blew against him in every way, as he insisted, but I shuddered to think of what sort of state he would establish if he took pro–Slavic Cossack ideology and Orthodoxy as its guiding principles. The *Oblast' Voiska Donskogo* may be close to majority Muslim now, and the Cossacks are greatly outnumbered—hardly suitable grounds for a Christian restoration. A desire for vengeance had to lurk in such aspirations. Moreover, his hope that the United States might intervene on the Cossacks' behalf was as divorced from reality as was President Bush's National Security Strategy of 2006 (issued several months earlier), which announced America's "ultimate goal of ending tyranny in our world." At Bespalov's remove, Bush's Strategy must have offered (delusional) succor, and I felt as sorry for him as I was ashamed of my president for giving false hopes to earnest advocates of democracy. In any case, U.S. assistance would delegitimize his efforts as soon as it became known, and make him look like a traitorous American pawn.

The corruption and repression Bespalov described do, of course, exist in Russia (and affect many more people than just dissidents), but the clever and determined do manage to circumvent them and succeed. I decided to ask Katya (a friend of a friend of mine in Moscow), whom I was to meet next, what she thought about the *Oblast'* and Cossack affairs. She had Cossack blood but was by no means suffering. She had, rather, worked hard (and honestly) to rise from poverty into the upper reaches of Rostov's middle class. She soon drove up to the hotel in her shiny new Japanese car and honked. I opened the door to find a tanned, shapely beauty in her twenties answering a call on a nine-hundred-dollar cell phone. Her garrulous six-year-old son in the back seat greeted me with a manly handshake.

"I'm sorry," she said, switching off the phone and patting the front seat for me to get in. "Let's go to a café for a chat."

She smelled deliciously of perfume, and her bracelets tinkled as she turned the wheel. As we drove down Rostov's bumpy back alleys to avoid the traffic jams on Bol'shaya Sadovaya Street, she told me her story. A native of Rostov (her great-grandmother was a Cossack), Katya had studied here and earned an economist's degree. She got her position as vice director of sales in a large local company not through *blat* or bribes but by landing a job that left her well positioned for promotion.

"People sometimes come into my office and see I'm a young pretty girl and don't take me seriously. But I prove myself to them. I never complain. I have great relations with everyone at work. I even have a Muslim boss, but we have no problems working together." She loved Rostov and had no desire to move to Moscow or anywhere else.

At Teatral'ny Park we left the car and found seats at a trendy outdoor café of the type that has popped up in cities all over Russia in the past few years.

Over mineral water and tea, I told her about my meetings with Bespalov and the ataman, though without mentioning names.

"Russians don't always see things in the best light," she said, shrugging. "They expect the worst. This pessimism is our national trait. But there have been worse times here—wartimes, times when there was nothing to eat, for example. So, if a healthy person wants to earn his living here, I see no reason why he can't."

"What if the government is making things hard because of someone's political views?"

"Things in our past have been much, much worse than they are today. Basically, no matter how bad people say things are now, I know *I* can always earn money and fend for *myself*. I don't concern myself with politics. I refuse to be pessimistic, but I do all I can to support myself and my son. Now I want a daughter. Giving life to another is a sacred joy." She was single, for now, and in no rush to marry.

A young boy walked up to our table and stuck out his hand, saying, "I'm hungry. Give me money to eat." His face was smeared with dirt, and his clothes were ragged, but he was too plump-cheeked to be taken seriously as a beggar. Katya refused him, as did I. He moved on to the next table.

Katya smiled. "He should be working, not begging. As a fifth-grader I washed floors in stores to earn pocket money. I always *worked* so as not to burden my family. If you really want to, you can always find work and earn your living."

"What do you think of Putin?" I asked.

"I respect him greatly. Things are improving with him in charge. There's at least less open corruption. People are afraid to take bribes." When I said I had heard the opposite, and brought up the recent cancellation of the last live political talk show, she shrugged again. "President Putin is a worthy head of state. For me things are better, and that's what I can say. I know how things are for *me*."

That was her testimony, delivered at ease, seated in a café filled with cheery diners and sippers of cappuccino. Her words were true, for her, no doubt. But happy people do not a revolution make.

3

Across a lumpy macadam diffusing heat absorbed from the taxing midmorning sun hurried perspiring passengers dragging checkered plastic suitcases and frayed nylon bags with Adidas and Puma labels (counterfeit, to be sure) toward their destination and mine: Rostov-on-Don's bus station. This was an unremarkable assemblage of sheet steel and glass panels that boasted, notably, novelties including orderly platforms with clearly lettered signs and a PA system announcing (intelligibly) bus numbers and arrivals. The passengers were mostly Caucasians, balding men, hirsute and short, dressed in synthetic dungarees and old tracksuits, often shod in pointy-toed fake designer shoes; many of the women, also hairy, were kohl-eyed, and their full-lipped mouths glinted with gold.

Caucasians brook categorization neither as Asians nor as Europeans. They come from the in-betwixt lands the ancient Greeks called *Kaukasos*, a formidable range of mountains that arose in the late Oligocene Epoch, some twenty-five million years ago, to form a high-altitude bridge from the Caspian to the Black Sea. The Greeks relegated these redoubts to the domains of myth, where Jason's Argonauts sought the Golden Fleece, and Prometheus, as punishment for giving mankind fire, was chained to a boulder to suffer the eternal predations of an eagle that devoured his liver.

In more recent times, Russians (preceded, as ever, by Cossack settlers) arrived to stay only in the nineteenth century, when, during the years 1801–10, they annexed Georgia, a Christian kingdom south of the Caucasus seeking the tsar's protection from aggressive neighboring Islamic states. This meant pacifying the fifty-odd Muslim peoples living in the Caucasus mountains—a bloody task that took decades (and, with fighting even now raging periodically in Chechnya, remains incomplete). In the nineteenth century, banishment to the Caucasus amounted to a death sentence. Today Russia's borders along the northern slopes of the Greater Caucasus embrace a mishmash of volatile ethnic republics. All in all, the Caucasian region is the most linguistically variegated on earth, the peoples of which, across the former Soviet Union, call to mind ebullient, if heavy-handed, hospitality, fierce codes of honor and blood feuds, and organized crime groups rivaling or exceeding Sicily's Cosa Nostra in reach and ruthlessness.

My next stop was to be the once grand resort town of Pyatigorsk, sitting on the Caucasus' northern hem, three hundred miles to the southeast of Rostov-on-Don. The Rostov-Pyatigorsk Bus 337, a decade-old but still serviceable Ikarus, careened around the lot and halted with a farting hiss by platform seventeen. The door swung open. Out hopped a potato-nosed man in his fifties—an bus company employee, judging by his blue trousers and white shirt. Passengers, bedraggled and sweating, hoisted their bags and began filing aboard. I joined them.

The bus is on time and looks decent, I mused pleasantly, *an augur for a smooth trip.* As soon as these words crossed my mind I hurried to repudiate them (as Russians do, so as not to jinx things) with the folksy apothegm *"Zagad ne byvayet bogat"* (One who predicts the future never gets rich), but I was too late. Just as I raised my foot to enter, a fat, gnarly-faced woman in blue seized my forearm and yanked me back onto the pavement.

"Just who do you think you are," she hollered, "you passengers, getting on the bus like this, without permission? Who told you to board! *Nu-ka,* get down at once! March! Down! Off there at once!"

A reverse exodus of bulky bags and sweaty backs ensued. But still she ranted on. "Who let you aboard, I ask you? You think we have no procedures here? What kind of herd of *beasts* are you?"

We might as well have been back in Soviet times. Such bile over nothing! I turned and peered into her short-lashed eyes, blue eyes set above a piggish snout, and shook my head at her gratuitous harangue. But, just as in Soviet times, no one resisted, no one objected. In fact, an older fellow, as he dismounted, even murmured words to the effect of "There, there, it'll be all right!"

She was still fuming. "Just who do they think they are!"

The potato-nosed man wrenching open the baggage compartment with a crowbar smiled. "Don't know, bunny rabbit, don't know! *Oy, oy, oy!*"

Once we were all down on the platform again, she ordered, "Form a line!" We did, and she readmitted us, checking our tickets, wheezing pulmonarily as she squinted at the computer-printed Cyrillic. "You just don't know what these passengers are capable of," she said.

"I do, bunny rabbit, I do," he said, slamming down the hood.

Once aboard, I settled into my seat in row two and surveyed the interior. The sun, filtering through red curtains, cast a hellish glow over threadbare black seats topped by soiled headrests. On the scratched glass partition by the driver's seat hung a densely worded placard entitled RULES FOR THE USE OF INTERCITY BUSES. In Russia, rules abound and they must be publicly posted, even if only to be flagrantly violated. Dangling above the rearview mirror was the usual holy triad of cheap plastic icons, the Virgin Mother and Child, Saint Nicolas the Miracle-Worker, and Christ. They stared down at us, their visages full of suffering. Just across the aisle sat a freshly perfumed Russian brunette in a candy-striped elastic dress, worn, as was immediately apparent, with a thong but without a bra, yet she attracted no untoward attention; this kind of dress in Russia is common, and men are used to it. Past my shoulders hustled soldiers carrying duffel bags and gallon-size plastic bottles of cheap beer (against the posted rules, but the harridan let them pass); following them came a contingent of brutes in tight polyester pants and shirts, their swarthy skulls shaved, their arms rippling with muscle, their fingernails black.

The driver jumped into his seat. He was, as they say, *staroy zakalki* (one of the old school), the salt of the Soviet earth—a hazel-eyed tow-headed man with noble features, a farmer's tan, and a reassuringly sober look. Last aboard was an old lady with gold teeth and witch-wild hair hawking Russian versions of *Men's Health* and *Glamour*.

"Gotta go! Climb on down, little bunny!" said the potato-nosed man, apparently the second mate. The old woman did, looking about in despair, her arms full of magazines.

We were soon hissing and clanking down a beat-up avenue colonnaded with shaggy maples toward a bridge over the Don, which was as reed-clogged as ever, its currents seeping toward the Azov like molten pewter under a painfully bright sky. As we rolled onto the steppes, I dozed off.

But not for long. Out in the feather-grass wilds somewhere north of Kushchevskaya, we slowed and approached a two-story GAI (highway patrol) tower, its batwing roof and narrow windows configured like a postmodern belfry on Dracula's castle. Out in front, a chubby young *gaishnik* looking anything but evil leveled his baton at our driver and pointed at the road's shoulder: *Halt!* The post marked the border of an administrative district, which meant a document check, at least in the turbulent Northern Caucasus.

Wherever and whenever such "checks" take place, they amount to little more than opportunities for officers to fleece the people they are charged to protect. They are as annoying (even dangerous, should one resist) as they are useless. In 2004 a van of armed Chechen guerrillas made it through well-policed Moscow to the Dubrovka Theater to seize eight hundred hostages; bandits of the same ilk had driven unhindered into Beslan to seize a school. (GAI officers pardon infractions, real or spurious, for a few rubles. To well-heeled terrorists they pose no threat at all.) Recently, President Putin's anti-corruption campaign had come into force, but this being Russia, the authorities were prosecuting not corrupt officials but citizens caught offering bribes.

We stopped. A wide-brimmed blue cap popped up at the head of the aisle. Inwardly I cringed, remembering that my hotel in Rostov had not placed a registration stamp in my passport. "You're registered in Moscow, so we have no right to register you here," the receptionist had told me. But being without one of many stamps in Russia invites harassment from the authorities. I should have insisted.

"Ready your documents for inspection!" ordered the baby-faced officer, his freckles orange on milky skin.

I handed him my passport.

He squinted at it and smiled slyly. "Come with me."

Away from the bus, by the GAI tower, he pointed out my incontrovertible violation, ignoring my explanation about the hotel's refusal to register me.

"Dzheffrey, Dzheffrey," he intoned, "this was your responsibility. You've broken the law. What are we going to do with you? How are we to resolve this issue?"

The driver had jumped down from the bus and was looking our way. My detention was delaying us.

"My papers are in order," I said, "as you see from the Moscow stamp in the passport, which is still valid."

"No, no! They stamped your *passport*. They should have stamped your *migration card*"—the wallet-size form foreigners must now carry stating their visa sponsor's name and other details. Naturally he dismissed my reasonable explanation on favor of his own (lucrative) concoction. He smiled and shook his head. "You're a violator."

"I'm sorry, but I have no control over which paper the authorities stamp." This I stated with a smile. Any gruffness on my part would only worsen things. "I really wish I could have persuaded them to stamp the card, you know? I'm as upset about it as you are."

"You're a violator nonetheless."

Bees buzzed over sunflowers behind him. The steppe swept away from the road in gentle swells, fertile and wonderful, a sea of verdure.

"Well, I can't release you without permission from my superiors. And they're a long way away. You understand. I would have to phone them."

"Please do."

His buttery cheeks and boyish eyes spoiled the air of menace he hoped to exude. He walked over to an ancient steel phone pegged to the post's wall. He made a show of dialing over and over and hanging up, glancing at me from the corner of his eye. Would I not offer him a hundred-ruble note and save us both this inconvenient charade? I thought, *No, I'll wait him out.* But then I noticed the bus driver again, standing arms akimbo across the road. I suffered an intimidating presentiment: I had thousands of miles of travel ahead and, surely, many checkpoints to cross.

"Well, I can't get through," he said with feigned fatigue, hanging up and pushing his cap back to reveal a freckled brow. "Come inside."

He swung open the door and led me down a steep steel staircase to a basement interrogation room with a desk and a chair in front of it, under a dangling bare bulb, just like in the movies. After I entered he shut the door. This was bad, possibly a prelude to a rough shakedown.

"Sit!"

I stayed afoot.

He scratched his stubble-free cheek. "So we aren't going to reach an agreement?"

What a relief! "I'll give you a hundred rubles," I answered.

"A *hundred* rubles?"

Had I insulted him by offering too little? Or was he one of Putin's anti-corruption *gaishniki?*

But he kept grinning boyishly. "Do you have a souvenir from the United States? Something, you know, *krutoye* [cool]?" All of a sudden he sounded like the kid he was.

"Oh, I'm sorry, I don't. I haven't been home in a long time."

"Really?" he exclaimed in a naively amazed tone. But before I could further parse his intentions, he pulled down his hat and frowned. "Okay, then just give me something *na pivo*"—for a beer.

A fifty-ruble note did the trick. He stood up, snatched the money with a grin, and handed me back my passport. *"Do svidaniya,"* he said.

I clambered up the stairs and hurried off to rejoin the bus.

SET AMID FIVE VOLCANIC HUMPS and sunflower-speckled steppes, with the mist-wreathed aeries of the Greater Caucasus walling off the southern horizon, Pyatigorsk ("five-mountain town," from the Turkic *besh tau*) spread ahead of us a fin-de-siècle menagerie of pastel-tinted stucco. Pyatigorsk started out in 1780 as Fort Konstantinogorskaya, a frontier outpost on the Podkumok River. Yet its mineral springs and exotic remoteness soon drew crowds seeking both a salubrious resort and the thrill of vacationing at the edge of empire. For nineteenth-century Russians, and then for free-spirited Soviets, the name Pyatigorsk would, however, most of all conjure up one flamboyant young litterateur: Mikhail Lermontov, the "Russian Byron" who penned some of the language's most stirring lyric verse (about nature, moonlit nights, and the fall of tyrants), as well as the Romanticist's bible of disillusioned youth, the novella *A Hero of Our Time,* the tale of a world-weary officer who absconds to the wilds of the Caucasus to assuage his ennui and meet his fate.

Lermontov was born in 1814 the son of an army captain of middling means in Moscow. When he was three he lost his mother; the loss scarred him, and it recurred in his writings. He was brought up by his grandmother in the heartland town of Penza, near the Volga. Early on he was afflicted with jaundice, which left him lonely and inclined to introspection, and so he focused his energies inward, on dreams of renouncing the world, on the liberating demesnes of fiction. His family took him, at age ten, on holiday to Pyatigorsk, where he met a girl who became his Beatrice; her memory he preserved in poetry, but she too was to disappear from his life. His father's death soon after confirmed in him his desire for escape, which manifested itself in verse he wrote as a literature student at university in Moscow.

In the nineteenth century poets were regarded as potential rebels who spoke truth to power and courted the hangman. As it would be at several points in its history, Russia in Lermontov's day was both ascendant and increasingly oppressive. Under the "enlightened" Empress Catherine the Great (whose reign from 1762 to 1796 saw half the population cast into slavery) and the repressive Alexander I, serfdom had expanded dramatically. The tsar's troops had marched into eastern Europe and assumed duties as the Gendarme of the Continent; they had crossed the Caucasus to annex Georgia; and Cossacks were pressing east to acquire Siberia. Then, in 1825 (the year of the Decembrist Uprising, the first attempt at establishing a republic in Russia), the ultrareactionary Tsar Nicolas I came to power. In shock and anger, he read Lermontov's *A Hero of Our Time* and took action against its composer, whose fate was to play out in Pyatigorsk . . .

I disembarked in Pyatigorsk heady with nostalgia, for I had my own history with both the town and its poet. In the early 1980s, before traveling to the Soviet Union for the first time, I had immersed myself in Lermontov's work, memorizing lengthy passages from Russian-language instruction tapes recorded by dulcet-voiced Soviet narrators. The combination of their impassioned recitals and the poet's concise yet dreamy verbiage did much to establish Russian, tender, evocative, and euphonious, as the dialect of my heart. Though far less worldly than Lermontov, I saw in *Hero* a plan of escape, a call to action. To answer it I went abroad and have never really returned.

When I reached Pyatigorsk in the summer of 1985, I fell in with merrymaking Russians who knew his oeuvre by heart and lived carpe diem on month-long employer-issued *putyovki* (free, all-inclusive tours in state rest houses). A tryst in the town's environs was, then, de rigueur, and I complied with custom; rich local red wines flowed through every poignant assignation. The cedar-embowered Lermontov Street, the creamy façades of Pyatigorsk's old-town homes, the breezes wafting fresh and piney from the fir-crowned crags of Mount Mashuk, gave the town a lost-world ambience I was to find nowhere else in the Soviet Union.

Now Pyatigorsk did little to revive these memories, at least at first.

Impoverished Caucasian migrants had replaced Russian vacationers. Smiles were few; policemen on patrol, many. Eager to reread Lermontov here, I searched bookstores for an anthology of his work. (I had not thought to bring my own.) In stultifying heat I trudged up and down streets cluttered with slot machine shops, vendors of cheap Turkish and Chinese clothes, and rancid-smelling look-alike cafés advertising beer and vodka and dumplings. In the town's few remaining literary vending points, translations of trashy American novels predominated; Harold Robbins outsold Tolstoy. Only in a used book store did I finally find a couple of volumes, which I bought immediately.

Books in hand, I set out, sweating and eager, traipsing along abruptly rising streets leading to the edge of town and the Lermontov Muséum Reserve, an estate beneath Mount Mashuk. I was almost the only visitor that day. The poet spent his last months in the simple stone houses and gardens here during his second exile. His "Death of a Poet" had occasioned his first exile to Pyatigorsk. Tsarist authorities interpreted as seditious his lines in honor of Alexander Pushkin (also killed in a duel, also a denigrator of tyrants), with their denunciation of courtiers as the "executioners of Freedom, Genius, and Glory" and his warning that they faced "God's judgment . . . a terrible judgment." Lermontov also excoriated the cowardice of the intelligentsia who failed to stand by Pushkin, the "*nevol'nik chesti*" (prisoner of honor), and their hypocritical remorse at his death.

A Hero of Our Time earned Lermontov his second and final exile (to be served in military service) to the Caucasus. Nicolas I read it in 1840 and declared it "disgusting, perfectly deserving of the vogue it enjoys . . . [filled with] the exaggerated portrayal of despicable characters that we find in today's novels." He pronounced it a "pathetic book displaying the great corruption of its author." The emperor hoped that an enforced sojourn in the Caucasus would allow the poet to "clean up his mind." (It must be noted that dissident writings in the Soviet era won their authors commitment to psychiatric hospitals, decades in labor camps, or worse. As bad as Nicolas I was, he paled in comparison with Lenin and his successors.) In the Caucasus, Lermontov acquitted himself well in combat, but, as a thunderstorm broke out above Mount Mashuk, he fell on its slopes to a duelist's bullet in July of 1840, not far from the bench on which I sat.

I wandered about the spare whitewashed chambers in which he lived, admiring the watercolors he painted, including the one that happened to grace the cover of my new edition of *A Hero of Our Time*. It was *A Scene from the Caucasus with Camels*—a reminder that in geography and fauna this new part of Russia had little in common with the slumbering north but was where the "Orient" began.

I walked back out into the garden. Mashuk's granite outcroppings cleaved the cerulean sky. I sat down on a bench and opened my volumes, finding lines that revived the melancholic passion that had impelled me to leave the United States and begin traveling twenty-four years before.

> *Beleyet parus odinoki*
> *V tumane morya golubom . . .*
> *Chto ishchet on v strane dalyokoy? . . .*
>
> *Pod nim struya svetleye lazuri,*
> *Nad nim luch solntsa zolotoy . . .*
> *A on, myatezhny, prosit buri,*
> *Kak budto v buryakh yest' pokoy*

> A lonely white sail flutters
> In the pale blue mist of the sea . . .
> What seeks he in that faraway land? . . .
>
> Beneath him run currents clearer than turquoise
> Above him flow golden rays of sun
> But he, ever rebellious, seeks a storm
> As if in storms there is peace

On and on I read. In the eyes of his beloved Lermontov discerns his own "past suffering and . . . perished youth"; in the Caucasus, he felt lonely, sad, and abandoned, with "none to whom, in an hour of soulful misfortune, a hand could be extended." "Years are passing," he wrote, "the best years!" but "if one looks within oneself, not a trace of the past remains." Reason cures the "sweet ailment" of passion. Life he considered a "joke, empty and stupid," and he asked, "What is a poet . . . without suffering? What is the ocean without a storm?"

When I first read those lines, they had spoken to me as had no other. They led me to a truth that I would seek to affirm through travel: our days are few, and to live them fully, before reimmersion in the Eternal Peace of our universe, the "peace that passeth all understanding," we must extinguish our flame through action. We must move ahead, never look back, and remember that "we are made for Joy and Woe," as Blake said.

Lermontov's Russia vanished with the Bolshevik Revolution of 1917; Pyatigorsk's easygoing decades as a workers' retreat ended with the Soviet collapse in 1991; and time was carrying me toward my own passing.

I closed my volume of verse, looked at Mount Mashuk, and got up to leave.

MOUNT ELBRUS is the Caucasus' highest peak, and I had hoped to observe it from the perch of the Intourist Hotel (where I was staying), situated on a promontory above town. But evening haze obscured its glacial slopes. Still absorbed in Lermontov, I nevertheless took a seat out at the almost empty balcony restaurant, the Saklya, and ordered dinner from the young waiter, reveling in my solitude.

He asked me what I was reading. I told him. He didn't seem to recognize the author. When I told him that *saklya* was Russian for a type of Caucasian hut found in Lermontov's works, he shrugged, not knowing the word. Loudspeakers soon screeched to life and a band assembled on stage to perform a deafening rendition of a *popsa* tune, spoiling any possibility of reading.

I told the waiter I was moving inside, where it was quieter. There, almost alone again, I chose a table in the blue-red glow of neon. But once more my presence sparked an assault of "entertainment." The lights dimmed, leaving only the red neon, and from crackling loudspeakers sounded "Ain't Nobody's Business." A lithe young woman in black stiletto boots, a white blouse, and a black tie tipped a raffish black fedora at me and mounted a stage with a silver pole in the middle. Her teeth and fingernails glowing in the ultraviolet light, she stroked herself and stalked the stage. She swung her hips to the music and, setting her eyes on mine, slowly flicked open buttons of her shirt; she turned around and bent over, smiling at me from between her sleek legs, showing me her black thong. She reached for the pole and whirled about it, striking poses, tipping her hat to me again and again. She was by any standard gorgeous, with a slender torso and modest bust, high cheeks, and a mane of shimmering russet hair, yet in Russia she hardly stood out. I had to make myself look at her, not only because she kept her eyes on mine but because she was obviously trying so hard, executing her moves with all the grace she could muster.

She was no different from any attractive girl I might have seen strolling down the sidewalks outside back in 1985, when, it seemed, everyone in Russia read and literature was in insatiable demand, and the notion that one day strip joints would pop up all over the country would have been laughable. I wondered if she would even know who Lermontov was.

I felt all at once alone, and far from home, wherever that was.

4

Under a cool gray sky the next morning, a taxi took me from Pyatigorsk out onto a two-lane highway heading east over plains, following the northern rim of the Greater Caucasus.

An hour after departure we flew by a red banner proclaiming, in white block letters on red, MAY THE FRIENDSHIP AMONG THE PEOPLES OF RUSSIA GROW STRONG AND PROSPER! Where the authorities saw fit to post such slogans one had to suspect trouble. We were in fact nearing the border with the republic of Kabardino-Balkaria, a predominantly Muslim entity of 790,000 cobbled together by Stalin from the lands of two rival peoples. The Kabardin, the majority, have Circassian roots and are denizens of the plains. Early on they allied themselves with Russia. The Turkic Balkar, the minority, fled into the mountains to escape the Tatar-Mongolian onslaught of 1237–38 and have largely remained there; they long fought off the Slavic invaders. Enmity between the two peoples ensured that once they were thrown together in a joint republic, both would look to the Kremlin to keep the peace —an illustration of Stalin's "unite and conquer" nationalities policy. Once the Soviet Union began disintegrating, the Caucasus erupted in bloodshed that hasn't entirely ceased.

Complicating matters has been the West's creeping intrusion into the Caucasus. After the Rose Revolution of 2003 brought a Western-backed liberal, Mikhail Saakashvili, to power in Georgia just to the south, the United States attempted to prize the country from the Russian sphere, initiating Alliance talks on NATO membership, but without much success. The Caucasus' problems, mostly internecine and ages-old, bear too intimately on Russia for the Kremlin to let the region loose; and the volatile nature of the Caucasians themselves would make them unreliable partners for distant Americans lacking the historical knowledge and cultural dexterity necessary to engage them.

We slowed for a police checkpoint at the border. I tensed up as the officers, squat and square-jawed, peered into our car. Would they haul me out, see my foreign passport, and demand to know what I was doing there?

There would have been a precedent. In October of 2005 (less than a year before my trip), in Nalchik, the republic's capital of 300,000, months of Islamist-related violence had culminated in a coordinated assault by three hundred Muslim rebels (apparently affiliated with Chechen armed groups) on three police stations, the airport, and other government buildings. Some attackers took hostages. Interior Ministry troops fought them off, killing ninety-five. (A total of 139 people lost their lives.) Soon after, the Russian secret police was tailing foreign reporters in town trying to investigate, and, it was rumored, beating up local officials who helped them. Chechnya was, after all, just fifty miles farther east. But certainly the mass impoverishment that followed the collapse of the Soviet Union played a role in the unrest. By 1999 the republic's industry (machine-building and metallurgy, mostly) produced less than a third of what it had in 1990; and local unemployment levels have, as a result, been twice as high as elsewhere in Russia.

But the officers waved us through the checkpoint, and even smiled. We drove into rich farmland and idyllic orchards. Gold-teethed women in gypsy scarves and floral skirts squatted at the roadside by piles of vegetables they were hawking to motorists; husky men on horseback trotted our way from far-off villages with non-Russian names such as Chegem and Etoko. My driver, Sasha, a former musician, switched on a Mozart tape, and the drama of the symphony accorded with the majesty of the ever-steeper mountains, the ever-denser deciduous groves. He raised the volume, clenching and unclenching his fist and softly pounding it in rhythm on the steering wheel. The music clearly transported him, as my first glimpses of Kabardino-Balkaria did me.

Sasha left me in central Nalchik at the cement-block Hotel Russia. A solicitous if gritty receptionist handed me a chit, which I took upstairs and surrendered to a *dezhurnaya* (floor attendant) in return for my key.

Roaring with the traffic of the adjacent thoroughfare, my room was all I had expected in such a town: a dirty window and sooty orange curtains, a synthetic tigerskin bedspread, long-unwashed linens.

But I was exhilarated. I had left ethnic Russia. The *real* Caucasus began here.

NALCHIK WAS CHARMING in a retro-Soviet way. Drivers on Lenin Prospekt, the main drag, slowed for pedestrians—a gentility unheard of in Moscow today but once common in socialist times. Streets were broad, clean, and smooth; sidewalks bustled with strollers. The Soviet version of Toys-R-Us, Detski Mir (Children's World), was still in business, though it now sold vodka, wine, sausage, and, upstairs, racy negligees, Kabardin ceremonial swords, and Balkar folk outfits. No women about were wearing the hijab. All in all, Nalchik resembled the resort town it had been during the Soviet decades, when its proximity to Mount Elbrus and various spas drew tourists from all over the country. The few police on beats, I noticed, were clearly Kabardin or Balkar (not Russian) and took no interest in shaking down pedestrians. They did, however, wear bulletproof vests and carry Kalashnikovs with the safety off.

In front of my hotel, on Maria Square, stood a bronze statue of Ivan the Terrible's eponymous Kabardin wife. The despot married the daughter of Kabardin Prince Temryuk in 1560 to cement relations with the Kabardin; Maria was the Christian name she adopted after conversion from Islam. No one had thought to tear it down once the Soviet Union collapsed. The Kabardin judged the winds of history and accepted Russian suzerainty in 1774; thereafter they largely favored the entrenchment of Russian rule in the Caucasus.

FRIENDS IN MOSCOW put me in touch with Lara, a Kabardin in her midtwenties who had once worked as a schoolteacher in Nalchik but had recently found a job as an accountant in Saint Petersburg and moved there. The afternoon of my arrival, Lara strode smiling toward me across Maria Square. She was dark-haired, slender, and dressed in a pink sweater and white slacks. Her eyes were drawn and prematurely wrinkled.

We took off down Lenin Prospekt. I told her how excited I was to be in Kabardino-Balkaria. I added that I was wondering how strong Islam was here; after all, the Kabardin had once been Orthodox Christian and had converted to Islam only in the eighteenth century, under the influence of Turkey. "Judging by people's clothes," I said, "I would hardly know I'm in a Muslim republic."

"Those are just appearances," she answered. "I believe strongly in Islam and observe its rules. I *would* wear the hijab, but after the attacks last year, people are afraid. There's a lot of pressure not to be openly Muslim."

"Pressure from . . . ?"

"Well, the authorities could suspect you of being a militant. They even arrested a pregnant woman for having no documents." (The law requires everyone in Russia to carry ID papers in public.) "They beat her up in the police station, and she had a miscarriage. Rumor had it that this was a provocation, to get us to rise up, but we didn't." She lowered her voice. "The attack last year, it was never explained. A couple of my students even took part. I couldn't believe it. They were killed in the assault, so I never found out why." She smiled all the time she was telling this, and her eyes darted about.

"So Islamic extremism is a problem here?"

"Well, when the war in Chechnya began, we were all very upset, you know. Planes full of Russian soldiers were landing in our airport. They just carpet-bombed Grozny. It was genocide. We feared we'd be next. Our young people started leaving."

"Because they thought war was coming?"

"That, and also because with our former republic president, there were no jobs and you had to pay big bribes to get work. Those who stayed have turned to religion. They just have to keep it hidden. So you don't find many women who risk wearing the hijab. Men who study the Qur'an can be arrested and disappeared. It happened to a friend of mine. They say the authorities are torturing them across the border in Russia."

Her words were chilling, and made the peace I saw around me now seem like a mirage. We stopped at a spiffy veranda café called Cherry and took seats beneath an umbrella. We were alone, aside from a couple of Russian waitresses. (Local Muslim women rarely take service-sector jobs that could compromise their honor.) We ordered lunch.

As soon as our meals arrived a tailless crow swooped down from the roof and perched himself on our table's edge, spreading his bulky wings, puffing up his breast feathers, and cawing and lunging after my french fries. The waitresses giggled but did nothing. The bird ignored my gesticulations and shouts, and when I swung at him he deftly fluttered aloft.

We began eating. But the bird knocked over the salt and pepper and tore apart the paper tablecloth; cawing, he lunged for my fries, bouncing out of reach each time I tried to cuff him. He fixed a gemlike black eye on me and opened his beak and stuck out his pink slivery tongue. *An omen,* I thought.

There was a ruckus across the street in Abkhazia Park (named after the Black Sea republic on Kabardino-Balkaria's southern border that was torn apart by civil war in the early 1990s and is still trying, with covert and not-so-covert Russian help, to separate from Georgia). Cars draped with flower wreaths were pulling in and disgorging musicians bearing drums and flutes and guests clad in tuxedos and gowns. They danced martial jigs and shouted and toasted, poured shots of vodka into tiny glasses and drank them, shouted again and drove away, to be replaced by more shouting partiers.

"Wedding guests," said Lara. "You see, the Abkhaz are our brother Muslims. So we supported them in their war to fight off the [Christian] Georgians. A lot of Kabardin fought and died there."

I shuddered at what such "fraternal" feelings of religious solidarity had led to here. In the early nineties incidents of savage ethno-religious violence broke out across the former Soviet Union: Azeris against Armenians, Ossetians against Ingush, Transdniester Russians against Moldovans, to name a few of the conflicts. I felt little sympathy for any of the parties, who let Stalin's choice of borders prod them into massacring their neighbors as soon as Kremlin control weakened—just as the dictator intended.

I waved off the crow and asked how Lara felt working as a Kabardin in Saint Petersburg.

"Well, there's a lot of pressure there to hide your Islamic identity. People sometimes say outright, 'Go back to your Caucasus!' They *hate* us for being Caucasians. Well, we hate *them* right back, you know? The police stop me all the time there; no sooner do I get done with one document check than I run into another." The fatigue in her eyes was well earned. "All this," she exclaimed, "and I'm a citizen of Russia! We just want to scream, 'Please, treat us like citizens!'"

We finished our meal and left the crow to tear into our leftovers and toss our silverware hither and yon. Back out on the sidewalk with the strollers and Kalashnikov-armed soldiers, Lara talked about the brutishness of Russian men; the soulful beauty of Russian women; and the Cossacks (whose descendants make up the majority of Russians here), whom she described as "not a people but a pack of exiles and criminals who are so militant because there's no substance to their national identity. They even stole their national outfit from us," referring to the *burka* cape and the conical *papakha* hat.

Yet her real passion was describing her own people and their character. She expressed it in contradistinction to that of other peoples. "We maintain our traditions, and Russians don't. We stand up when an elder comes into the room. We never argue with our parents, unlike Russians. We're not like the Chechens, who can invite you home and treat you like family and then trick you. Chechens are even proud of how much they deceive others." The Balkar were a "petty" people not worth saying much about. She summed up, saying, "We Kabardin are pretty much the royalty of the Caucasus, like the British royal family, with its traditions," she declared.

"A pretty militant group of royals you are, it sounds to me."

"Oh, no! We would never start a fight with anyone! That isn't part of our national identity."

It was getting dark, and so time for Lara to head home. We agreed to meet up the next day.

MY CELL PHONE RANG. Timur, a local gas station owner whom friends in Moscow had recommended I meet, was on his way over to the Hotel Russia to pick me up and, he said, "show me a good time." He spun around the square in a silver Mitsubishi Pajero SUV with tinted windows and a dashboard resembling a spaceship's console.

Timur was in his thirties, but he had a baby face and bouncy brown hair that made him look younger. He cut a beige figure at leisure ensconced in his SUV's black interior. He had a soft handshake and an even softer, self-effacing demeanor.

"Impressive car," I said, after introductions.

"Oh, I'm soon going to get, if all works out, a, well, a . . . an . . . *Infiniti*." This he pronounced as "een*feen*eetee," bashfully averting his eyes, as if the mention of such an exalted vehicle elevated him above other mortals in a way that could not overtly be acknowledged without appearing immodest. "What do you think of that?" He bashfully turned away again.

"Well, it must be a great car."

When he had recomposed himself, he said, "We have this restaurant I'd like to take you to. The Bochka"—the barrel.

The Bochka was just that: built of wood and shaped like a beer barrel on legs, with a few trellised pavilions scattered around outside for more private meals. We would eat inside, in the barrel's cool belly. We ordered *shashlyki* (lamb kebabs) and beer, which the Russian waitress, dressed in the flouncy skirt and white ruffled blouse of an Oktoberfest maiden, brought us cold, in half-liter glasses.

"We're sitting here in the Barrel and everything looks normal, doesn't it?" he said. "But the secret services are at work and extremists may have shaved their beards and still be plotting." We bit into delicious lamb on ribs. "The day of the attack was really bad. I had just dropped off my kids at school. Then my brother called me and told me what was going on. So I hurried back to school. There was shooting all over the place and the troops had their guns trained on cars. Everyone was thinking, *Could there be another Beslan?* Anyway, at school the teachers had herded all the kids into the central courtyard, where they'd be safe from stray bullets. I grabbed mine and we ran out. After I got them home, my neighbors called and asked me to pick up their kids too. So out I went again into the shooting. But you see, the people didn't support the rebels. Their purpose was to awaken fury here in sleepy Kabardino-Balkaria. But they failed."

Everything *seemed* so normal here now. Yet Timur reminded me that Bespalov's words about Russia being a tinderbox might be true. We chomped through a basket of lamb and ordered more, with more beer as well. Politics hardly interested Timur. That Putin had canceled local elections and now appoints the republic's president upset him not at all. ("We had the former president for twelve years. We couldn't get rid of him. Maybe a Kremlin appointee will be less corrupt.") He had little reason to object: his aim was to make money, support his family in style, and run his business, all things he could do now, with the Kremlin appointee, more easily than before. He had found his niche in Putin's new order and had no reason to wish for change, certainly not change in the interests of abstract concepts like "democracy" and "human rights." The een*feen*eetee was enough.

AT ELEVEN THE NEXT MORNING, with my head still fuzzy-feeling from the unsterilized beer, I again found myself at the Bochka, but this time outside, in one of the pavilions. Lara and her friend, a Kabardin professor named Ahmad, had picked me up in his Audi. In his fifties, Ahmad had something of the kinky-haired, roly-poly satyr about him; his ruddy complexion and springy gait suggested an excess of libidinous humor. He spoke Russian with a coarse accent that puzzled me, for Kabardin was a melodious language that sounded like the call of whippoorwills.

Light from the late-July sun filtered in through the pavilion's trellis, as did the cloying smell of flowers from the adjacent park. Comely Russian waitresses ("You are so beautiful!" Ahmad said to one, and to another, "My God, you're such a sweetie!") were adding to the plethoric spread of food and booze that he had ordered in my honor: piles of *shashlyki* sprinkled with onion slices, heaps of tangy Kabardin goat cheese, mounds of tomato and cucumber salad lathered in locally pressed olive oil. Bottles of vodka stood next to tall bubbling glasses of Terek beer.

At the Bochka, Ahmad was a big man because he knew the Big Man himself, the owner, Muhammad. Muhammad dropped in wielding a bejeweled cell phone and sporting black sunglasses and a designer leather jacket (despite the heat). After chatting in Kabardin with Ahmad and Lara, he addressed me in Russian.

"We should be more like China. The great thing is that they kept socialism but allowed private property. Now they're thriving and everyone fears them."

"Do you really think you can keep socialism and have private property? And is fear so good?" I asked.

He stared, perplexed, at me. Lara cut in. "Who would want to live under the Soviet system anymore? That's not an answer to anything. We want to develop."

He must have been unaccustomed to retorts of this sort. A boss in the Caucasus is the Boss, the Eurasian equivalent of the African Big Man. Ignoring my remark and Lara's rejoinder, Muhammad bent over the table and asked for her phone number. She gave it to him, but his dark glasses hindered his view of the keys on his cell phone, and he had to punch it in repeatedly before he got it right. That done, he abruptly wished us *bon appétit* and walked out.

"Ah," declared Ahmad, leaning back in his chair and putting his hairy arm around Lara's pink shoulder. "I don't know about you," he said to me, "but I'm for love, *physical* love, with girls, *young* girls." He squeezed her and pressed his red sweaty cheek to hers. She tittered nervously. "What about you?"

"Oh, well, who isn't?" I said.

He squeezed poor Lara again. "Well, let's drink to love!"

Having had beer the previous evening, I wanted nothing less than to drink before noon the next day. But in the Caucasus refusing hospitality can cause real offense. He reached over and started to pour me vodka, but I demurred politely and grabbed a Terek.

"Good choice!" said Ahmad. "It's the best beer in the country!" He stood up, as did Lara, so I did so too. With his glass raised, he pronounced a few words about the succulent joys of physical love, and then recited a rousing poem in Russian called "In the Kindness of the Kabardin," a militant ode to the hospitality the Kabardin proffer the unannounced guest, with lines about the undying friendship of the Kabardin, their readiness to help a new friend in need, their unparalleled skills in toasting, and a finale lauding their worthiest attribute: modesty. We clinked glasses and drank.

My hosts then segued into a joint discourse on the superiority of the Kabardin, their proudly shared roots with the Adyghians and Circassians (Caucasian peoples with nearby republics), their unique tongue ("No other people has a language like ours," said Lara. "We have one sound that takes five letters to write"), their sterling character and valiant history. They described fierce Kabardin warriors in high black boots and sweeping black capes; men in black *papakhi* canted rakishly over stern mustachioed countenances; brave Kabardin teens armed with daggers; virtuous Kabardin women covered from chin to ankle in embroidered dresses, their heads wrapped in shawls reaching down to their waists—the very picture of Caucasian nobility.

This all sounded wonderful, at least on the face of it. Every people takes pride in their heritage, but this pride, especially in the Caucasus, often conceals prejudice, even enmity for "inferior" neighbors—in this case, the "petty" Balkar (who, incidentally, also wore *papakhi*, capes, daggers, and so on). Moreover, what fruit had all these outstanding features borne? The Kabardin had not even possessed a written language until Soviet times. Under Stalin's direction, Soviet authorities, as part of a nationalities policy that aimed to foster ethnic identity and thus encourage rivalry, had set down Caucasian languages in Latin and Cyrillic. My companions' discourse told me they had succeeded.

I tried to phrase my objection politely. "I'm just wondering, as an outsider, what is the Kabardin legacy to the rest of us humans? Besides just being excellent hosts and having such a language and so on?"

Said Ahmad, "I just read you our national poem. Doesn't it tell you anything?"

"Yes, it's beautiful and inspiring. But what have the Kabardin *done?*"

"We're all Muslims, so we're all one people," he said. "We once had a kingdom stretching from the Black Sea to the Caspian."

"Really? I've never heard of such a kingdom."

"We had feudalism back then, so we were divided into principalities. But you see, all the Adyghians and Circassians are *really* Kabardin. And of course you know what Napoleon said about us?"

"No."

"'I would trade fifty French soldiers for one Circassian!' It's true —check the history books! You can *never* know our history, or even appreciate it," he announced. Its grandeur was immense, ineffable.

Each time I ate a kebab Lara dropped another on my plate; each time I finished my salad she heaped on more. Waitresses ceaselessly replenished our table's cornucopia, each receiving lustful plaudits from the professor as she evaded his grasping hands. "You have such beautiful eyes," said Ahmad to one, reaching for her face. She dumped her load of *shashlyki* into our basket and slipped out.

Lara said, "Ahmad's right about our history. I was visiting with an Ossetian girlfriend. I saw a book on her table about the history of the Nart people."

"The Nart?"

"We're Nart, really—I mean, the original Adyghians were Nart. Anyway, I said to her, 'Hey, you're studying our history! *We're* the Nart!' She had the *nerve* to say the Ossetians were the true Nart."

"Just think about the poem I read you," said Ahmad. "It says it all."

(I later learned that "Nart" referred to a cycle of epic poetry, probably of Iranian origin, concerning the mythical doings of mountain deities. The Nart epic, as far as is known, came from the Ossetians, whose language belongs to the Iranian group but spread across the region, and thus could be claimed by no one people.)

We toasted to the Nart.

"So," I said, "I gather that the Adyghians, the Nart, and the Circassians all speak Kabardin?"

"Of course not," answered Ahmad. "Kabardin and Circassian are the same, but it's unintelligible to the Adyghians. The Kabardin language is unique, as we've been telling you." This was a meaningless if contradictory pronouncement—every language is unique in its own way. But I forswore pursuing the question. "And by the way," said Ahmad, reaching around Lara's shoulder again, "did I tell you? I'm for love, *physical* love. With, with—"

"With young girls," I said. "We've heard."

Ahmad squeezed Lara, who was too respectful of her elders to object. He then went on to relate the legend about how the Kabardin got their fertile land on the plains. When God was distributing plots to the Caucasians, the Kabardin were the only people not to beg for their share; hence, he rewarded their pride with the choicest terrain.

"That's wonderful," I replied. "But I'm just wondering. Why's there been so much bloodshed in the Caucasus? It seems real civilization would have taught people to get along."

I was right, they told me. But the Kabardin's rotten neighbors—from the piddling Balkar to the Georgians, "who produce nothing but fake wine and have only mountains; what would they be without our brother people, the Abkhaz, and their land?"—spoiled everything.

"Then why not re-draw the borders?" I asked. "After all, Stalin drew them, and he's been dead since 1953."

"Because the only thing worse than these borders would be trying to change them," answered Lara. "People have moved all over the place and mixed. No one would give up his land or his home. There would be chaos and bloodshed."

"I propose we drink to peace," said Ahmad. "If you have peace and health, you can buy all the rest you want in life!"

"To peace!" I said, and we clinked glasses.

A couple of hours later they dropped me off at my hotel. Unshaven men in dark glasses and grimy tracksuits and rubber sandals were sloughing around in the dingy hall by my room, smelling of sweat. Tired from the beer and so many *shashlyki,* I lay down on my hot bed and closed my eyes. I tried to ignore the deafening clamor of traffic outside.

But my cell phone rang. "Get ready for a real Kabardin party!" said Timur in a shockingly chipper voice. "My relatives are celebrating the birth of their daughter. I'm coming to get you!"

Within half an hour he was knocking at my door.

*

IN THE NULLIFYING HEAT of early afternoon, thirty-five or forty revelers sat around a long table set on a shaded patio next to a courtyard, the men on one end boisterous, the women on the other restrained. A *tamada,* or table master, presided. He had a trim mustache, waxed-back salt-and-pepper hair, and bright blue eyes. He was handsome and reminded me of a portly George Clooney.

I was not the first to have this idea. "Meet our Kabardin George Clooney!" said Timur, seating me to the *tamada*'s right. George turned out to be his nickname. Timur, sitting on the other side of me, leaned over and whispered in my ear: "You must ask the *tamada*'s permission to do anything: to drink, go to the bathroom, even to speak. This is our tradition."

"Okay," I said.

"Now, please, meet our historian!"

Across from me sat a brawny perspiring fellow in his middle years. His face was pink from vodka, his pupils dilated. He cleared his throat. "Clooney, may I ask our new guest a question?"

Yes, said George.

"What are you exactly?" he asked me.

"I'm a writer."

"I mean, what's your nationality?"

"American."

"No. What's your *blood?*"

Distressed that even a historian found knowledge of ethnic background so critical to initiating a conversation, even here, at this party, I told him about my roots. When I got to my Sicilian grandmother he perked up.

"Oh, Sicilian! *Zdorovo!* [Excellent!] Was she in the Mafia?"

"Of course not." I tried to explain that such a stereotype offended honest Sicilians, but he cut me off and said something to Clooney in Kabardin. Clooney authorized him to make a toast.

He stood up. His gruff accented Russian sounded as though it might have issued from a Kabardin Don Corleone. "I was, dear guests, using 'Mafia' in a positive way. Sicilians are dear to us all here. We think Sicilians and the Kabardin have a lot in common. You Sicilians are like us, hot-blooded and honor-bound. And like us, you're clever, much cleverer than ordinary Americans! Let us drink to Sicilians!"

We did. Soon after, the celebrated father, a lanky youth in gangsta jeans, showed up with a swaddled baby girl. Dad took his progeny from reveler to reveler; all, including me, stuffed a few thousand rubles (about $120) in her blanket, as was the custom.

The *tamada* raised his glass. "Please, say a toast in Sicilian!"

I thought of trying to put together something in Italian with the words *vendetta, omertà,* and *Corleone* but decided it was ridiculous.

"I would actually like to toast to your hospitality," I said in Russian. "You've made me feel very much at home."

"The Sicilian is at home with us!" shouted the historian, pounding on the table. "He feels like he's in Sicily! Bravo!"

"Bravo the Sicilian!"

"Bravo!"

We downed our vodka.

The party was ending. I thanked everyone for the hospitality. With a farewell nod of permission from Clooney, Timur arose and so did I. We walked unsteadily out to the car.

"Is it safe to drive after so much vodka?" I asked.

"No problem at all," he replied. "I know all the cops. Everyone here is my relative. No one would dare stop me!"

We peeled out into traffic, invincible in his space-age Pajero, kings of Nalchik's heat-warped roads.

5

In the blood-drenched thirteenth and fourteenth centuries, Tatar-Mongolian horsemen rampaged through what is now the republic of North Ossetia-Alania and drove most of the prosperous Ossetians from their black-earth farms on the lowlands up into the Caucasus' infecund rocky heights. (The Ossetians are an Iranian-Caucasian people that adopted Christianity from the Greeks and Georgians in the sixth century. Half of them now dwell south of the border, in Georgia, in the republic of South Ossetia—another Russian-backed entity trying to break free of Tbilisi.) Shortly thereafter came the brutal razzia of Timur (a.k.a. Tamerlane), which wrought mayhem on those who stayed behind. So it does not surprise that the Ossetians welcomed the Russians, who in 1784 founded Vladikavkaz (translation: "Rule the Caucasus") as a fortress from which to secure their grip over the region. Under the tsars' protection, the Ossetians descended from their high-altitude villages to farm the *chernozem* anew. They have, by and large, served as Russia's allies ever since.

Yet today Vladikavkaz's most conspicuous landmark is not a church but the century-old Sunni Mosque, a blue-domed, brick-walled jewel of a temple with two mighty minarets and, of all things, a crenellated roof recalling the Kremlin. Standing in the center above the frothy glacial currents of the Terek River, the mosque embodies the contradictions inherent in the Russian Empire's expansion, an expansion led by divinely sanctioned Orthodox monarchs whose mission of territorial aggrandizement burdened Russia with dominion over restive, non-Christian peoples. Muslim migrants from Kabardino-Balkaria were among the first non-Russians to settle in Vladikavkaz. There is still tension between ethnic and religious groups. Now and then bomb blasts, either terrorist- or *mafiya*-related, hit markets and shatter the calm. And just a few miles north sits Beslan, where in 2004 Muslim rebels took a school hostage, and 331 people, mostly children, died.

Underlying the current instability are the mass deportations of 1944. Stalin suspected Ossetia's Islamic neighbors (the Chechens, the Ingush, and the Balkar, among them) of collaboration with the Nazis and exiled them en masse to Siberia. After Stalin's death, Khrushchev allowed the deported peoples to return, but religious animosity and ethnic hatred simmered on. After all, Stalin had spared the loyal (Christian) Ossetians but sent Muslims packing. The recent Beslan massacre incited the Ossetians to blame (and hate) the Chechens and Ingush even more fervently.

To this day Ossetians retain unrepentant pride in Stalin, their most famous half son. Ioseb (Joseph) Dzhugashvili was born to an Ossetian mother and a drunken, abusive Georgian father in Gori, a town in central Georgia. A seminary student and a talented poet, young Joseph soon fell in with Marxist revolutionaries, adopted the nom de guerre Stalin (Man of Steel), acted as a bank robber and hit man for the Bolsheviks, and eventually became a cohort of Lenin's. In 1922 he assumed duties as general secretary of the Communist Party. Lenin passed away in 1924, and Stalin, taking a decade or so to consolidate absolute power (mostly by imprisoning or murdering potential rivals), ruled the Soviet Union till his death in 1953, killing millions but transforming his backward agricultural country into an industrial superpower with nuclear weapons and a GDP second only to that of the United States. It is Stalin the statesman that so many in Russia still admire, not Stalin the butcher.

An Ossetian named Aslan gave me a lift from Nalchik to Vladikavkaz through burgeoning fields of corn and tomatoes. In a throaty voice, he growled out his admiration for the supreme *vozhd'* (leader). "Whatever people say about Stalin, he was a powerful politician. At the Tehran Conference, Churchill and Roosevelt agreed before meeting him not to rise when he entered the room, to show their disdain for him as one who *supposedly* was such a dictator. But when he walked in, they jumped to their feet! He made such an impression! Oh, Stalin! And of course more Ossetians, fifty-one in all, were awarded the medal Hero of the Soviet Union than any other people!"

Once settled in to my hotel in Vladikavkaz, I accepted an invitation to escape into the mountains. Genri Kusov, an Ossetian historian, author, and Soviet-era television show host whom I had arranged to meet, invited me to what he called his *khizhina* (hovel) high in the Caucasus, near Dargavs, City of the Dead, a village famous for its open tombs. His friend Astan agreed to drive me there.

Astan, a local businessman, picked me up from my hotel the next morning in his white Volga. His Ossetian-accented Russian was thuggishly inflected, flat-voweled. (Stalin spoke this way, and so rarely addressed the Soviet public over the radio.) Hook-nosed, faintly pockmarked, and in his late forties, Astan nevertheless had a dignified air about him. We rolled south out of town down a rutted highway, toward the Caucasus, a looming massif of jagged scarps and green slopes crowned with clouds, at once awesome and intimidating, for centuries the abode of bandits and blood feuds. Through its granite fastnesses the Russians, in the 1900s, had blasted the Georgian Military Highway to connect Vladikavkaz with Tbilisi, a hundred miles south as the crow flies.

As we neared the first gorges he sped up, swerving to dodge trucks and ever more numerous cattle. In fact, soon cows stood here and there every ten yards or so, pensively chewing cud, presenting Astan with an obstacle course, which he ran with perilous alacrity.

"What are all these cows doing on the road?" I asked, gripping my seat as he hit the gas and yanked the wheel.

"They stand out here to get away from the flies."

"Oh. Maybe we should, you know, slow down, because we might—"

His cell phone beeped. He fumbled the handset from his shirt pocket to his ear, saying *Da!*, and then shouted in guttural Ossetian, swinging the wheel with one arm to maneuver around cows and slowpoke trucks.

"*Chort!*" (Damn!), he exclaimed, losing the connection and looking up just in time to swerve away from a sixteen-wheeler barreling toward us in the oncoming lane, which we had invaded. Then he took his eyes entirely off the road and scrutinized the phone's tiny keyboard. He tapped out a number and began shouting into the mouthpiece again. More furious last-second evasive maneuvers followed.

As we skimmed the brims of ditches and just made it back onto the tarmac to cross bridges, I had to say something.

"Shouldn't you keep your attention on the road? I mean, look at all these ditches and trucks!"

"You know," he said, raising his voice enthusiastically, "I had this German policeman friend here once. I took him out driving. He told me he'd make a fortune in his country if he could fine a driver for all the laws I break! A fortune, and that's in euros!" His phone beeped again. "*Chort!* Another text message!" He yanked the wheel just in time to miss an abyss. "Ever been to Germany?"

We soon left the cows behind and motored upward into chasms, alone on the road, with the mountains (mercifully) cutting off his cell signal. ("*Chort!*" Astan said, returning the handset to his shirt pocket.) The air cooled and I closed my window. Valleys now swept away, deep and grassy in places, leaden and rocky in others, dappled with shreds of mist. We wound toward the sky through thinning groves of oaks and pines arrayed precariously on cliff sides. The Caucasus took on a haunted, Brothers Grimm look. Stone shepherds' cabins spied down on us; fog obscured the distant depths of abysses; and crags at times cut off the sun. Astan slowed and took turns cautiously.

Around noon we bounced off the highway onto a dirt road, trundled along it for half an hour, and cut through a valley hamlet. The people, grizzled mustachioed men and shepherd boys with staffs, looked up and regarded us with vague alarm, even hostility.

"Thieving is in people's blood up here," said Astan warily. "It used to be an honor to steal a stallion. Nowhere is the code of honor stronger. Our *abreki* [outlaws, in tsarist days] were *honorable* men, *true* men. By God," he said, his voice hoarsening, "we Ossetians are the *justest* people on earth!"

I asked how justice and thieving went together. He explained that for countless dark centuries before the Russians came, Ossetian clans plundered their rivals (which made theft "raiding" and therefore honorable), and blood for blood was the law. Some have seen in Stalin's Terror manifestations of the same ancient code of vengeance.

We turned on to a rocky slipshod track that wended over a barren declivity toward a wooden hut standing alone, like a sentry's outpost, on a grassy outcropping above the valley. A stream burbled far below. Genri, graying but spry, in a floppy hat, trotted up to greet us, hoe in hand.

"Welcome to my *khizhina!*" he said as we stepped out.

Twenty minutes later we were reposing on benches in his yard in the shade of a rowan tree, by a rough-hewn oaken table set with a feast fit for those famished by exertions in such thin air: *samogonka* (moonshine); a bottle of Dagestani cognac (reputed to be the best in Russia); and plates stacked with freshly grilled chicken, fragrant hunks of country bread, fat cucumbers from his garden, cups of *adzhika* (a hot sauce concocted from red peppers, tomatoes, onions, and garlic), and locally curdled *brynza,* a briny white cheese made from sheep's milk. Our thirst we would quench on rainwater Genri had gathered in a barrel. Across the valley towered the stark anvil summit of Watsilla, the legendary home of the Ossetian god of thunder and lightning. (Christianity never quite overcame all the Ossetians' pagan beliefs.)

An eagle screamed and described arches in the piercing azure. I inhaled air so fresh, it seemed to singe my lungs. Only the buzz of bees disturbed the silence here on earth. My appetite awakened in full.

"I wish I could offer you more," said Genri. "But an avalanche washed away my garden. We're eating what's left." He poured us shots of cognac and raised his glass. "I propose we toast to Kshaw, the Almighty, so that we have peace and no more war."

"*Kshaw*'s Ossetian for 'God'?" I asked.

"Kshaw is *our* god. We leave everything to the mercy of Kshaw. We don't lock our houses out here. The mountains and the air we're breathing are Kshaw's gifts. We Ossetians were animists, after all, even after we adopted Christianity."

Genri had a soothing voice, a cultured manner, and a subtle charisma that had worked well on camera, relaxing his interviewees and intriguing his viewers. His Russian was flawless, lilting with Muscovite intonations. The cognac went down smoothly, and we dug in to the food. Quail sailed over and flitted about our feet.

Astan took a deep breath. "Ah, give me a hammock and a cabin like this—I'd need nothing more. Civilization corrupts people. I hate all the genetically modified food that comes from America. When I first saw American chicken legs being sold in our markets, I said, 'Drumsticks *can't* be that fat! They've fed the chickens hormones!'"

Genri's chicken was lean and tangy—no hormones there. The *adzhika* set it deliciously afire.

"These mountains could be paradise," I said. "It's a shame there've been so many wars here."

Genri pushed back his cap. "Before the Caucasian War"—the twenty-five-year-long battle Russia fought with the Muslim mountain peoples that ended in 1859 with the capture of the resistance leader, Dagestan-born Imam Shamil—"there were no ethnic conflicts here, and there was a fair amount of intermarriage. But then the Georgians, fearing Ottoman Turkey and Persia, sought protection from Russia, and the Russians had to find a way to reach them. So Peter the Great attempted to go around the Caucasus, by the steppes of Kalmykia—a dangerous and impractical route. But then he learned of this Christian people, the Ossetians, high in the mountains. He found us, and we've been allies with Russia ever since. The Russians fulfilled their promise to us—which is unusual, I'll admit. They gave us land on the plains and let us descend."

"So the Caucasian War caused all the strife, all the Christian-Muslim hatred here?" I asked.

"Yes. The outside powers, the Turks on one side, the Russians on the other, used Islam as a weapon to divide people."

"But then Stalin exiled so many people and did so much damage. That contributed too," I said.

"There's more to it than that. Stalin understood that Lenin had made major mistakes. Lenin gave republics to peoples who never had them at all, like the Abkhaz and the 'South Ossetians'"—now in Georgia, and resisting governance from Tbilisi. "How can a people name itself the 'South' Ossetians? We're all just Ossetians. So then all these so-called local national elites began demanding power for their 'republics.' Stalin needed to crush them, and he did so in the 1930s, with the purges and the Terror."

"Well, 'needed' is a word one might dispute."

"He killed off the national elites because he needed absolute power to rule Russia as a despot."

Astan clenched his fist. "Stalin did what he had to do. Russia needs a strong ruler to unite it."

I had heard this pronouncement so often that I let it slip by without comment. In the Russian context, "strong ruler" invariably connotes an enthroned assassin who, acting in the name of the state, victimizes those objecting to the often absurd, deleterious policies he imposes. In discussing Russian history, the need for a "strong ruler" amounts to a default position; one hardly questions it, and events always seem to bear it out. Yet the despot-as-savior, it must be remembered, appeared only as a response to the Tatar-Mongolian yoke. Kievan Russia brooked no autocrats and was fractiously democratic.

"So what should Stalin have done differently?" I asked Genri.

"He should have created republics based on territory, not ethnicity. All these peoples have a right to their own states. Why not, if they want them? Since 1991, I don't see the state as guilty per se, but rather as having made stupid mistakes."

"Such as?"

"Look, the Russian Empire was unwashed and uncivilized, but the Bolsheviks achieved something. They established an equality of sorts. Ask any Soviet minister who his parents were, and he'll tell you peasants or workers. That's an accomplishment. In Soviet times there were Chechen generals, *Chechens!* [Even the first leader of the Chechen rebel movement, the late Dzhokhar Dudayev, had been a general in the Soviet Air Force.] The point is, the Soviets educated people on a secular basis that helped dampen their religious and ethnic hatreds."

Astan cut in. "See, we had a *good* life in Soviet days. What has the West given us, *what?* Pornography and sex. When Garry Kasparov"—the former world chess champion now leading the democratic opposition to Putin—"came here talking about the need for democracy, we threw *stones* at him! We wouldn't let him speak here! *Nobody* believes the liberals anymore. They just want to create problems and get rich off other people's grief. You've seen it over and over again in Russia: some liberal buys a factory but then closes it and throws thousands of workers into the street, leaving them to starve. I ask you, shouldn't those factory owners be executed? Sure, Stalin collectivized agriculture and nationalized industries, but the people got something from it!" He took a breath as anger inflamed his eyes. "Democrats gave us *nothing. All* of us love Stalin. He took over Russia and launched her into space and gave her nuclear weapons. Only political prostitutes, traitors, thieves, and degenerates dislike Stalin."

Genri was unperturbed by this ill-reasoned outburst, the statement of an extreme, but now somewhat popular, point of view. "To solve problems," he said calmly, "we need the state to assure us of a living wage. We need a level economic playing field. We need a *real* free market. When people occupy themselves with their businesses and begin earning money, they forget their ethnic grievances. But in any case, if things ever do explode here, it will be because outside powers stir them up"—a not-so-subtle reference to the new Great Game and the role played in it by the United States, which had just helped Saakashvili to power in Georgia and thereby aroused anger among pro-Kremlin folk in the Russian Caucasus.

Astan leaned over to me. "If you want my opinion, I still don't see why we can't undo all the privatizations the state fobbed off on us in the 1990s. How can a Khodorkovsky or a Gusinsky"—two Yeltsin-era oligarchs, the former now imprisoned in Siberia, the latter in exile—"legally become a millionaire overnight? They stole their fortunes from the people, that's all. I'm a businessman, but I'm at heart a *Communist,* a *decent* Communist. What I absolutely don't need is President Bush coming here and telling me how to live. I'm no bandit, I'm honest, and just because I'm a Communist doesn't mean I don't know what's good for me. We *laugh* at Bush here whenever he talks about democracy!"

The eagle screeched overhead. The water rushed blue and foaming in the stream below, cutting through brilliant green swards.

"Well, I think, in the end, that all the state has to do is assure people of a decent living," Genri said, returning a note of sanity to our talk. "I'd like to propose a toast, a traditional Ossetian toast. May our enemies prosper so they have no need to attack us!"

We drank to that.

We talked and feasted until the sun began to sink. Eventually I grew sleepy from the tart cognac and fresh air. After I thanked Genri for his hospitality and insights, and wished him luck in salvaging his garden, Astan and I drove down around the mountain to the City of the Dead—a lonely scattering of stone huts on a slope. We climbed among them, peering through doorways inside: rays of sunlight fell through the gloom onto largely intact skeletons, onto tibias and skulls and femurs and ribs; it appeared that their owners had crawled inside to die on top of one another. The graves date from the fourteenth through the eighteenth centuries. Little else is known about them.

Astan was quieted by the mournful sight, and found in it evidence of Ossetian self-sacrifice. "See how people were in those days?" he said. "These people had diseases. They crawled up here and died in solitude so their families wouldn't get sick."

A breeze sang through the cracks of the sepulchers. Unrecorded deaths from centuries past, bare bones and wind, rock and sky. From the crags and Dargavs I took away a different message, one evocative of the all-encompassing Truth, the eternal peace that will dawn when, one day, mankind will cease to exist, no more enmities shall be held, no more codes of honor or vengeance reign. A pair of shaggy Caucasian sheepdogs barked at us from the village below, their heads giant and wolflike. Villagers had emerged from their huts to stare at us. The sun was dropping. It was time to go.

THE NEXT DAY back in Vladikavkaz I visited the Terek Cossack Museum on the main drag, Peace Prospekt. The museum, the creation of a meticulous Cossack in his sixties named Dmitry Dmitrievich, consisted of one dusty room, dimly illumined by sunlight seeping through grimy windows. Dressed in a careworn flannel shirt and baggy chinos, wearing horn-rimmed glasses, balding and skinny, and with just a few blackened teeth left, Dmitry beheld me with rank suspicion when I knocked on his door. On seeing his reaction I felt a pang of regret at having come. The Novocherkassk ataman's rants came to mind, and Astan's angry proclamations; I had no taste for more. But I explained myself. He warmed to me when I told him of my recent reenactment of a Cossack explorer's expedition on the Lena River, and invited me in.

Puffing a cheap Russian cigarette, he ambled about his museum and showed me its exhibits. The shelves overflowed with household items from Cossack villages; quill-inscribed edicts covered the walls, with tsarist-era maps and censuses and records all asserting the predominance of Cossacks in this part of Russia, the Terek oblast (until the revolution). He exhaled acrid smoke and related the Terek Cossacks' history. Ivan the Terrible founded the oblast by decree in 1577, when the first Cossack settlers arrived. The Cossack-administered territory comprised what today are Ossetia and Alania, Ingushetia, Chechnya, Dagestan, and Kabardino-Balkaria. The last ataman in office escaped the advancing Bolsheviks and fled abroad, but in 1945 the British handed him back to the Soviet authorities, who executed him. Dmitry told me all of this matter-of-factly, often shrugging, his voice tired but his diction precise.

"I chose every item you see here and brought it here myself. I've done all this out of love for the Cossacks. But as soon as I'm gone, it will all be snatched away. That one Cossack trunk alone is worth fifty thousand dollars."

I asked what he thought of the Cossack revival of today.

He raised his eyebrows. "Yeltsin and Putin have issued so many orders reviving us, but they're all marked 'to be carried out as local authorities see fit.' Officially the law on repressed peoples rehabilitated us"—restored legal status after Stalin's purges—"but other rehabilitated peoples got land and money for their sufferings. We Cossacks got nothing at all."

"What would you like?"

"Well, you know, an Ossetian is living in my ancestral home today in a village near here; I've gone there and seen him. My grandpa spent ten years in the prison monastery Solovki, on the White Sea; when they arrested him, they gave his property to this Ossetian. But what's the use in my complaining to him or trying to sue him to force him out? Four generations of Ossetians have grown up there now, in my house. The Bolsheviks let the Ingush rob us and kill us off; and when they dispossessed us, these robbers took over our houses—they even killed us as we fled. Now the Cossacks are divided into various groups and subgroups. We're powerless."

"So you see no way to revive?"

He shrugged and said something unintelligible. He opened a cabinet closet and showed me his *Cherkesska* (Cossack dress uniform), which he had sewed himself following original patterns; it included a dagger that he had forged with his own hands. He hadn't known how to sew or forge but learned just to assemble this uniform. He put it away and invited me to have a seat by his desk.

I would put my question differently. "What does being a Cossack *mean* nowadays?" I asked.

"Once we were the tsar's military caste and we served him loyally. Nowadays 'Cossack' means saying 'My grandfather was a Cossack,' no more. We were once the best-equipped troops of the tsar's army, but we're nothing now. The Soviets instilled in us all the idea that you get your salary whether you work or not. We're too lazy to be revived because revival would mean work. No one wants to work. But anyway, who needs us these days? Why should we go around patrolling with the police? What's the police for, then, if they need us? It's just silly. We have a modern government now. 'Cossack' is just a word." He shrugged and lit another cigarette. "Just a word."

Dmitry had pursued his passion and preserved what he could of his Cossack heritage. But he recognized, wisely, that it belonged in a museum, not on the streets. How could a government ruling over a multi-ethnic, religiously diverse people in the twenty-first century make use of the Cossacks, whose identity rested on blind allegiance to the tsar and Orthodoxy, when Russia had overthrown one and outgrown, by and large, the other?

He fell silent and fiddled with papers, giving me to think he had work to do. I thanked him for his time and left.

On the way to my hotel I reflected on all the anger I was hearing on this trip (and had heard over the past fourteen years in Russia). Often what really riled people was not that they were living so poorly, but that others were living so well. Settling scores now would only mean some dispossessing others, and would set the stage for further conflict. But how little do we need to survive on this earth, and how much we can share! Even if we are born into cultures encouraging us to seize land or demand justice or kill age-old enemies, we are all, as humans, organically the same. We are not heirs but chance possessors. We need humility, not anger. We can always renounce and move on. Dmitry had done that, and it was a good sign—if others would follow him.

There was little evidence any would.

6

The midmorning sun of August inflamed the Terek, transforming its waters, pleasantly blue-green and rippling only a few hours earlier, into sheets of incandescent glitter. On emerging from my hotel I squinted at them, then felt the air, and my heart sank. A lengthy, circuitous, and nerve-racking journey lay ahead of me, and such punishing heat would not help. I was to leave Vladikavkaz for Makhachkala, the capital of Dagestan, on the Caspian Sea. In other times, getting there would have been easy, and meant traveling just 160 miles due east down a federal highway. But that highway happens to run through Chechnya, which Moscow, to squelch a separatist movement, invaded in 1994 (and again in 1999) and which has famously degenerated into a sui generis post-Soviet Hades, a clan-run furnace of anti-Russian revolt, Islamic insurgency, *mafiya* fiefdoms, and corruption that many Chechens have since abandoned.

The Kremlin claims that Chechnya, following the second Russian invasion, has been "normalizing." Putin supports (in fact, appointed) its thirty-three-year-old president, Ramzan Kadyrov, son of the rebel-commander-turned-Kremlin-loyalist Akhmed Kadyrov, who held the same office until he was shredded by a bomb blast in 2005 at a Grozny parade. The Kadyrov *teip*, or clan, still rules, with backing from Moscow, to the extent that anyone or anything can govern this satrapy of primordial chaos. (Chechens, long before the Soviet era, were notorious outlaws living by laws of blood vengeance.) Chechnya remains aboil with crime, kidnappings, bandit raids, and sporadic, if diminishing, battles between federal forces and diehard guerrillas. Apart from progress reports about the wise reign of the Kadyrov scion and Grozny's rebuilt center, Chechnya has mostly disappeared from state-controlled newscasts in Russia, and few in Russia, except the Chechens, seem to care much about it. Some Russians perceive Moscow's struggle to hold on to the republic as a battle to forestall the breakup of the Russian Federation; others cite corruption, arms sales, and a local oil pipeline as motives for the continuing conflict. In any case, Russian troops control border checkpoints and let foreigners in only with special permission, and then only on troop-escorted tours. Few non-Chechen Russians will venture there for any reason at all.

So, public transport in the region avoids Chechnya. Since the resulting roundabout, 250-mile bus ride to Makhachkala would involve negotiating at least a dozen police checkpoints and could last eighteen hours, I decided to hire a cab for the trip. But even this proved tough to arrange. "Dagestan is another Chechnya!" said the taxi dispatcher, before hanging up on me.

SHE WAS RIGHT. In fact, Dagestan, not Chechnya, raised the original banner of Islamic revolt against Russia in the Caucasus, soon after Tsar Alexander I acquired the territory from Iran in 1813. Leading the first insurgents in holy war was a Sufi Muslim named Ghazi Muhammad, whom the Russians assassinated in 1832. Two years later his followers elected a replacement, the erudite, Arabic-speaking Imam Shamil. Imam Shamil declared Dagestan's independence in 1834, and, commanding fanatic, superbly trained Dagestani and Chechen forces, launched assaults of astonishing ferocity against Russian positions across the Caucasus until 1859, when he finally surrendered and called off the jihad. Alexander II spared him, exiling him to Kaluga, a small town south of Moscow, and even let him make the hajj to Mecca in 1870. There he died a year later, a hero to the Caucasus' peoples. His portrait, showing his bearded and turbaned visage, inspires Islamic rebels to this day.

Guerrilla movements linked with Chechen rebels plague Dagestan still. Between January and August of 2006 (the year of my trip), some two hundred Russian soldiers and special-ops troops had perished in the republic. A number of villages had fallen into the hands of Islamic fundamentalists, including Gimry, Imam Shamil's birthplace, and are now suffering the cruelties of sharia law. In Makhachkala itself criminal gangs routinely detonate bombs in markets to settle scores; gunmen with obscure affiliations battle police and the military; and rebels use nail bombs to blow up Russian troop trucks on the highway into town. Foreigners and Russians have been kidnapped, tortured viciously for months, and then murdered. The dusty barrens and craggy fastnesses of Dagestan are desperately poor; in fact, it is the most impoverished part of Russia. Only 15 percent of the republic's land is arable, so Dagestanis tend to eek out a living raising animals, as they have for centuries.

But being so close, I had to go. Dagestan's notorious history of resistance, even the wild sound of its name (meaning "Land of Mountains" in Turkic), exercised a pull on me no less powerful than that of the Congo. I arranged to be met in Makhachkala by a Dagestani acquaintance of my wife, and resolved to take my chances.

If I could get there, that is. Astan called around and finally found me a taxi for the reasonable fare of $150. At nine-thirty in the morning, a serviceable European passenger car pulled up in front of my hotel. Two drivers climbed out, reeking of cigarette smoke, with hacking coughs. Slavik was skinny and rodentlike, with dirty claw nails and greasy rumpled hair; Sergey was perspiring, fat, and bald, with a hoarse voice and two days' growth. Both had smokers' yellow-gray teeth. They wore tracksuit trousers, frayed nylon shirts, and sandals over fuzzy black socks.

I introduced myself. They told me straightaway they were Ossetians, and so Christian; they let me know that a drive to Dagestan was an excursion into a barbarous Muslim realm sane folk did all they could to avoid.

"Bandits, corrupt police, you name it," said Sergey. "And the road there is hell," added Slavik. "We want to get in and out as fast as possible. You must have a hell of a good reason for going there."

"Oh, I've got to see a friend of my wife's," I replied, putting my bag in the trunk and hoping to ward off further questions. "Family business."

Sergey took the wheel first and drove us north, out of town, onto sun-washed, black-earth plains, the southernmost fringes of the boundless *dikoye pole*, the "wild steppe" of the Volga-Don where, for centuries, Cossacks had fought off nomads and Tatar-Mongolians from the Golden Horde. Heat haze soon shrouded the land. Sergey hit the gas, telling me he wanted to reach Makhachkala by nightfall. He and

Slavik lit up, filling the cabin with bitter smoke. I was glad of the speed; I wanted to make good time and put this misery behind me.

But we soon drew up on the border between North Ossetia and Kabardino-Balkaria, marked by steel-and-glass shack checkpoints sunk in shrubs and bushy low trees by a stream. The Ossetians let us through without stopping us. Twenty yards farther on stood the Kabardino-Balkaria post.

Sergey snarled. *"Stakan naley-ku!"* (Please fill up my glass!, rhyming with *"As-salam 'alaykum,"* the Muslim greeting "May the peace be upon you"), he blurted out, laughing. "That's what I tell these bastard Muslim cops when they try to get a bribe out of me. They say they're Muslims but they all drink, the pigs! Get ready!"

"They'll stop us?" I asked.

"Sure. The pigs'll see our Ossetian tags and know we're from the wrong side of the border."

Sure enough, an officer stepped out of the hut to wave us over with his black and white baton. Plump and swarthy, with pancake-size sweat stains under his flabby arms, he took his time to walk over. Sergey, however, didn't deploy his derisive greeting but silently handed over his driver's license, keeping his eyes fixed ahead. Wheezing, perspiring, the officer thumbed through it and then snapped his fingers for the vehicle's registration paper. After sniffing at this, he peered under the hood and in the trunk, rifling through their rusted car repair oddments. Saying nothing, he returned our papers and let us go.

We were on the road again, flying across wastes broiling and glare-suffused. Sergey and Slavik passed no car without letting loose a smoky-breathed expletive at its driver. They lit up ceaselessly, steering with their elbows as they fumbled with matches and cigarettes, even on turns, even overtaking trucks. "Bastards! Scum!" they shouted, as an acrid haze of ash settled into my sweaty pores.

The sun hit its zenith and the heat had me gasping through the open window. The road deteriorated, yet we maintained speed, swerving around wrecked stretches and potholes, shooting down the tarmac through hayfields, by haystacks, honking to force aside hay-loaded mule carts piloted by veiled women and dead-eyed, square-jawed men in fedoras and old baggy jackets. At first the scene put me in mind of eastern Turkey and the Anatolian Plateau, but then it didn't, and I couldn't say why.

"Skoty poganyye!" (Cursed buggers!), shouted Sergey at the prolifer-

ating checkpoints. Every five or ten miles, *gaishniki* caught sight of our Ossetian plates and waved us over for a fifteen-to-twenty-minute inspection, repeating the same document and hood and trunk checks, always finding nothing and letting us go. A fifty-ruble note slipped into proffered papers would have quickened our passage, but with the posts so numerous, such bribes would eventually consume all their profits.

Then, "*Skoty poganyye!* Up ahead's the Russian border post!" Sergey announced.

Certainly they would detain us for a good long while, I assumed. Entering Russia proper from the Caucasus had to be serious business. But after just a glance at papers, the officers lifted the red and white crossbeam and we rolled ahead into the corn and hayfields of Stavropol' region.

I felt good at being back in Russia, but my relief didn't last long. We began taking turn after unmarked turn down ever-bumpier gravel tracks, passing lumbering wrecks of cars, bouncing through villages of eye-searing squalor—tumbledown huts of cement and rusted steel, collapsing wooden cabins, trash-strewn yards and stray dogs, bare-fanged and half starved. Men in soiled sweatpants hoed the mucky sod of garden plots; obese women in Islamic headscarves squatted by the road, spitting out sunflower seeds and staring at us.

This was a Russia I had never seen before, not far removed geographically from eastern Turkey, but—now I understood the difference —without any redeeming hint of the traditional, without the proud, noble smiles of the Turks. When we stopped to ask for directions, answers came through rotten teeth as if through mouthfuls of marbles, and with much tortured gesticulation. Russian here was a foreign language. The Slavs manning the GAI posts, I thought, must feel as though they'd been banished to the Middle East.

Soon a *gaishnik* appeared and waved his baton at us.

"The sons of bitches!" grumbled my drivers simultaneously. "The bastards! These Russians *really* hate us!"

How many times had we been stopped? Six or seven. Of the four hours we'd been on the road, at least an hour and a half we had spent at checkpoints.

The officer was a Russian Herman Munster, tall, bulky-shouldered, clumsy, and long-faced, his GAI hat perched atop an oddly rectangular skull.

We pulled up by him and halted.

"Grazhdane!" (Citizens!), he said, saluting us. "Out of the car!"

He pulled apart the seats, picked at the upholstery. "Oh, Christ," Sergey said under his breath. "We'll never get to Makhachkala with bastards like this every ten kilometers."

Officer Munster examined their papers and got to my passport last. "Oh-ho! An American? How can it be?"

I smiled and shrugged.

"Say," he said, returning my smile, "I've got this brother in the States, on a work-study program. Tell me, can he stay on once it's over?"

Sergey rolled his eyes.

"Well," I said, seeing no way out of a forced chat, "he'll have to find an employer and leave the country to reapply for a new visa, as far as I know. I—"

"He won't bother with all that, I think," said Munster. "He'll just overstay his visa. What I really want to know is, is your government hard on illegals?"

"Oh, Jesus, we don't have time for all this blabber!" Sergey cut in. "We've got to move on!"

"I'm afraid he has a point," I said.

The officer was unmoved, and not surprisingly, after Sergey's outburst he prolonged our discussion. I explained enough about labor laws and visas to satisfy him. He nodded, said thanks, and returned my passport. He shook my hand and saluted, and wished us well.

"The hell with him!" barked out Sergey, once we were moving again. "You shouldn't waste your time. They'll screw you any way they can."

"Well, they *are* people, after all," I said. "If they want to, they can detain us for hours or even days. Anyway, I wasn't going to begrudge that *gaishnik* a talk with one of the few foreigners he's likely to see on this beat."

"I'll never give these thugs a single ruble. If they sense weakness they'll screw you for every kopek you've got. I *never* submit. I'll sic the KGB on their corrupt asses," he said.

We drove on in silence. Sergey confronted the GAI every day on the job, and its often venal officers cost him time, money, and nerves. Of course, he lacked the authority to sic the KGB or anyone else on them, and all he could do was curse them (well out of earshot). But I didn't and *wouldn't* react to them as he did. No matter how corrupt or annoying others are, we can choose how we respond to them.

Farms soon disappeared and the steppe began again, here stretches of semidesert empty save for browned-out feather grass and the rarest of willows. As we neared the Bazygausky Sands, the land dried up even more. Hot wind blasted in through our open windows, chapping my lips, pelting us with grit. Sergey switched on his old cassette player and *"I LIKE TO MOVE IT MOVE IT!"* screeched forth, but Lermontov's poem of exile came to my mind.

> Farewell, unwashed Russia!
> Land of slaves! Land of masters!
> Farewell to you, blue uniforms,
> And you, people loyal to them

DUN-COLORED DEAD LAND swept away from the road, its most distant expanses meeting the sky; above us hung cumulus clouds, battleships of cotton floating on roving currents of hot air; and dust devils spun by, as if in search of souls to seize. Desolate, alienating harbingers of Central Asia . . . Whatever the map said, this was no longer Russia.

Slavik took the wheel. Sergey climbed in the back and yawned, exhaling foul breath, smoked a cigarette, and stretched out to sleep. The road improved. We sped ahead down a highway curving only rarely, the heat soporific, the glare wearying.

Somewhere near the settlement of Tersky, a dot in the sand-blasted wastes ahead resolved itself into a guard shack. Sergey sat up and rubbed his eyes. "Oh, screw them! This is a bad post. The cops there are real *skoty.*"

Sure enough a *gaishnik,* tamping down his high-brimmed hat, stepped out to the road and waved us over. Slavik shot past him and slammed on the brakes, leaving the officer with a five-minute walk to reach us—a breach of citizen-*gaishnik* etiquette. In Russia, drivers usually stop near the *gaishnik,* grab their papers, and jump out smiling to shake his hand, hoping to ensure a more lenient reception (and less onerous demands for a bribe).

"Screw his mother," Sergey said through clenched teeth.

"Get out of the car and come with me," ordered the officer after checking Slavik's papers. Slavik quickly obeyed.

An hour later Sergey and I were still there, waiting in the sun for Slavik, battered by ever-hotter winds and dust devils, caked in grit. The officer objected to Slavik's not being registered to drive Sergey's vehicle—an open-and-shut case, it seemed.

Sergey burned through four or five cigarettes. "I'm going to tell that goddamned officer," he said, "'Show me where it says you can detain him for that and I'll pay you your fucking fine!' But he *can't* show me 'cause the law doesn't say any such thing."

"Are you sure?" I said. News of changes in laws enacted in Moscow often took months, even years, to reach the provinces.

"They took that clause out of the new law. The fucker doesn't know that or he doesn't care."

"Well, how much does he want?"

"Five hundred fucking rubles. Traffic out on this damn road's so light, the *gaishniki* milk their victims for all they can. But we'll wait him out."

Had another car showed up, offering the *gaishnik* a chance for easier booty, perhaps he would have released us. Just as I was about to get out and pay, Slavik ran up and jumped in. "I gave him two hundred rubles and he let me go!"

"The hell with him," grumbled Sergey. "Why'd you do that?"

"No, really—he could take my license. He showed me the law."

"Look, let's get out of here before he changes his mind!" I said.

Sergey pounded his fist on the dashboard. "Let me catch that corrupt bastard in Ossetia and I'll throw a grenade at him, the son of a bitch! If he tries to come to Ossetia I'll smash in his skull! I'll disembowel him!"

We pulled out and sped ahead toward a horizon bristling with gas and oil rigs, beset by dust devils, with every mile taking us into hotter, more hopeless terrain.

AROUND SIX IN THE EVENING we were racing across the Nogay Steppe, dustbowl plains mottled with a drear scant growth of dead grass, dotted with scurrying balls of sagebrush. Kalashnikov-wielding men in blue camouflage waved us through a two-story steel compound—the exit border post for Stavropol' region. A few miles on was a dilapidated entry bunker marked DAGESTAN, where officers, short, swarthy, and grumpy, registered us and let us go.

As the sun set I perked up. Darkness would become these barrens. From the west a reddish-pink haze seeped across a turquoise sky. The land greened slightly, and ripe melons soon covered the earth in sloppily planted rows. Turkic-looking shepherds and cowherds with high brows and short black hair dawdled along the road, prodding their flocks with switches; and mud-brick houses sunken into the earth replaced the more or less modern hovels we had seen since Vladikavkaz. We were penetrating a new, non-Russian world. I thrilled recalling Lermontov's verse; I inwardly churned, roused by the novelty of the scene.

An hour or two after nightfall we hit Makhachkala, a mess of clogged lanes as chaotic as an oriental bazaar, enrobed pedestrians wandering into traffic, kebab carts trailing plumes of smoke from roasting lamb, a confetti spray of lights glittering on the Caspian's luminescent cobalt waters, and, to our great pleasure, balmy, if humid, maritime breezes. Men were short and wiry and swaggering, yet when we asked them for directions, they stopped and smiled and helped us in primitive Russian, and wished us well.

We arrived at the walled-off compound of my hotel, the Lux. I paid Sergey and Slavik and we said a quick goodbye so they could hit the road back. I got out, exhausted, yet excited with the Middle Eastern scents and scenes, black with exhaust grime, my shirt speckled with sweat salt, and shouldered my bag. From an unseen minaret on the corner, a muezzin wailed out the nighttime call to prayer, the last of the day.

7

I awoke to the taunting, boisterous yelps of seagulls. Drafts warm and briny teased my window's curtains, gauzy yellow filters irradiated by the southern sun and spangled with glints from the sea, which spread glaucous and frothy beyond the minarets and apartment buildings and satellite disks. Save for the oil and gas tankers chugging along the horizon, I might have been somewhere in the Muslim Mediterranean, anywhere but Russia. In fact, Makhachkala is closer to Tehran than to Moscow. Before there even was a Moscow, before Kievan Russia had embraced Christianity, Syrians arrived here (Makhachkala was then the Khazar capital, Semender), bringing a new faith called Islam. Only when Peter the Great fought Persia in the 1720s did the Russian presence begin.

It was to be a bloody one. A century later Lermontov wrote:

> *V poldnevny zhar v doline Dagestana*
> *S svintsom v grudi lezhal nedvizhim ya*
> *Glubokaya yeshcho dymilas' rana*
> *Po kaple krov' tochilasya moya*

> In the midday heat of a Dagestani ravine
> I lay motionless, a bullet in my breast.
> The deep wound steamed still, and
> My blood flowed out, one drop at a time

Dagestan in the poet's day was a savage realm of conquest and guerrilla war where many of the tsar's most daring soldiers lost their lives. In 1844 the Russians founded the *Ukrepleniye* (Fortification) of Petrovskoye on a hill above Semender. Only in 1921 did Petrovskoye become Makhachkala. For all its apparent exoticism, Makhachkala is a Soviet appellation concocted from the given name of a certain Makhach Dakhadayev, a local revolutionary. Eighty-one ethnic groups make up the population of Russia's most diverse (and fractious) republic. But however much blood is shed here, large deposits of oil, gas, and minerals (so far little exploited) ensure that the Kremlin will do all it can to keep Dagestan in Russia.

I dressed quickly and went downstairs to meet Murat, my Dagestani friend.

An hour later Murat and I stood shading our eyes from the wicked sun atop a rocky promontory, surveying the cluttered white seaside neighborhoods of Makhachkala below; behind us towered a wall of bleak sandy mountains slashed with gorges. Freckled, strawberry blond, and patchily bearded, and dressed in baby blue trousers, a pressed white shirt, and pointy white elf designer shoes, Murat had an affable manner that straightaway set me at ease. Born in 1965, he had received a Soviet education and so spoke fluent Russian. As the owner of profitable gas stations in impoverished Makhachkala, Murat was a Big Man.

His family, like most in Russia, had been buffeted about by the bloody tides of history. One great-great-grandfather had died in exile in Archangel; Chechen bandits had murdered another. Before the revolution, his mother's relatives had employed forty servants. The Soviets dispossessed them and threw his mother and grandmother in prison. His father they banished to Siberia.

He recounted all this without a trace of bitterness.

"Is there bad blood between Chechens and Dagestanis?" I asked.

"No," he said, lighting up a cigarette. "We may be the only people who get along with them. I don't mean they're perfect. I think they were planning to collaborate with the Nazis and probably did prepare a white horse as a gift to Hitler," he said, bringing up an old rumor. "So Stalin had his reasons for deporting them to Siberia and Central Asia [in 1944]."

"Did he deport the Dagestanis too?"

"No, but he was going to. Somehow, though, a clever Dagestani minister got Stalin's ear and persuaded him not to touch us."

His cell phone rang. He answered, speaking a Turkic dialect close enough to the Turkish of Turkey that I could understand much of what he said. This I found thrilling, and it made me feel even more excited to be here.

When he hung up I addressed him in Turkish. He smiled and replied in Turkic. "Well, I'm a Kumyk, you know. Our language is eighty percent the same as the Turkish of Turkey. The Kumyk are the third-largest people here, after the Avar and the Dargin." He went on to explain the ethnic balance observed in the republic's ministries, where fourteen languages have official status. Returning to Russian, he said, "We once used Arabic as our written language so we could all communicate. But now Russian is our lingua franca. We couldn't get along without it. We were all brought up on Soviet culture here."

The call to prayer sounded, mingling with the cries of seagulls and the faint din of cars and horns from the city below. It was Friday noon, and time for the sermon of the week.

"Oh, let's get going," he said.

We hurried down over the rocks to his Volga, parked on the last stretch of road. Before he got in, he dispensed with his dying butt and lit up again; I would never see him without tusks of smoke streaming from his nostrils. As he puffed and we drove down into Makhachkala, he talked about how the Soviets tried to extirpate religion.

But then he surprised me.

"The Communists forbade all kinds of truths in the Qur'an. For example," he said, snorting smoke, "they forbade us from learning about the jinn"—spirits that, according to Islam, may be good or evil, and supposedly dwell among us.

"Ah, you believe in jinn?"

"Of course! They're in the Qur'an. If it weren't true, the Communists wouldn't have banned it. Anyway, I know about them from my own experience."

"How's that?"

"Well, this cousin of mine back in my village, she had what we call in Kumyk a"—here he lit up anew—"a *jinn er.*"

"What? A genie husband?"

"To be exact, an *invisible* genie husband. That's what we mean by *jinn er* in Kumyk."

We were now honking and proceeding slowly, fording crowds toting folded-up prayer rugs.

"Forgive me," I said, "but if you couldn't see him, how do you know he existed?"

"The villagers *did* see him once, when he *chose* to show himself. That's the whole point: the *jinn er* can only be seen if they want to be. There're devils and jinn all over the place, just like the Qur'an says."

"Okay."

I didn't want to say more, for fear of offending him so soon after our meeting for the first time. But he must have sensed my incredulity.

"Really, this isn't something I'm making up. The whole village says it's true."

"Well, maybe. I mean—"

"And that's not the only truth the Communists forbade. They never wanted us to hear about our yeti either."

"The abominable snowman? It's a hundred degrees here!"

"Well, out in our village we have this yeti that came down from the mountaintop, where it's a lot cooler. I know this for a fact. My grandfather tore off a clump of his hair. As everyone knows, if you steal a yeti's hair, they never leave you. We had this yeti working on the farm. I'm not saying it was nice having him around, mind you."

"Well, if he was abominable, I imagine not."

"Yetis like crushing people to death, using their giant arms and famous wedge-shaped chests. And of course the female yetis have these really long tits they throw over their shoulders when bathing, and . . ."

In Russia, Murat's loony tales didn't really stand out. Conspiracy theories abound, psychics enjoy cult followings, many prefer folk healers to regular doctors, and suspicion of all "official" truths is a sign of sophistication. Reality is for naïve bumpkins.

We pulled up behind the Central Mosque. It resembled an Ottoman shrine, with wizard-hatted minarets, manifold blue domes, and high arching windows. No surprise there: Turkey partly financed it. Murat asked me to wait by the car and discreetly approached one of the skull-capped caretakers, who gave me a censorious look and shook his head. It turned out that I, an infidel, would not be allowed in during services, so we stood out on the granite esplanade.

"Please don't forgo prayers on my account," I said, wondering if, with his Soviet upbringing, he could really be religious enough to attend mosque.

"Oh, it doesn't matter. I'm a believer, but I think everyone should decide on religion for himself. We're not Wahhabis here. All that Wahhabi extremism we have out in our mountains comes from young men returning from studying Islam in Arab countries. No matter how many imams here say they want to close down our saunas"—brothels, really—"deputies in the National Assembly own them and profit from them, so that will never happen. Whoever has the most cash is elected. Religion only goes so far here."

Murat went on to state the well-known "benefits" of Islam: It prohibited killing. Prayer, with all its strenuous prostration and genuflection, is exercise. Ablutions keep people clean. Counting the ninety-nine Arabic names of God on stringed beads teaches arithmetic. Anger, pride, and greed are "the worst of sins."

Potbellied men, some unshaven, were hurrying by, sweaty, winded, and jovial, clamping down their skullcaps and clutching prayer rugs and Qur'ans.

Murat knew many of them. "There's our banker! This one's a militiaman! That guy is one of our big lawyers!"

Morose-looking youths with scruffy beards were flooding past too, removing their shoes (and releasing a sour footy odor into the hot air) as they stepped inside, where room soon ran out. The crowd overflowed onto the esplanade, and we had to step back. Barefoot little boys circulated, hawking sheets of scavenged wallpaper as substitute prayer rugs for those who arrived without. The head imam would later tell me that attendance at Friday services had grown from a few middle-aged men in Soviet times to eight thousand and counting now. The average age of worshipers was now between twenty and twenty-five, the most radical age—a portent for Dagestan's future.

One sees similar scenes of public piety all over the Middle East, but rarely in Russia. The imam, unseen by us, deep in the shadowy cool of his *mithrab,* soon commenced chanting the Qur'an, and segued into his weekly sermon, "The Jihad [Struggle] with Oneself." He spoke in Russian, inserting key words and Qur'anic citations in Arabic. ("Studying Arabic is all the rage now," Murat whispered proudly.)

"True joy and happiness come from struggling with oneself," the imam said in a measured baritone, "within the framework of sharia and while taming one's passions and desires, that is, one's *shakhvat*"—from the Arabic *shahwa*, or lust. "Eating when hungry, sexual relations with one's lawful spouse, and sleeping for purposes of rest bring a man pleasure. When a man enjoys these things within the framework of sharia, with the *proper intention,* he even receives rewards from them. . . . Alcohol, drugs, sexual relations outside wedlock, striving to acquire material and other goods by any means, which are all so common now . . . stem from the lack of struggle with oneself." His voice rose as he condemned gambling, brothels, tobacco, and amusement parks as recent, post-Soviet, and therefore illicit, phenomena—his idea of morality clearly accorded with the prudish Communist ethos once enforced here. All, he thundered, were manifestations of *shakhvat*, "Satan's most frightening weapon," the Muslims' addiction to which brought on disunity, weakness, and conflict, especially (for some reason) in Palestine and Lebanon. He demanded a return to Islamic principles, and reminded his audience, "God almighty has elevated Muhammad's *umma* [community of believers] above other *ummas*," and the "Western way of life" must be rejected in order to find God's favor. He finished with, "Embellish the body of Islam and make this world a flaming pit for Zionists and the other enemies of Islam who tirelessly drink the blood and sweat of Muslims! Amen!"

"Amen!" repeated the worshipers.

"Amen," said Murat quietly, though he had not been praying.

There was nothing seditious here, little that was political, and no call to holy war; certainly the security services kept close watch on Makhachkala's imams. One might have heard the same homily in any Cairo mosque. In fact, a Russian Orthodox priest might replace "Islam" and "sharia" with "Christianity" and "the Ten Commandments" and deliver much the same (anti-Western) discourse in church up north. Resentment of the West now amounts to an ecumenical faith across Russia.

"So what did you think?" I asked Murat.

He shrugged. "What he said was true."

The sun beat down. As the worshipers donned their shoes and gathered up their rugs and scraps of wallpaper, we climbed back into the Volga. Murat flicked on the air conditioning, reposing in the shade of his tinted windows, and lit up.

"Like to get a bite to eat?" he asked.

"Sure."

We pulled out into traffic, our white Volga puny amid black and boxy armored Mercedes SUVs and jacked-up Cherokees with tinted windows all.

MURAT'S HANGOUT, and Makhachkala's elite lair of leisure, was the Viking, a dimly lit restaurant that, with its stained wood interior, shabbily curtained booths, and Oktoberfest waitresses (all Russian) in red aprons and white blouses, would have been unremarkable anywhere else. But here it stood out, offering both an air-conditioned retreat from the Dagestani sun and refuge from mean streets: in just a few hours, I had witnessed two explosive arguments in guttural Dagestani dialects, and the lurking presence of camouflaged troops didn't reassure, either.

The staff greeted us with a restrained chorus of *Zdravstvuytes!* We climbed ladderlike stairs to Murat's aerie—a table set atop a lookout platform a good ten feet above the ground floor. Tatyana, our waitress, mounted the steps behind us, huffing. Like the other waitresses, she looked more matronly than maidenly.

Murat pulled out a fresh pack of cigarettes and lit up, ordering us a bottle of Lezginka cognac, a kilogram or two of mutton *shashlyki*, bowls of salad, and hunks of cheese. "I'm going to show you real Dagestani hospitality," he said.

He turned in his seat and surveyed the patrons arriving down on the lower level. As in Islamic countries, many took Friday afternoons off here. But Makhachkala being in the former Soviet Union, people did so less for reasons of piety and more to start partying early. He identified those he knew by their ethnic group. "That one's a Lezgin. This fellow's an Avar. Over there's a Nogay . . ." He might have been reciting a list of Russia's historic adversaries, the warriors of steppe and hill so vividly brought to life in the verse of Lermontov and Pushkin.

"All these different peoples come and drink in one spot?" I asked.

"Dagestan is diverse, as you know. We all get along really well here, despite our ethnic backgrounds." My raised eyebrow prompted him to add a qualifier. "I mean, aside from the bomb blasts and shootings."

"Who gets killed?"

"Usually local officials. Killing's how people settle scores here."

"How many have been assassinated so far this year?"

He counted till he lost track. "Anyway, the problem is simple. The police arrest some guy. They send him to jail; he does his time and gets out. But Makhachkala's a small place. So he hunts down the one who put him in jail, and, well . . ." He took a drag on his cig. "I've come upon terrible scenes here, right after bombings, guts and blood and limbs strewn all over." He shuddered and looked away.

Half an hour later Tatyana reappeared, panting, at the head of the stairs, bearing an opulently laden tray of dishes arranged around an amber bottle of Lezginka. Our order would have surfeited a gathering of five or six: piles of goat cheese, a heap of sizzling ribs and chops, bowls of greens doused in olive oil. "Dagestani hospitality," Murat said, proud of feasting traditions considered bounteous even in Russia, where sating guests is a sacred duty. Friends in Moscow had warned me, "Caucasian hospitality is wonderful—if you can survive it!"

We toasted and knocked back shots of Lezginka, which went down smooth, with a chestnut fragrance. We then attacked the mutton—the most succulent I had ever tasted. All at once it seemed I hadn't eaten in weeks.

"So," Murat said, chewing lustily, "I've arrived after attacks and seen it all: cut-off arms and ripped-off legs and severed heads." He gnawed on a rib and spat out a sliver of bone. "Just recently they put a bomb in this guy's car, in his seat's headrest." He bit off a chunk of flesh. "Blew up and decapitated him. The government creates killers here, forcing them to sit on bottles."

"Sit on bottles?"

"Of course. They arrest you and throw you in jail. They grab you and strip you and stand this bottle on a chair and force you to—"

"I get it, I get it. Let's drink to our never having to sit on bottles."

We raised our glasses. Murat blew over his left shoulder and downed his dose.

Footsteps on the stairs. A slender, soigné fellow, curly-haired, with penetrating black eyes set on me, stepped cautiously up to our table and greeted Murat. He wore a classy leather jacket and a Zegna shirt.

After introductions (his name was Nabi, or "prophet" in Arabic), he lifted his glass and narrowed his eyes, which were still on mine. "So, you're American?" he said flatly. "I'd like to propose a toast to Americans. To those who come to enjoy our Dagestani sunshine."

Murat and I stood and raised our glasses.

"Thank you," I said. I moved to drink, but Murat didn't.

Nabi wasn't finished. "How wonderful Americans are," he said in a steely tone, still looking at me. "Americans, that is, who come to make *peace*, not *war*, not to stir up our peoples and set them against one another."

"Well, I come in peace."

"If you dare fight us, we'll never surrender! We'll all die together, but surrender—*never!*"

We drank and all sat down and resumed eating, I under Nabi's circumspect gaze. A tall, paunchy youth named Sultan joined us and light-ened the mood. Murat poured him a shot of cognac. Americans, they agreed, should butt out of Russia's "sphere of influence," fold up their seat at the table of the new Great Game, and stop using their NGOs to support opposition parties, as they had in Georgia, Ukraine, and Kyrgyzstan. And woe to any who *dare* mess with the Dagestanis.

"We have a joke," Murat said. "We hear that China is going to invade Dagestan with a billion soldiers."

"And?"

"And our only concern is, where will we find room to bury them all!" Laughter and glass-clinking and macho gulps followed. "Allah Allah! *Kitay gitti!*" (China is finished!)

"I don't think the U.S. is planning to invade Dagestan anytime soon," I said in Turkish, which evoked smiles and mild exclamations of surprise from the newcomers: speaking Turkish, I became a brother, at least as long as the cognac buzz lasted.

"Putin's great," announced Murat. "Things are *much* better with him in charge."

"Really?" I replied.

Eyes widened all around the table. How could I have asked?

"Why, he's ordered society," Murat said. "Call it authoritarianism, KGB rule, who cares? What matters is that people get their pensions on time and workers get their salaries. He put an end to the chaos of the Yeltsin years."

Nabi rose and lifted his glass. "Makhachkala is a *great* place. You know why?" he asked me. "Because *I* live here! Ha! No, seriously. In Russia, you can be someone's relative today, and tomorrow they kill you. In Russia you're not *protected*. But here it's different. We know everyone. In Dagestan you're *safe*. Let's drink to that."

I felt hot, flushed, intoxicated. I began sensing that Dagestan was indeed different from other places I had seen so far on my trip; it was more alive, simmering with an energy (revealed by Nabi's comments about America) that, nonetheless, could definitely spark violence. I wasn't sure that I felt safe. But a weariness with alcohol was creeping over me; since leaving Moscow, I'd been fêted almost every day. This was, however, not the time to say no, and I honored Nabi's raised glass. Certainly here more than anywhere the epigrammatic, Stalin-era adage still held true: *"Ne p'yosh, zalozhish!"* (If you don't drink [and therefore remain sober enough to remember what we're saying], you will inform on us [in the morning]!)

Downstairs a singer had arrived and a band was tuning up. Nabi shouted an order for a song he wanted dedicated to me. A woman, invisible from our aerie, performed "Listen to Your Heart" in slightly accented English.

Nabi leaned over to me. "For us a guest is made of *gold!*" He lowered his voice. "However, we *hate* Bush here. We're *all* against Bush and the war in Iraq. You don't know what you've got yourselves into."

Murat cut in. "You can see on Bush's face that he's a bad person, bad. He's not worthy of sitting here with us to drink a *beer.*"

"Let alone Lezginka!" said Sultan.

"I would like to say something," Murat announced, sweat trickling down his freckled brow. "September eleventh was a visitation from the Almighty. God gave us the attacks of that day as a lesson to remind us that he exists, that we're all his children, all children of one god. It's not just we in Dagestan who live on a powder keg, it's all humanity now. For the first time, Americans can feel that for themselves."

It was risky, but I responded that while I basically agreed with him, I believed in no revealed religion; if anything, I was a Buddhist, though a Buddhist who rejected reincarnation and any other intrusions of the supernatural into a philosophy based on compassion and nonviolence.

A moment of silence ensued. Had I damaged my credibility by introducing a note of heresy? (Islam ranks Buddhists as heathens, unworthy of even the second-rate status it accords to Jewish and Christian "People of the Book.") To my great relief, Murat said he found much to like about Buddhism. Sultan was skeptical, but Murat persisted, evincing a knowledge of the teachings that could only come from reading and reflection. In no other Islamic country had I heard such a calm, frank exposition of a rival faith, and for this I credited Soviet secular education.

I got up and climbed carefully down the steps and found Tatyana. I ordered a song for Nabi, a traditional Azar tune, the sort of rousing flute-and-drum instrumental to which a *papakha*-coifed mountaineer could stamp out a dance in high black boots, arms akimbo, sword in teeth, his defiant gaze fixed on the heavens. On the way back, I caught the eye, thick-lashed, moist, and inquiring, of the singer, whose dark hair framed an olive-complexioned face of startling beauty.

Up in the aerie more libations were proposed, and soon we were shouting, toasting, declaring our hatred of tyrants, and professing desires for peace in Turkish, Russian, and Kumyk. Such solidarity! Such élan! Dagestan seemed wild and free, my tablemates heroes, exemplars of liberty untouched by Soviet domination. Murat promised to take me up into the highlands, to Gimry, the birthplace of Imam Shamil, where I would meet Dagestanis at their most noble and traditional. Hurrah! We drank to that. Hurrah!

The singer appeared at the head of the steps, and we calmed down. Sultan stepped out to offer her the seat next to me. Refusing a proffered shot of cognac—she was on the job—she spoke to me in fluent English.

"I wanted to meet you," she said, brushing her heavy locks away from dimpled cheeks. "I can't sing Dagestani songs, you know, because I don't know the language. I'm not from here."

"No?" I said.

"I'm Azeri and Armenian."

"You're very beautiful," I said, feeling the words coming out too quickly because of the Lezginka.

"Well, I'm from a typically mixed Soviet family. Mixed blood produces the most beautiful children and the smartest too, no?"

Tatyana huffed up the steps to replenish our piles of *shashlyki* and cheese and switch our empty bottle of cognac for a new full one. Murat and Sultan poured more rounds and dug in.

The singer glanced about. "You have civilized friends."

"Thank you. Ah, what exactly do you mean by 'civilized'?"

"Other people here . . . others in this republic . . . are *savage.* In Dagestan we're completely unprotected by law—we're at the mercy of clans and gangs and thugs and killers. You might not see this. But you need connections to do anything, anything at all. One wrong move and they kill you."

"How's her English?" asked Murat.

"Wonderful," I said, hoping he could not understand her.

She clenched her small fists and said in a voice smoldering with desperation, "I can't *stand* it! I want to get out of here and live freely. I want to immigrate to Canada." She stood up abruptly. "I'm sorry, I have to work. I'll sing a song for you."

Just before her head dropped beneath the top step she shot me a look inscrutable and searching. A minute later she sang "Without You."

"What was she so upset about?" Murat asked.

"Oh, nothing. Wants to go to Canada."

"Oh."

We raised our glasses and toasted to Canada. Her words highlighted how my status as a visitor here was shielding me from the reality of this place, which was, cognac and toasts aside, bomb-splattered guts and blood feuds.

At two in the morning, a full twelve hours after arriving, we walked out of the Viking into a city of few street lamps and many dark empty streets. Murat was still surprisingly sober; I felt severely fatigued, but not really drunk, thanks to the way they had paced the toasts. (Here as in Russia, one drinks obligatorily to toasts, but not on one's own.) And as in Nalchik, no *gaishnik* would dare arrest Murat for driving under the influence—he had connections, he knew everyone.

Murat and I climbed into his Volga and set out for my hotel. The main boulevard was illuminated, but not the lanes branching off it, onto which we turned.

Headlights soon flashed behind us, bouncing with the potholes. Murat glanced in the rearview mirror. We turned and the lights turned too. He accelerated and took a sharp left down a pitch-black alley. The lights drew closer.

"What's going on?" I asked. I thought, *We should have stayed on the main road! Maybe this is a kidnapping!* All of our feasting suddenly seemed wildly imprudent. We would make the perfect targets: we were unarmed and had been drinking, and surely everyone in the restaurant had learned of my nationality.

Murat pulled over, as did the other car.

"Who are they?" I asked.

"Wait here."

They cut their lights. The blackness was total.

He jumped out and was gone. I could see neither our pursuer, nor the street ahead, nor Murat.

Ten minutes passed, twenty, and no sign of Murat. Hot, humid sea air seeped through my shirt and I sweated. I pulled out my cell phone and pondered calling for help. But whom would I call? How would I describe where I was? If I made a run for it, where would I go? And what, if anything, was really wrong?

Just as I was about to climb out and confront our pursuers, Murat stuck his head in the driver's side window.

"Talk to this man about going to Gimry," he said in a strangely hoarse voice.

A blue-shirted paunch appeared in the window, and then its owner, a police officer who resembled a corpulent Nabi (he must have been an Azar as well), peered in. I offered my passport but he ignored it.

"You want to go to Gimry," he said in an accusatory tone. "Don't even try. Our mountains are dangerous and the people up there bad. You could be kidnapped for ransom or worse. Three commandos have just gone missing today up there. My advice to you is, simply put, *leave*. Do you understand me?"

"Yes," I answered.

"You do get my drift?"

"I do."

"Okay then, *do svidaniya*."

Murat got in and started up the car. "Sorry," he said, "but our Gimry plans are off. I'm really sorry."

"No problem."

At first I felt betrayed. Murat must have told the officer everything about me. The officer probably ordered a background check on me over the police radio—hence the delay. But I immediately renounced my grudge. I would leave and Murat would stay. He had good reason to keep on good terms with the authorities (such as they were in Dagestan).

I thought of the singer and her desperate eyes.

AT TEN THE NEXT MORNING Sultan and Murat showed up at my hotel in an aging black BMW. It was hot, much hotter than the previous day, so hot, in fact, that after all the booze of the previous night I felt dizzy on stepping outside. They had a surprise in store for me, they announced as I got in the smoke-filled car. *I sure hope it doesn't involve drinking*, I thought, foggy-brained, almost retching at the notion of more alcohol.

We were soon flying down a crowded two-lane highway, swerving around trucks and dodging Ladas, heading south, the Caspian to the left brilliant, aquamarine, and glimmering in the merciless white light. This was once the camel-trod Dagestan Corridor, formerly a caravan route leading from Russia to Baku, across the border in Azerbaijan. All I could think of now was fresh air, but when I opened my window Sultan objected: drafts, here as in Russia, are believed to cause illness. He flicked on the air conditioning, but it spewed out only tepid currents of recycled smoke.

They took calls on their cell phones, shouting in Kumyk and repeatedly lighting up. Sultan as a result drove one-handed—no mean feat with a stick shift. Caucasians have earned infamy in Russia for their macho, and frequently lethal, driving habits. Near misses followed swerves, lunges left came after gravelly skids on the shoulder, and we often swung back into our lane just in time to avoid a head-on collision. We ended up passing a car passing a car; in a dusty haze drivers in all three vehicles honked and shouted in Kumyk—curses? Dares? I clutched at the dashboard, but Sultan chuckled.

"He's a great driver," Murat assured me.

We finally pulled in to the town of Derbent and cruised down into the center, which resembled Damascus, with its sandy hues and bustle of donkeys, its veiled women and mayhem of vendors and smoking *shashlyki* stands. We took a right and bounced up steep alleys, passing scenes that looked straight out of a Syrian medina. We stopped beneath gigantic dun-colored ramparts.

"Naryn Fortress," Murat said. "It's older than time."

The sun beat down. We mounted hot steps to a palatial stone arch set in the lowest granite wall of a fortress covering half the mountainside. A young woman arose from a seat in the shade. She was kohl-eyed and sultry, her slender curves filling a tight peach knee-length dress, but she had hidden her hair under an Islamic headscarf. Still, luscious raven locks peeked out. Her name was Ayna and she would be our guide.

Naryn Fortress was massive and impregnable, a stone behemoth baking in razoring light. As we ascended the walkway, our steps heavy in the heat, Ayna rattled off facts. Naryn had been constructed in the sixth century B.C. to guard the Dagestani Corridor. Derbent appeared around 300 B.C. The Arabs seized it in 728, the Tatar-Mongolians in 1220. Dagestan's peoples adopted Christianity from the Byzantines, and thus came late to Islam.

Naryn consisted of forty-five miles of walls that were fifty-five feet high and ten feet thick—heavy enough to absorb blasts of modern artillery. Herodotus, Plutarch, Pliny, Marco Polo (who noted it was called the "Gate of Iron"), and even Alexander Dumas had visited. Peter the Great's arrival in 1722 spelled the beginning of Russian domination, which commenced in earnest only in 1813. In 2003 UNESCO had named Derbent's old town and Naryn World Heritage Sites.

Ayna's historical excursus left me marveling: how could such a monstrous fortification be so little known in the West? And I wondered about her. She was confident, beautiful, learned, and professional.

How was life as a modern woman—another legacy of secular Soviet rule—here in Derbent?

We stepped up to a giant hole in the rock-littered earth. I peered over the edge: it was lined with stone but concave.

"This was Naryn's dungeon," Ayna said. "Prisoners would serve life sentences in there. They would be lowered in on a rope, thrown their food and water, and never be allowed out. It was never cleaned. They died, and the new prisoners had to live with corpses. The dying died on the dead, on and on."

A gruesome thought. I noticed my two companions were less intrigued than red-faced and sweating from the ascent and the heat, and, no doubt, from our previous day's debauch, plus their multi-pack-a-day habit; they were in fact ready to heave. I decided not to prolong our tour by asking further questions.

Ayna led us back to the main gates, and we said goodbye. I gave her a healthy tip for her services. She accepted it gracefully and wished us well.

"And now for our surprise," said Murat, rills of perspiration trickling down his squint-wrinkles. Sultan leaned on him to keep from falling over.

"What? Naryn wasn't the surprise?"

"No! Get in the car!"

We drove down through town to a complex of placid grassy lots around private white booths on the sea. The Oasis Restaurant. Here the maritime damp fused with the heat, and it was tough to breathe. I checked the temperature with my pocket thermometer: 108 degrees.

A waiter showed us to our reserved table, which was set with—what else?—vodka and cognac, lamb and cheese. I opened the window: in drifted sweltering wet sticky air, so I closed it.

"Shall we?" said Murat, unscrewing the cap on the vodka bottle and looking at me.

"Oh, no, I can't. Really, I'd love to. But—"

The road back to Makhachkala, with all its dicey perils, flashed in my mind's eye.

"Oh yes, you will."

So, I did.

8

The rigors of revelry had finally wrecked me, as had the heat. I awoke the morning after our Derbent feast weak, wobbly, and woozy. The seagulls outside my window had gone silent, but my room's air conditioner was rattling loudly in a failing bid to defeat the 110-plus-degree temperature. Makhachkala (and the rest of southern Russia) was now languishing in thrall to a record heat wave, the worst since World War II.

Murat called early to say he was on his way over to pick me up for another feast at the Viking. I broke the rules of Caucasian hospitality and bowed out, avowing illness and the need to conserve my strength before boarding the train that evening for Astrakhan. (In fact, I wasn't fit to go to Astrakhan or anywhere else. But any delay in my departure would only end, one way or another, drowned in Lezginka, and I just couldn't handle that.) He understood, and promised to drive me to the station. I then hobbled down to the ticket office, which was mercifully near the hotel, and bought a bunk to Astrakhan aboard the Makhachkala-Moscow Express. "Express" was a relative term; it would take fourteen hours to cover the 375-mile distance. The Express was said to be prone to breakdowns and rebel bomb blasts, but there was no better train in Dagestan. I splurged on a first-class ticket, reserving a sleeper in the "car of heightened comfort," and, feebly, hoped for the best.

*

"OH, YOU SHOULDN'T HAVE," I told Murat, reluctantly accepting a plastic bag bulging with four bottles of Dagestani cognac as we pulled into the station lot that evening. "Really."

"You'll need something for the road."

"But four bottles?"

We climbed out of his Volga's smoke-befouled cabin into a Bengali blaze to confront a scene reminiscent of Partition and the mass flight of refugees. Throngs of heavyset scarved women and short, swaggering men surged up the steps, dragging tawdry bundles and taped-together suitcases; following them, glancing about fearfully, were boys in skull-caps and little girls with babies lashed to their backs. Up on the platform the police checked papers (Murat greeted them in Kumyk and they waved us through); troops, clad in camouflage and wielding Kalashnikovs, loitered, stone-faced, in groups of three and four. Pie sellers and bun peddlers intoned nasal chants, and one-eyed goiter-throated beggars whined for alms. The poverty on display was disquieting, and I realized that since arriving I had hardly spoken to anyone outside Murat's well-heeled Viking clique.

We found the Express, which from the outside looked much the same as any provincial Russian train—which is to say, dilapidated in a homey, bearable way. Murat checked my ticket.

"Oh, you've got a seat in the car of heightened comfort!" he said with a nod of approval. "Come on!"

We located my car; being first-class, it was up near the engine, away from the crowds. He tossed aside his cigarette and hoisted himself aboard, groaning, for some reason, as he reached the top step. I grabbed the railing—it was hot, and I yanked back my hand.

"Come on up," he said. "It's still a little warm in here, but enjoy it while you can. You've got the Kalmykia Desert to cross. Hand me your cognac."

I did, and climbed smack into a wall of broiling air reeking with latrine smells and sweat; the car must have been baking in the sun all day. Suddenly I felt nauseated, and I staggered down the hall after Murat.

"So, here's your compartment!" He turned and addressed someone inside it. "Please accept a passenger!"

I looked in. Four leathereen bunks, soiled white nylon curtains, finger-smudged windows—a compartment typical of an outback train, but hotter than anything west of Rajasthan in July. By the window sat a Russian woman soaked in sweat, red-faced, middle-aged, and beer-bellied. Perspiration beaded on her cropped hennaed hair; her khaki T-shirt was a wet tent sticking indecently in places to rolls of fat; her sallow pudgy arms were blotched with psoriasis. She had a lumpy nose and ferret eyes; her stubby toes were jammed red into plastic sandals. She was breathing audibly, as if struggling for air. The compartment smelled of her breath.

Murat stowed my cognac under the seat. "You've lucked out," he said to her. "You'll be sharing your compartment all night with this American!"

"*American?*" she said, doing a double take at me. "Oh, shit!" She shook her head and looked out the window. "Well, I guess he's better than some fucking aborigine. Let him in."

Ignoring the racist remark, Murat (an "aborigine," of course) shook my hand and wished us a good ride. And then he was gone down the hall. He jumped down onto the platform, wiped his face with a handkerchief, and hurried off into the crowd.

"Well," she said, "take a seat. Name's Nadia." She chuckled, her laugh catching in phlegm and ending in a cough. "You're going to have to get used to me," she said, using the familiar *ty* form of address, which should establish intimacy—just what I was afraid of. "I'm no God-sent gift to you. I smoke a lot, drink too much, swear all the time, and I'm rude as hell. You're just going to have to put up with me. And I'll tell you why. I—"

The conductor, a chunky Dagestani woman whose wavy black hair fell in wet hanks over her kind eyes, rapped on our door. She checked our tickets, shot the Russian a suspicious look, and turned to leave.

"For God's sake, switch on the air conditioning in this rolling crapheap, will you?" ordered Nadia in a wildly rising voice. "We're in fucking first class here!"

"I can't do that till we're moving," the conductor answered calmly. "The air conditioning works only when the engine's on."

She left us to check more tickets.

"Oh, shit," said Nadia, shaking her head in an exaggerated way and laughing. Her eyes were pink, as if set in sockets of goo. She was, I then realized, thoroughly intoxicated.

She wheezed, making gurgling sounds. I myself felt short of breath. I tried to open our window, but it had been welded shut. I moved to try the one in the corridor, but Nadia grabbed my forearm, her fingers like prehensile sticks of hot greasy salami. "It's no use. They're all welded shut." I gently pulled my arm free and slumped back onto my seat.

The train eked and hissed and we edged out of the station. No comforting whir of air conditioning accompanied our departure. Slums of mud houses and bony cattle and children skipping down dusty streets slid by our now steamed-up window.

Nadia laughed to herself again. She hauled a khaki duffel bag from under her seat, unzipped it, and pulled out a bottle of white wine, a small plastic bag of hardboiled eggs, a hunk of ham, and a loaf of dark bread. She flicked the bottle with her forefinger. "Drink with me," she commanded.

"Thanks very much, but I'm feeling a little off."

"This'll cure you."

"I really thank you very much, but I'm not feeling—"

She stood up. "What the *hell's* wrong? A lady's asking you to drink and you shouldn't be rude and refuse! And all this food's going to spoil if you don't help me eat it!"

"I'm really sorry, but I can't."

She glowered over me for a moment, but then she sat back down and shook her head, splattering sweat drops. "Fuck. Well, mind if I drink alone?"

"Be my guest."

She tossed the food back in her sack, zipped it up, uncorked the bottle, and set a plastic cup on the tiny table between us. "I drink white wine. I prefer it to vodka." She poured some and gulped it down. "You look like a cultured type. I was afraid they'd put me in here with some *skot* [beast] and I'd have to listen to his stupid banter and smell his stinking feet all night. The Dagestanis, these aborigines, they're savage. They're, they're . . . you have *no* idea. There're killers all over this asshole of a republic, bloodthirsty, tribal, murdering killers." She gulped down more wine. "May I ask you, kindly, what the *fuck* you're doing down here?"

"I'm traveling across—"

"I hope you wrote your will before coming. Count yourself lucky no one kidnapped you for ransom or raped you and cut you to pieces. It happens all the time here."

"I was visiting Dagestani friends."

"You think that Dagestani guy is civilized? You know nothing." She rolled her eyes and poured herself more wine. "For God's sake, what *bullshit!* Just look at this craphole they call first class."

The conductor walked by. I asked her to turn on the AC.

"Oh, sorry, I forgot!" she said, and trotted back to her station.

Forgot? Soon dust showered down from a vent and a tepid breeze blew through the compartment. We coughed. It was still better than nothing. I leaned back, my head throbbing, suppressing nausea, and closed my eyes.

Nadia refilled her cup and gurgled down its contents. "Look, I'm in the army down here. My husband and I are stationed out in the mountains. We can hardly leave the base! Rocks and sand everywhere, rebels, shooting and killing, and beasts, beasts all around! All the time!"

A toggle-eared Dagestani man walked by, slowing to drop a bundle of magazines on the seat—a common peddling technique used by deaf vendors on Russian trains. You choose what you want and pay him when he returns.

"Oh, that fucker is deaf, is he?" Nadia said. "Right. I'll shout 'hundred rubles' and he won't be so deaf. Look at how well these Dagestanis live, all on Moscow's money! This fucking republic doesn't contribute anything, they produce nothing, they just take subsidies. Savages, thieves, and bandits! The Caucasians are the type of loyal family men who go to whores and if they like a guy's sister, they'll say, 'Hey, she's your sister! So give her to me free!'"

This was nonsense, to be sure, reflective of widespread Russian prejudices. But I was too weak to argue back. Moreover, a sort of weird rectitude transpired through her rants, which she delivered in grammatically correct Russian. She reminded me of *bichi* (a wry acronym meaning "formerly cultured person" but also the word for "scourge") I had met in the hinterland, educated people beaten down by life in Russia who fought back by drinking themselves to death and making everyone around them miserable. Even if I had been strong enough to tell her to shut up, I would not have.

The deaf peddler stepped back in.

"Hun'red rubles, you!" shouted Nadia. "Hun'red rubles!"

He didn't respond, but picked up his magazines and left.

"Where're you going now?" I asked.

"I'm heading up to my uncle's in Moscow, and then on to see relatives in the Baltics. Haven't been there since the Soviet Union fell apart.

The Balts've finally *deigned* to give me a visa, the bastards." She snickered and drank more wine. "The army pays for my ticket. Some vacation, right?"

Outside the steppe rolled by, wearying dun wastes speckled with stones and sagebrush clumps motionless in the torrid air. Behind it all was a translucent sky, as if sapped of all color by the heat.

She fumbled in her purse and produced an old camera. She crossed over and sat next to me and, holding the camera at arm's length, snapped off several frames of us.

"American, you say."

"Yes."

She returned to her seat and upended her wine cup. "I hear Condoleezza talking about democracy and that retard Bush telling us how to live, and I say, 'America, shove your democracy up your *ass* and stop lecturing us!' You meddle in other countries and fuck them up and then scold *us* about human rights. Shove it! I once thought Americans were a great people. But what kind of great people elects a fucking retard *twice* as president? You c'n tell by the look on his face that he's a moron, a brainless cretin, but you elect him anyway!"

Many now express views like hers, and not only in Russia. But in Russia, where strength and cleverness are revered above all else, they mattered. Disdain for an America perceived as weak and stupid would embolden Putin in his confrontation with the West.

"In fact," I said, "a lot of Americans would agree with you. And neither election was clean, especially the one in 2000."

"Oh, yeah? So he rigged the votes, so what? I know all that. But you didn't protest, you didn't fight back. Look, I'll tell you one thing and you'd better listen." After emptying the last drops of wine into her cup and setting the bottle on the floor, she leaned over and put her face to mine. "Russia is getting *stronger*, Russia is *rising*, and you're just going to have to *get used to it*." She sneered. "We've got thousands of clever people in this country, *brilliant* people, scientists and schemers, and make no mistake about it: they're out-and-out *bastards*. We live like shit, sure, but we don't give a damn. Like it or not, we're getting stronger, and we're no fucking pansies. The Yeltsin days are over. We're not taking any more orders from Bush or anyone else."

This kind of talk wasn't entirely untrue. Russia's Hobbesian human jungles hone ruthless talents of survival, and its poverty anneals the masses to discomfort; whereas Westerners, or so Russians think, are spoiled, fragile, and spineless. A predatory government forces Russians to develop tactics of evasion and subterfuge, while Westerners indulge their fancies in law-bound societies that permit frivolous pursuits and childish dissent. These are gross generalizations, but in some ways they hold up; Russia is much stronger than it looks. Certainly the Nazis had underestimated Russia (weakened by Stalin beyond the point of no return, they thought) and met their end here as a result.

She opened another bottle of wine and continued her rant. "The only good thing Yeltsin ever did was appoint Putin as his successor. 'Cause of Yeltsin, I have to work as a janitor on base, and I've got a *teaching* degree. I, I had *dreams.* I'm a *teacher* by education for Christ's sake, and look at my life! I'd . . . I'd . . . I'd like to grab a gun and just start shooting and kill everyone, all the thieves and scum I have to live with, I'd kill them all!" She upended her glass again. She sat back and belched, and her head wobbled. "By the way, how do I know you're not a spy? How do I know the KGB isn't listening to me now? How . . ."

She dozed off in midsentence and her head drooped. Feeling increasingly ill, I was glad of the silence.

Night fell. The train rocked north, penetrating the Caspian Depression, the eastern fringes of the republic of Kalmykia—the semidesert homeland of 300,000 descendants of the Mongols who migrated here in the seventeenth century. The cattle-breeding Kalmyks were peaceable Buddhists, but Stalin exiled them all to Siberia for alleged cooperation with the Germans. The Kalmyk steppes were surely hotter than Makhachkala, but now, bathed in moonlight, at least through the window they radiated a silvery cool.

We had stopped several times, and the conductor had forgotten to restart the AC. The heat in the car was not abating. My head throbbed, my gut ached, and I needed air, fresh air; I was dizzy and feeling desperate, almost claustrophobic—a sensation I had never known before. Something was snapping in me, and I shuddered. *I've got to ride all night in this foul, roasting crate, and I can't stand one more minute!*

I gripped the metal bunk bar and pulled myself to my feet. I went out to the conductor's station at the car's end, passing two or three passengers in the hall. I found her arguing in Kumyk with several other sweating train employees.

"Excuse me, but what's wrong with the AC?" I asked. "We're roasting alive in here."

"Oh! I forgot!" She threw a switch and tepid air blew from a vent above us, preceded, as ever, by puffs of dust that made everyone cough.

They resumed their talk. I stood there pondering in silent rage how she could forget. I was seething, soaked in sweat, and sore all over, feeling close to breaking.

As I turned to limp back to my compartment, a woman grabbed my arm. She was a Dagestani my age, with mascara on her lashes and milky skin, comfortably plump in a sun dress.

"Excuse me, you feel okay?" she asked in rough Russian. She moved her hand from my forearm to my fingers. "Oh, your hand is cold! You have blood pressure problem?"

Her eyes were wide and warm. I told her that, in fact, since my mother's death the previous year, I had suffered mild bouts of hypertension. But I took medicine and so there was nothing to worry about. As I said all this, I wondered at my openness to a stranger.

"Oh, but maybe this is an attack," she said. "I have high blood pressure, so I know. Wait one minute—I get my measuring machine."

She scuttled back down the hall.

The conductor stepped out, apparently having overheard our talk. "Are you okay?"

"I think so." Their concern quickly, inexplicably, alleviated my distress, and the relief stunned me.

"How's that drunk Russian woman treating you?" Her eyes too were wide with warmth.

"She talked a lot, but she's fallen asleep."

"I can have her thrown off the train. Just tell me."

"No, no, that won't be necessary."

The woman returned with a blood pressure monitor, which she fastened around my wrist. It beeped and flashed a reading. "Yes, see? You have blood pressure. Drink my herbal tea now."

She handed me a plastic cup and I drank its warm, bitter contents. She stood with me, her hand on my forearm, looking me in the eye. "Better?"

"Why, yes. Thank you."

She kept her warm wide eyes on mine but periodically consulted the readout on her machine. "*Oy, oy, oy,*" she said, shaking her head.

The train pulled into a lonely station on the Kalmyk steppe; giant beetles circled madly around the platform lights, now and then, strangely, crashing to the ground and flopping about. Up and down the train conductors wrenched open the doors and a dozen or so passengers tumbled out, all sweaty, some drunk, others staggering and exhausted by the heat.

My Dagestani savior and I stepped out too. Here the air was, at least, a little less hot. I had never before poured out my heart to a stranger, but I did now, telling her of my mother's sudden death and how it had thrown me. She listened, her eyes beautiful, heavy-lashed, answering *da, da,* and touching my arm and checking the blood pressure reading. She never asked me where I was from; we never learned each other's name.

When the brakes hissed we reboarded and said good night. The train inched into motion. Back in my compartment, two young Dagestani women, slender and comely and with manes of black hair, were settling in to the upper berths. They had brought textbooks, which they read by flashlight.

Nadia mumbled, half awake, "You're not such a bad person, Jeff. Everything will be okay."

She dozed off.

I looked out the window. The train rocked on across the heat-stricken steppe, under a full silvering moon, and moonlight glinted on the rails, rails leading away into a hot, dark infinity. How lost we all are, how alone! The only remedies, while we're here, are kindness, the touch of a hand, the warmth of compassionate eyes. All else is illusion.

Nadia resumed snoring winy exhalations, her mouth open, her jowls sagging, her forehead perspiring. She might have been the embodiment of Soviet degeneracy—fat, drunk, and crass, spouting bile and bigoted invective. But she had not begun life this way. Her country had shaped her as mine had me.

I lay down and fell asleep as the Dagestanis above were flipping through their textbooks, making notes in the margins, studying for a better life.

JUST AFTER DAWN the Makhachkala-Moscow Express creaked into Astrakhan, sixty miles north of the Caspian Sea, at the head of the Volga delta. The heat wave here had kept highs at 110 degrees for a week. The station was awash in oppressive orange sunlight; the heavy-leaved trees seemed to exude steam. I stepped out into the swampy air, finding breathing difficult. The sky, even this early, baked and smothered. Rain must have fallen during the night, and the lingering dampness was infernal.

I WOULD LEAVE in the morning for Kazakhstan, to begin the Central Asian leg of my journey. I had little idea of what to expect there, but I hoped, most of all, to leave behind the anger and ethnic hatred I had met with almost everywhere I had been in Russia.

9

Leaving behind the Volga inflamed with the August sun, and skirting the Astrakhan kremlin's walled-off trapezoid grounds, my dented yellow Volga taxi turned down Lenin Street and bounced toward the highway running east to the Kazakhstan border. Ivan the Terrible had built this kremlin here on Zaichi Bugor, the highest land in town, in 1558, after smashing the Astrakhan khanate two years earlier and ending centuries of Tatar-Mongolian slaving raids into southern Russia. The kremlin cathedral's green onion domes and gold crosses, jutting above the walls and now hazy in the steam-bath heat, must have struck the surviving Muslims in town then as an insufferable affront in land that had belonged to the Abode of Islam for three hundred years. Nevertheless, Astrakhan afforded Moscow access to the Caspian, and soon grew into a frontier outpost of Russian Orthodoxy and a center of commerce as trade with Persia, India, and the states of the Caucasus flourished.

During the Soviet era, Astrakhan was industrialized and turned into a major builder of and service center for ships; but the countless millions of jars of fish and caviar (caught in the Caspian) bearing the city's name have enduringly associated it with seafood in the minds of most Russians. The boom has since passed. Today, here and there along the Volga's marshy, midge- and mosquito-ridden banks lies rusted industrial detritus: ship hulls, tires, and shells of automobiles, all exposed to the searing southern sun and corroded into inutility by the perennial damp. Steel-and-plank docks abound with black and white cutters moored under wraps of soggy hemp, as if never to sail again. Neverthe-less, Astrakhan is a spirited city where Tatars, Kalmyks, Russians, Ka-zakhs, and others trade and live side by side in relative harmony, as they did in Soviet times, without the ethnic tensions now plaguing so much of Russia. In fact, migrants from the Caucasus and Kazakhstan are so numerous that one might believe Central Asia began here.

WE CROSSED A BRIDGE over the slack brown currents of the Kutum River and slowed, lurching through Russia's most pervasive, enraging bane—the traffic jam. There are traffic jams everywhere, of course, but those in Russia originate in injustice and corruption, and so madden like few others. Sirens screeched from official black sedans as their driv-ers forced their way ahead of crumbling Ladas and decade-old Moskvi-ches, many stalled in the heat (at ten in the morning, it was already 100 degrees), competing with SUVs and overloaded Soviet trucks spewing forth a miasma of lead and carbon dioxide. *Gaishniki* delayed traffic further, pulling over vehicles (but never the official sedans, and rarely the SUVs), checking documents, exacting "fines." Anyone with cash could run lights, drive on the sidewalk, speed the wrong way down one-way streets, whatever—and, if stopped, pay up and be gone. The rest of us simply bumped along and sweltered.

My driver, Khakim, was half Kazakh, half Russian (as were many in this border region), and jovial; his amiable banter made the irritating delay tolerable.

"It's incredible," he said, "over there, in Atyrau"—the Kazakh city I hoped to reach by nightfall. "There you don't have traffic jams of rotten Soviet cars, no sir. There you've got jams of BMWs and Audis. The economy is booming. We like to say Atyrau is another Las Vegas, with casinos and restaurants and beautiful women. It's all because of the Tengiz oil and gas fields out in the Caspian."

"I've heard it's a dump," I said. "From friends who were there in the nineties."

"That was then. Now, with energy prices so high, they have so much money they don't know what to do with it! I go there a lot so I know."

We both soon sweated through our shirts; grit from exhaust stuck to our skin and scratchily coated our throats. Drivers around us were leaning on their horns, creating an infuriating, high-decibel, multitonal ruckus, but Khakim ignored it; in fact, he smiled and frequently ceded the way. It seemed he took life as a joke—the only way to keep one's sanity in a country where hope of reform is dead, the rich are thieves, the poor losers, and deceit is institutionalized, given officers of enforcement and seal-emblazoned codices of plunder.

Away from its historic center, Astrakhan is a foul spread of mechanics' shacks and cement vendors; rubbish-strewn lots of yellowish earth; Caucasian migrants, low-browed and hairy-backed, in tracksuits; and hulking Russian women with heat-frizzled hair. We crossed bridges over the Volga and its delta effluents, and reedy marshes closed in on the road, emitting vaguely fetid vapors.

Khakim chain-smoked as I checked my passport and visas. Would the newly terrible relations between the United States and Russia affect my reception at the border? I wondered.

He offered me a cigarette. I declined.

"Don't smoke?" he asked. "Maybe it's better not to. I had five brothers and lost 'em all to heart attacks. Imagine: I'm now the only survivor of my family." He coughed hard and lit up again, his lungs wheezing. He wasn't angling for pity. In Russia early deaths for men are the rule, mostly owing to widespread overindulgence in booze and cigarettes and to the cardiovascular troubles they provoke. Everyone knows this now, but people still smoke, saying, with a fatalistic shrug, "*Tvoy kirpich tebya vsegda naydyot.*" (The brick meant to land on your head will always find you.)

Finally we broke free of the town's vehicular jam and shot out onto a lightly trafficked road across scrubby desert splotched with hanks of feather grass, the sun burning in our faces. A half-hour later we passed through the one-goat village of Karaozek and back out onto the empty steppe, where we drew up on the border—a complex of prefab buildings in decent repair, surrounded by a barbed-wire fence. There seemed to be something at once absurd and fitting in this frontier post out in the middle of nowhere, dividing nothing from nothing.

Khakim slowed for the "queue"—an ancient truck and a silver Lada station wagon—then pulled up in front of a closed steel gate. No one official-looking was around. He honked. Still no one. He got out and rattled the gate. The dry mechanical drone of cicadas and the buzzing of flies grew louder in the heat.

"Hey! Is anyone here?"

Out walked a tall customs officer in a crisp white shirt and green trousers, his high-rimmed green forage cap canted forward.

"Could you let us through?" asked Khakim. "I've got an American with me."

The officer swung open the gate and we motored ahead, jumping the other two vehicles. Then we stopped.

"*Zdravstvuyte!*" said the officer, grinning at me as I climbed out. "U-S-A? *Vashington*?"

"That's right."

He shook my hand.

Khakim saluted me. "Well, good travels!" he said, and was gone.

"Can I see your papers?" the officer asked politely, as if I had a choice.

I handed him my passport but kept to myself the currency declaration form showing, with a validating stamp from customs in Moscow, that I had legally imported (and therefore had a right to export) four thousand dollars in cash. Why let him know how much money I was carrying unless I had to?

But he never asked for it. Instead, he scrutinized the visa and looked up at me, furrowing his brows in mock suspicion. "Smuggling any contraband today?"

"No. But please feel free to check."

I opened my bags—a small green soft-sided suitcase and a blue knapsack with camera gear and slide film. He glanced at them, nothing more.

"Okay, all's well. So walk on up the road to passport control. And have a happy journey."

We shook hands again. I shouldered my bags and trotted the next hundred yards to another jumble of steel-roofed, white-brick buildings. However bad relations with the United States are, I concluded, they had done little to spoil the *personal* attitudes of so many Russians, even officials, toward Americans.

The Lada station wagon rumbled up and preceded me to the booth. Its driver, an agitated Kazakh in his fifties, was soon shoving passports through the window slot, but the officer inside refused to accept them: the electricity had failed and his computer was down.

"How long do we have to wait?" asked the driver. "Just exactly how long?"

The officer turned his back without responding and stepped away into the darkness of the booth. The driver looked at me. To my surprise, his eyes, set in sun-wizened sockets, seemed amused, his scrunched-up features almost comical. His spry demeanor told me he was an operator — a useful person to have around at a border.

"You look like you need a lift to Atyrau?" he said. "Give me your passport."

I did. He slipped it in with the three others he was holding. His Lada was, in fact, a taxi, and we settled on a hundred-dollar fare for the 190-mile trip. A Russian father and son were his other passengers. The son, an eight-year-old with green eyes, bent down to pour water into a cup for a mutt panting in the booth's shade. The father, in his thirties, was crisp, sporting a crewcut, and smoking avidly, glancing about impatiently.

The lights came on and the officer stamped our passports. We all jumped in the Lada, and, at an unseemly high speed, drove a hundred yards, bounced across a pontoon bridge over the muddy, narrow Buzan River, and drew up to another silty Volga effluent. There we rattled aboard an aged five-car ferry, which chugged us across the water to the Kazakhstan side — an elaborate border post with an overarching roof, vehicle inspection pits, and a knot of grim officers in dark uniforms waiting for us with their arms crossed. Beyond them stretched more nothingness, sandy and bleak.

Inside the inspection building fans creaked, stirring the hot fly-infested air. A young officer, his uniform patched with sweat, walked around to a side door and entered his glass-enclosed booth and slammed the door. He took my companions' passports, flipped through them to a blank page, stamped them, and slipped them back through the slot.

He then took mine. He looked up at me and back down at the picture several times.

"You are American?" he asked in Russian, leaning back and giving me a dull look.

"Yes."

"Then what kind of passport is this?"

"American."

"No, I mean, why isn't the passport number perforated on the cover?"

"Well, I don't know."

"Why don't you know, huh? Why don't you know?"

"It's an American passport. I'm sure of that. Take a look."

He grabbed a magnifying glass and began examining my photo, now and then daubing his sweaty eye print from the lens. Then he flicked back to my Kazakhstan visa.

"Oh!" he said, now really alarmed. He peered through the glass again. He asked me to explain—though it was all written there—where I had acquired the visa (the Kazakhstan embassy in Moscow), where the consular officer's signature was (right where it should be), what its dates of validity were, and so on. I smiled, showing no displeasure; even a modest expression of annoyance could cause further delay. The taxi driver patted sweat from his forehead and looked impatient. Probably he regretted having offered me a ride.

After twenty long, hot minutes of redundant queries, glass-peerings, page-thumbings, and the subjection of my passport to a special light, he stamped it and shoved it back through the slot, saying nothing.

"Come on!" said the driver. "Let's go!"

We all jumped in his car, with me in the front seat, father and son in the rear. We sped through the gates and out into barrens of sand, scrub brush, and salt flat, terrain far harsher than the steppe on the Russian side. At customs it had been 110 degrees, but the heat was still mounting. We were descending back into the Caspian Depression, eighty thousand square miles of broiling steppe that sinks as low as six hundred feet beneath sea level.

"My name's Murtaza," the driver announced. "But you can call me Kolya"—short for Nikolay.

Faraway brown blobs wobbling in heat haze resolved themselves, as we approached, into shaggy, double-humped Bactrian camels, the likes of which I had not seen since 1998, in western China. Doing sixty, seventy miles an hour, we bounced from side to side on the almost deserted highway, skirting potholes and chopped-up stretches, every half-hour or so shooting past rock and cement villages far poorer than anything in Russia, each preceded by a cemetery of fenced-off, tombstoned graves. Furnace blasts of wind bore down on us, driving dust devils and tumbleweed clumps, fusing sky and earth into a blinding gaseous mass; my lips chapped and my throat dried up.

"You like to sweat?" Murtaza asked me.

"What?"

The macadam degenerated into a scarred dirt track. And this was the road to Kazakhstan's oil capital! Dust poured through the windows, which we rolled up urgently; but more dust flooded through the dashboard's ventilation slots. (The air conditioning didn't work.) Murtaza shut them, leaving us airless. Sweat popped out all over me and I soon felt I would gag, choke—I needed to breathe! Ahead, fulminating banks of dust billowed out from a lumbering convoy of trucks; clouds of blowing dust assaulted us from the north, enshrouding us in a fulvous choking fog. We swerved, just missing camels. I pictured us ramming one of the beasts, his massive body crashing through the windshield, bludgeoning us with his coarse-haired bulk. When the dust fell away distances opened into mirages of glaring sky and flats of tremulous dazzling silver.

We shot on. In the closed inferno of the car I felt short of breath and clammy, suffering an urge to vomit; I gripped the door handle. I wondered, with all the oil billions rolling into Kazakhstan's coffers, why the government couldn't spend a few dollars on building decent roads for its citizens. But in one of the most authoritarian countries in Central Asia, the answer was clear: an autocrat would hardly feel accountable to anyone but himself and the security services that keep him in power.

The little boy in the back seat was gasping and pale and lolling his head. The father was less bothered. "What do these Kazakhs *do* around here to make a living?" he asked, incredulity sounding in his smoke-hoarsened voice. "Who would live out here?"

"Oh, once they raised camels and sheep," Murtaza said. "But now they earn their living off oil."

We hit the tarmac again and rolled down the windows. I sucked in hot air; the dryness caught in my throat and I coughed. Breaks in the dust curtains revealed oil rigs and industrial parks, skeletons of steel and cement fouling this wasteland even more than nature had. The sky cleared but new dust devils spun along, like awful geysers of grit. We bounced over the warped road between them as on waves at sea, the car creaking, threatening to tear apart.

As one agonizing hour passed into the next, I pondered just why this desert seemed somehow worse than the many others I'd seen. The romance of the Bedouin and the lost kingdoms of Africa invests the Sahara with historical grandeur; Marco Polo's *Travels* mythologizes the Gobi; and even the American Southwest had garnered fame as home to outlaws and gold seekers. But Kazakhstan's emptiness stands for nothing, evokes nothing, arouses no sentiments other than revulsion, a primitive fear of death by thirst. It is Hell without its Dante, unredeemed, sand and salt and rock and no more. Even worse, in Soviet times the Kremlin had designated the northeastern part of Kazakhstan a nuclear testing ground—the Semipalatinsky *Poligon*—and conducted 129 surface detonations and 348 underground blasts. Their effects on residents' health (cancers, birth defects, and stillborn gargoyle babies among them) are still being documented. Somehow, the land's natural desolation invites human desecration.

Around five-thirty, ten- and fifteen-story buildings edged over the horizon, forming a low, blocky skyline. The road improved. We slowed and eased into a traffic jam. Atyrau, Kazakhstan's main Caspian port city, was then upon us, a farrago of casinos and restaurants and construction lots, a frontier post high on oil, some twenty miles inland from the sea and straddling the Ural River—the waterway that, according to Russian tradition, divides Europe from Asia.

The Russian and his son got out at an oil company's gated complex. Murtaza drove me to the Chagala Hotel, on the Ural's European bank. Masked in grit and sweat salt, parched and dizzy, I presented my miserable self at its reception and timidly asked for a room.

I HAD EXPECTED little from Atyrau (population 150,000). Yet the fenced-off grassy grounds of the Chagala offered me unexpected comforts both human and material. The hotel was a new, clean, air-conditioned Western-style affair housing mostly oil company expats, and was outfitted with cable television and the Internet. The staff, a friendly crew of professionally attired Kazakhs and Russians, never once regaled me with the *what-the-hell-do-you-want* service-sector "charm" of the former Soviet Union. Its location enchanted me: beyond the perimeter fence, the Ural River meandered through landscaped banks, glittering with the desert sun at noon, glowing with the pastels of an azure sky and orange-tinted cumuli in the evening. The green and blue glass skyscrapers on the Asian shore would have been unremarkable in Manhattan or Moscow, but here, especially compared with the low, shoddy warrens of the Russian towns I had just seen, they heralded growth and progress and new life.

The original inhabitants of the steppes around Atyrau were nomads called Sarmatians. They didn't last long. Two millennia ago, cattle herders of Turkic stock, availing themselves of novelties such as carts and domesticated horses, set out from somewhere near China and roamed west over the steppes of Eurasia, initiating a mass migration that would reach the Caspian, absorb the Sarmatians, and, of course, culminate in the arrival of Genghis Khan's armies. In the thirteenth century Genghis Khan's son, Batu Khan, who razed much of Russia and ruled the Golden Horde, founded the first city in these parts, Saraichik, thirty-five miles to the north of Atyrau, on the Zhayyk River.

Located on a trade route running from Europe to Asia, Saraichik prospered as the Golden Horde's capital, with straight streets, earthen palaces, and cupola-topped mosques and bathhouses. But the Horde fell apart in 1391. In 1395 Timur and his army invaded Saraichik and destroyed it; in 1580, the Cossacks did the same. But none of the marauders found much to hang around for, and Saraichik rose again, to become the capital of the Kazakh Horde, holding sway over land from the Irtysh River, in Siberia, to the Danube. The Kazakhs, however, pressured by the assaults of Dzungar nomads, accepted Russian protection in 1731. Anti-tsarist revolts broke out in the following century as the Russians restricted Kazakh grazing and fishing rights, but all were repressed.

The Kazakhstan government has chosen to present the Turkic ancestors of the Kazakhs as wise and noble, as men who built magnificent khanates and kept the roads safe—"[forefathers] . . . held sacred in the people's memory" (according to Atyrau's official website). Yet the town museum depicts them as wild-haired, tangle-bearded, yurt-dwelling ruffians in pointy helmets and suits of mail clutching hatchets, swords, spears, and whips—as barbarian warriors, in sum, whose battleground was the steppe. Little in Saraichik's history suggests that it was ever more than a primitive clay outpost.

Civilization—no other word fits—dawned only with the arrival of the Russians. Atyrau arose independently of the Kazakhs as the Russian fishing town of Nizhni Yaitsky Gorodok, in 1645. Soon after, it took the name Gur'yev (and would only become Atyrau in 1992, after independence) in honor of a prominent local Russian trader, and later served as a Russian military advance post. Until the last years of the Soviet era, the town subsisted off the bounty of sturgeon and black caviar hauled in from the Caspian.

Then came oil. Kazakh herders living around Atyrau had long cured skin diseases using the petroleum bubbling up in places through their salt-encrusted lowlands. Prospecting began in the late-nineteenth century, but the Soviets built the rigs we had passed driving in only in the Brezhnev era. In 1979 exploratory drilling began offshore, but oil and gas really started flowing in 1991, when Chevron joined with the Kazakh corporation Tengizneftgaz to invest in technology and boost production. Two years later, a consortium of the world's largest energy companies (including Agip, British Petroleum, Shell, Mobil, and Total, plus Kazakhstankaspiishelf) stepped up prospecting in the Caspian, and in 2001 opened a pipeline from the Tengiz field to the Black Sea. Another pipeline will service China. Oil and gas companies are planning to invest $130 billion, and eventually hope to pump seventy-five million tons of oil per year; Kashagan, the biggest field, will come on line in 2010. With oil, gas, and their byproducts accounting for 58 percent of Kazakhstan's exports and powering an annual economic growth rate of 8.5 percent, Atyrau is the modern-day Silver City of Kazakhstan. And the money has only begun to roll in.

WHAT DOES ONE DO in a boomtown set smack in the middle of a Dante-less desert hell? Party, as do the other condemned. I washed up and went down to the hotel bar to begin. The maroon carpet was spotless, windows were heavily curtained, the lighting, soft and artificial. A dowdy but talented Russian musician in a peach dress played a sonata on a new piano; two giant plasma TV screens showed BBC with the sound off; and here and there around the room sat British and American men in their middle years, staring in silence, heads tilted forward, at tall, fizzy glasses of beer. The scene was soothing and anodyne—just what I needed after such a violent ride in.

At the bar I ordered a beer.

"New in town?" asked a voice with a British accent.

I turned to face a Brit my age puffing on a cigarette and sipping a Heineken, with froth on his mustache. He had blue eyes and curly gray-black hair; the beginnings of a paunch slouched over his chinos. We started chatting. Evan, as I'll call him here, worked for a foreign oil company drilling in the Tengiz field and spent many of his off-hours (or perhaps even days) here at the bar—the only entertainment in town, aside from another bar, he said with a wink, that he would tell me about if he got drunk enough.

Evan had little to say about his job but a lot to impart about life as a married-back-home, bachelor-in-Atyrau expatriate. His first concern involved keeping his three cell phones straight: one for the job; a second for the wife in Britain; and a third for his Atyrau girlfriends. Drinking too much could lead to confusion and dire complications.

An older Englishman sitting next to us warned me to watch my step off the hotel grounds. "It's these gangs of Kazakh youths that'll give you trouble. They don't like the expats flying in and snatching up their girls. They've robbed and beat people up just down the corner. Rumor has it that an expat was just murdered outside a nightclub here." Rumor was about all they had to go on. Fear of the locals kept most of the expats locked in their Chagala pen outside work hours.

"He's right," said Evan. "Atyrau's the final frontier, so you've gotta be careful. Anyway, I know these girls are only out for money. Back home, a girl selling sex wouldn't be someone you'd want to know. But here life pushes them into it. They can be well brought up and educated and clever. With no hard edges. In fact, they find a lot of you Americans to be funny types, inviting them out to dinner, asking them about their life's goals and plans, things only Westerners think about. I suppose it makes sense. Americans don't know much about other countries, unless it's one they happen to be bombing, so they probably can't really ask them intelligent questions anyway. These girls're clever and just want to know the bottom line. I can respect them for that. They deserve respect, and I give it to them."

He finished his beer and got up, telling me, "You can't go out and get blasted every night working here; you've got to keep yourself under control. I'd take you to the *real* bar for expats, if it were Friday. But it's over in bloody Asia."

"The real bar?"

He gave me the address, drank his dregs, and said good night.

The receptionist called me a cab. Outside, columns of moonlight were falling between thunderheads, probing the Ural's dark currents. A taxi took me on a high-speed trip across the bridge into Asia, down thoroughfares clogged with SUVs, and into the center. We turned off the main street onto a gravelly lane, to the Green Hotel.

A Turkish pop tune was playing at its bar, a dark and modern hotel watering hole with a prefab interior. Three plump Kazakh hookers in chintzy evening dresses sat slumped on stools, sucking on cigarettes and ogling a pair of middle-aged expats whose glassy red eyes told me they had been there a long time.

In English I asked one of the guys to let me through to the bar.

"You're late! Late as usual!" said he, a Brit with a pointy shaved head and a Newcastle accent.

"Excuse me?"

"You're American, I take it."

"Yes."

"I'm Herman," said the other fellow. "From Switzerland."

Herman had beery eyes and a doughy face, a sloppy belly and a plumber's mustache. He looked around and tried to focus. "You like the women here? You know what? I don't."

"Why not?"

"I don't like the people of Kazakhstan. Because"—with his fingers he drew the skin around his eyes back into slits—"because it's in my *blood* not to like Orientals. I can't help it."

"That's ridiculous," I said. "How—"

"Please don't tell me I should try to understand them as people. This is not possible. It is genetic. I worked for an oil company in the Niger River delta too. I cannot understand the Nigerians either, *we* cannot understand, *we* cannot understand because they are *totally* different."

"I doubt you've really tried or even care," I said, regretting having come.

"Aw, lay off it, you poof," his friend Bart told him. "He always goes off on the same rant and forgets what we're here for. I can tell you I *love* these Russian girls." He glanced again at the two clearly non-Russian Kazakhs. "They have nothing but they give you everything. British chicks just wanna fuck and splash."

"Splash?"

He raised his beer to the Kazakh women. "Splash, mate, *splash* eighty-dollar bottles of perfume all over 'emselves!"

He stepped away and sat down between the women. The Swiss gulped his beer.

Soon the Brit returned to the bar. "I may or may not go with those girls," he told me.

I suddenly found myself deeply bored, yearning for Yana and her soulful confessions, missing Murat and his erudite Buddhist banter. *Maybe I should leave.*

A bearish, baby-faced Kazakh guy walked in. He almost knocked me over as he pushed through the bodies to the bar. He apologized, smiled at me, shook my hand, and apologetically flicked his forefinger against his neck—the Slavic gesture meaning "Let's drink!"

When he found out I spoke Russian, he pulled me away from the others and began to talk effusively in mangled but intelligible Russian. He was a laborer but his concerns went far beyond the quotidian.

"Let's drink," he said, his words thick with Kazakh glottals, "to the great United States and a strong Kazakhstan!" We clinked glasses. "You're not real American. You a Jew?"

"Why?"

"With Russian like yours, you're a Soviet Jew who immigrated to America."

I explained who I was.

"Oh! I have much to tell you. I, I . . . well, I'm afraid to talk, the KNB"—Committee for National Security, the Kazakh KGB—"could be listening."

"I'm not a spy."

He looked both ways. "Come away." He pulled me to a corner near the door. "Kazakhstan is a dictatorship. [President Nursultan] Nazarbayev won the last election in 2005 with ninety-one percent of the vote. That's impossible. Only *Stalin* could win like that." By rigging the vote, he meant.

"Yes, but who objected?" I asked.

"The point is, only *Stalin* could win like that. I can't talk freely, or the KNB will arrest me. We build our homes and then the government declares them illegal and seizes them and beats us. Is that democracy? But your Vice President Cheney shakes Nazarbayev's hand and calls him partner! *Why?* It's not fair!"

In May of 2007 (after my trip) the Kazakh rubber-stamp parliament abolished presidential term limits, which amounted to anointing Nazarbayev president for life. The Bush administration, wishing to maintain access to Kazakhstan's oil supplies, quickly applauded the move as "a good step forward for democracy in Kazakhstan." Yet despite Cheney's handshakes and the United States' repeated cajoling overtures meant to win Kazakhstan over to its side in the new Great Game, Kazakhstan's closest trade partner and strategic ally remains Russia; and Putin and Nazarbayev meet monthly. Kazakhstan's historic and family ties to Russia, plus its 34 percent Slavic minority, make any break with Moscow illogical and fraught with danger.

The Kazakh raised his voice. "No one cares about the *people* of Kazakhstan, they only care about our *oil and gas*. But we're *people* here, not oil, not gas, but *people*. We need our *rights*. But look at our region—rights are difficult here. Next to us we have China. We hate the Chinese. We Kazakhs are fifteen million and the Chinese a billion and a half, so how can we fight them? They come here yakking in their yak-yak language and act rude and try to dominate us. The Uzbeks we hate too. The Russians we respect. They taught us to drink vodka, which was good, but not how much, which was bad. But they work hard and are smart." He paused. "Ah, are you a Republican?"

"No, independent."

"Because it's dangerous to be a Democrat since they're in the opposition, right?"

"No, not at all."

"Well, I'm a member of Ak Zhol"—the Bright Path, the main anti-Nazarbayev opposition party that in 2004 won just one seat in parliamentary elections and split the next year, with the majority of its members adhering to pro-business policies little concerned with human rights. "Just for saying that the KNB could arrest me and throw me in jail and torture me and come after my family."

Was his fear of the KNB justified? Ak Zhol posed no threat to the regime. Some in Kazakhstan suspect the government had rubbed out Altynbek Sarsenov, an Ak Zhol leader, but nothing has been proven and Kazakhs have been less than fired up over the issue, probably because new pretenders to former Soviet thrones have often turned out to be just as corrupt as the old. Apathy among the electorate, induced by decades of Soviet rule, has much to do with keeping Nazarbayev in power.

And his power is considerable, even by regional standards. Nazarbayev has ruled Kazakhstan since Soviet times, when he was the local Communist Party boss (which gives him, if nothing else, the advantage of being known to his people). The CIA World Factbook sums up his hold over the country: "President Nazarbayev arranged a referendum in 1995 that extended his term of office and expanded his presidential powers: only he can initiate constitutional amendments, appoint and dismiss the government, dissolve Parliament, call referenda at his discretion, and appoint administrative heads of regions and cities." In this and other elections, Nazarbayev's government has pressured directors of parastatal enterprises to "get out the vote"—for him, of course. And they have.

Nazarbayev's leadership style is that of a sober, authoritarian CEO who wants to keep profits high and discord low. There isn't much of the latter anyway. (Besides Ak Zhol, Hizb ut Tahrir, the Islamic fundamentalist party, has some support in the provinces, but its membership is limited.) Officially Nazarbayev did win the latest elections with 91 percent of the vote, but even the exit polls conducted by the U.S. embassy in Almaty awarded him 83 percent.

Alcohol began slowing down my friend's words and clouding his eyes. He looked around, as if to see who might have been listening. "I want to leave. You come?"

I thought perhaps he wanted to confess something too seditious for the many ears at the bar. We walked out into the warm dark, which now, oddly, was smelling of exhaust and humming with idling motors from somewhere nearby. He pointed to a two-story home behind a wall, modest by Western or even Muscovite standards. "There you see it. A rich man is building a house the size of my apartment building, all for *himself.* Just like in tsarist days, the rich are thieves. It angers me. You don't have such thieves in America, I think."

"Of course we do. But how do you know the house builder's a thief?"

"How can he get money for such a house in our country? Only a few get the oil money."

"Well, he must be one of the few."

"I don't like it."

We ended up in a dark, smoky lot—the source of the motor noise. All around us taxis were idling. In each, besides a driver, sat pairs of girls, mostly village Kazakhs, plastered with rouge and reeking of cheap scents, gravel-voiced, smoking, in counterfeit designer jeans and sweat-stained halters. They were why he wanted to leave the bar.

"You want a girl?" he asked.

"No thanks."

He walked around the lot, checking out the hookers. He finally called over a flaxen-haired Russian with stubs of gray teeth and a wrinkled slab of belly hanging over pudenda-high jeans. Her mascara-smeared eyes drooped and her toes were dirty in her sandals.

"*Da?*" she said. "Oh. You know the rules." She blurted out a practiced spitfire patter. "*Bez anala, bez orala, s rezinkoy*" (No anal sex, no oral sex, and with a condom). "And only in our apartment."

"Hmm." He dismissed her offer with a disappointed wave.

"You can go with them, you know, but don't let them take you back to their apartment. They rob you there."

We walked on back to the hotel and said goodbye.

THE NEXT MORNING I stepped outside into a punishing sun bath, hundred-degree heat, and scorching sandstorm winds—a fine summer's day in Atyrau, the expats said. I decided to stop by the Ak Zhayyk

Hotel and buy a train ticket to my next destination, Aqtöbe, formerly Aktyubinsk, some 275 miles to the northeast. (The Chagala's staff warned me that lines were always bad at the railway station, but the upscale Ak Zhayyk had its own ticket booth.) I raised my hand and hailed a gypsy cab—a red Japanese-made compact. The driver, who was in his thirties, had an unusually broad face for a Kazakh.

We got to talking. I mentioned Atyrau's almost complete lack of vegetation, and he snorted.

"What do you expect from these Kazakhs? They were just nomads out in the desert. They don't know what trees are."

"You're not Kazakh, I take it."

"Of course not! I'm Korean!"

Ruslan was his name. He spoke fluent Russian and had a no-nonsense curtness about himself. Fleeing poverty in Korea eight decades ago, his grandparents had immigrated to the Soviet Union, which, he said, "turned out to be not such a good idea. They were arrested in Stalin's time, back in the 1930s"—at the height of the Terror—"and dispossessed, and exiled all the way to a village north of here, out on the steppe. They were just tossed off a truck in the middle of nowhere, with nothing at all. They would've died if it weren't for the Kazakhs, who were compassionate. They showed my grandfather how to build a house out of mud, for instance."

Educated as an oil engineer, Ruslan, though living in the Kazakh petroleum capital, drove a gypsy cab. "I don't know anyone important so I can't do anyone any favors worth hiring me for. I have no uncle in the mayor's office to get me a job in the oil sector. Try finding work here without connections! It's impossible! Anyway, I pull in a thousand bucks a month just driving this cab, which is twice what I'd get in an oil job as a local hire." (Kazakhstan's monthly per capita income was $770.) "I'd never get the money expats get. But anyway, everything in Atyrau is twice as expensive as in Almaty, because of all the oil money and inflation, and even on a thousand, I'm barely getting by. We don't *live* in Atyrau, we *survive*. It's a disaster."

Five-story Soviet apartment blocks, sagging and sooty, alternated with rectangular Soviet-era office buildings. Kazakhs, and here and there a Russian, walked heads down in the blowing incandescent grit.

"But this town was a dump before, from what I've heard," I said. "You can't be saying it would be better off without the oil."

"No, no. Oil and development are good, I grant that. But everything is corrupt. Our local government steals the funds the federal government sends us. What can you expect? Nazarbayev doesn't want to give up power; he's been ruling since Communist days; he doesn't want to give the young *their* chance. All the officials are the same old Communists. They can't change: for seventy years people had to steal from the state to survive, not work, but *steal.* So that's their habit. Everyone *steals.* Only my children's generation will be able to change this."

Now new buildings glinted and flashed in the desert sun, turning the street into a tableau of glare and fumes and right angles of blue glass and steel. The words on the municipal website came to my mind:

> In Atyrau every stone seems to be a living testimony of the past. Over thousands of historical monuments, archaeological, architectural, and monumental structures . . . remind progeny of the great spiritual heritage left behind by their ancestors.

The traffic lights went dark and we slowed to a halt in a jam of used foreign cars. Simultaneously all the drivers leaned on their horns, and some rolled down their windows to shake their fists at the traffic cop, who waved his baton and whistled and shouted back in Kazakh, all as gusts of dust whipped through and whirled about. Ruslan started cursing. "Look at this fucking mess. This fucking city."

I spotted a supermarket twenty feet ahead, so, availing myself of the delay, I jumped out to see what they had. But it was dark inside; the guard by the door told me that the neighborhood's electricity had "gone out again."

"This place is like Lagos in Nigeria!" I said to Ruslan, climbing back in.

He shrugged. "See what I mean? Our lights go out all the time. There's no order to our development, just thieving, and we're without basic services. Out in our villages—you saw a few if you drove here—people are dying from polluted water and TB, a disease of poor people. But we're earning so many millions from oil! It all started back in 1996. You know, originally the federal government took all our oil revenues and left us to survive on our caviar and fishing industries."

Glare from a skyscraper and oil turrets on the desert horizon caught my eye. "What's that?"

"That's the ANU complex"—the Atyrau Petroleum Directorate.

"The ANU actually did us some good. They made the foreigners invest-ing in our energy build roads and infrastructure, so what development you see here is thanks to them. Out in the villages people have nothing. They drink and steal cattle and kill. They move here and they kill here too. We just had a mass murder, our first. A gang from a village killed a man and his wife and all their kids, just to rob them. You see, these Ka-zakhs have no history, no culture, nothing behind them they can use to orient themselves now. They're not really even Muslims. They only set-tled in Soviet times, because the government made them."

The jam loosened. To avoid traffic, we made a couple of quick turns. We would take the long but less congested way to the hotel. We sped along a road by the steppe; women in floral dresses and scarves squat-ted on the shoulder selling melons. SUVs barreled past, honking to force smaller cars out of their way, showering dust over the women.

We swung through what Ruslan called Zhilgorodok—a residential community. The five-story apartment blocks were the same as those all over town, but aging poplars provided them with shady alleys and a liv-able ambiance.

"The Russian constructors who built this town also built themselves a decent neighborhood, didn't they?" he said. "You see, Russians know what green means and how to preserve nature." He shifted in his seat. "If you don't mind me saying so, if Russia really *does* get its act together, it will *bury* the United States. A country that can build a city on swamps"—Saint Petersburg—"can do *anything.*" This minor divaga-tion took me by surprise, but it made sense: Russia was the empire he knew, it was rising again, and he would have little reason to like the United States, an enabler of the corruption that hindered him finding a decent job in his profession.

Next came the "cottage districts" where bland, two-story homes stood on separate plots of land. "This is where our elite live," he said. Finally we shot past the "American Village"—a guarded compound of suburban-style yet still modest homes, behind a wall. "Your country-men live apart from us," Ruslan said. "But nowadays Kazakhs can move in there too, if they can afford it."

Finally, the Ak Zhayyk Hotel.

"You staying here?" he asked as we pulled in.

"No. I'm buying a train ticket to Aqtöbe."

"What? *Train ticket!?*"

"Yes. What's wrong?"

"You haven't got a chance. They're all sold out."

"How do you know?"

"They always are. Especially these days. They're so cheap, they sell right away."

"Well, if I can't get a ticket, would you drive me?"

"*What?* Have you seen our roads?"

"I'd pay you well."

"Sorry, but no. The roads would break apart my car. You can die out there in the desert. I'm really sorry. No one will drive you from here."

"Well, I'm not going by plane."

"As well you shouldn't. Have you seen our planes? If you survive the flight you'll only regret how much they overcharged you."

"Then I'd better just try for a train ticket."

"As you like. But there are no tickets."

We said goodbye.

Inside the Ak Zhayyk's slick modern lobby the heat was unbearable except in front of the single standing AC unit, which poured icy air onto the bar. Behind it, in a sort of alcove, a queue of five or six people fanning themselves with paper scraps led up to a window where a train schedule was posted high and in small type.

Excusing myself to those in line, I approached the window, wanting to check the schedule.

"Get away from my window! Get away!" the ticket lady shouted at me in a high brittle voice. She was an old Kazakh woman, an unrehabilitated Soviet shrew-functionary of the type long gone in Moscow. I ignored her and tried to read the type, but I couldn't. "Get *away!* And the rest of you, leave this line immediately! I can't serve all of you today! I've told you! Get away!"

No one budged. I took a spot at the rear of the queue. It took her half an hour per customer. Ticket issuance involved consulting a computer that froze, scribbling out numerous supporting documents, and making phone calls (rarely answered on the first or second try) to the station office to confirm seat availability. And just when she finally seemed ready to slip a ticket through the slot, her cell phone would ring and she would turn away again to chat with her daughter about which vegetables to buy in the market that day.

No one objected to her scolding. She wielded small but important powers, and Kazakhs, being former Soviets, were accustomed to sub-mission in things big and small.

Two hours later I was still there, but second from the front. After the shrew's fifth or sixth cell phone call, the middle-aged Russian man ahead of me had had enough.

"Where's the complaint book, dammit? I want to file a complaint!" The cashier began filing papers. "You can't behave this way! We've been here for two hours and you've sold three tickets! How dare you!"

"I'm doing my accounting!" she screeched, and turned away from him.

"Then say so and close your damn window, you old bitch!"

She grabbed his passport from her counter, shoved it through her slot at him, and shrieked something in Kazakh. He took it and left.

As I tried to read the schedule, which was finally close enough, ster-torous breathing sounded from behind me, and I smelled sweat and sour breath. A Kazakh man of sixty or so in a grease-streaked track-suit elbowed me aside. Huffing and wheezing, he tossed his passport through the window slot. His fingernails were caked with crud, his hair was thin and matted, and mucus-soaked curly locks flowed from his mashed red nose.

She began to serve him, not me.

"Take your place in line, sir!" I said to the intruder.

He shot me a hard look. "I come yesterday, no serve, wait all day."

"We all have our stories. Please, take your place in line. It's not fair to me or these others ahead of you."

My protests were in vain; the cashier issued him a ticket. *"Kakoye khamsvto! Kakaya khamka!"* (Such rudeness! Such a rude woman!), the woman behind me murmured.

My turn came nevertheless. "I would like a ticket to Aq—"

"No tickets! All sold out!"

"You didn't even let me finish my sen—"

"No tickets! All sold out!"

"Wait a minute, I—"

She returned to her filing.

A Russian fellow from the line said, "Oh, you should just go to the station."

"Why? I heard it was worse there."

"Of course it is, if you go to the *ticket booth*. So you don't go to the ticket booth, but to the *dezhurnaya po vogzalu* [station manager]. You bribe her with five hundred tenge"—about four dollars—"and she'll get you a luxury seat in a sleeping compartment from here to Almaty! That's what I'd do, if I had the money."

Artificially low prices resulted in sellouts to sharks. The station manager, said the man, was in on the scam.

So I took a cab over to the railway station. I went straight to the window marked DEZHURNAYA. There a smiling, adorable Kazakh woman giggled when I asked for a black market ticket.

"Well, hmm, that sounds awfully illegal." She batted her eyes. "But if you come tomorrow at nine in the evening, I'll give you the ticket."

"Is five hundred tenge your price?"

"What, me, take money? Don't worry about that. I'll be glad to be of help. For free."

I told her I would be there the next day.

10

The next evening at the appointed hour I returned to the station and rapped gently on the *dezhurnaya*'s window. The curtains ripped open and I faced not my soft-spoken savior but a hulking termagant with a unibrow and a trombone bass.

"Ah, hello," I said. "The other *dezhurnaya* asked me to come tonight for my ticket to—"

"No tickets! All sold out!" she thundered back.

"Yes, but she said—"

"I don't know what that other *dezhurnaya* was talking about!"

"She said she'd get me the ticket herself and—"

"That's illegal!"

"But," I objected politely, "I'll make it worth your while if—"

"Get away from my window! No tickets! No tickets!"

She flung shut the curtains. The aluminum door to her cabin banged open and she stepped out with a thud, her sweaty bulk shrink-wrapped in a polyester uniform. She grabbed a black and white baton, jammed an official-looking cap on her perspiring noggin, and turned to me.

"I've got a train to meet!"

She set off waddling down the passageway leading under the tracks.

I stood speechless in the heat, paralyzed between despair and rage. How was I going to make it from here to Beijing if I couldn't even get to Aqtöbe? (Ruslan had been right: I couldn't find anyone to drive me.) Fifteen years had passed since the Soviet collapse, and *look* at how people lived! Everyone, or at least most people in this goddamned country, suffered from this ticket scam. Why didn't anyone *do* anything about it? To be sure, *real* reform would consist not of rising GDPs but of improvements in basic state services (railways in Kazakhstan are still government owned), of the banishment of the absurd and spirit-sapping Soviet-style corruption from daily life. Whatever the country's rulers were doing, they were not bettering the lives of their citizens. And their citizens were not fighting for change, but only submitting.

A young Kazakh couple approached me and, in oddly deferential tones, asked me how they could get tickets—they had a sick relative, a family emergency, and just had to get to their village.

"I'm sorry," I answered. "I haven't the faintest idea. I'm a stranger myself. I can't get out of here either."

They slumped away.

With nowhere else to go and nothing else to do, I stood and waited for the *dezhurnaya* to return.

An hour later she did. She climbed into the booth, shut the door and locked it, and flung open the curtains.

I tried a different approach.

"I'm really, really sorry to bother you again. I'm a foreigner here, an American. I understand I should follow procedures, but as you say, there are no tickets. But I've got to get to Aqtöbe. It's a family emergency. My wife's Russian but her mother, who refuses to move up to live with us in Moscow, has had a stroke. If, somehow, there's anything at all you can do, I'll be happy to reward your kindness."

She sighed. "You're not some kind of fugitive, are you, trying to avoid showing your passport at the ticket booth?"

"Not at all. They're just out of tickets, as you know."

"Of course they are. It's summer and everyone's traveling. But you're acting like a fugitive, lurking around here and trying to bribe me. Let me see your documents." I handed her my passport.

I pointed out my visa and registration and entry stamp. Everything was in order. She sighed again, blowing damp locks away from her brow, drew shut her curtain, and stepped out.

"Sick mother-in-law, eh?"

"Really sick."

"Come with me to the train. You can arrange it yourself with the conductor. I won't take your money. There are plenty of spaces on the train and no bribes are necessary."

We walked through the underpass and emerged onto a platform where a train marked AQTÖBE stood idling. A sensuously corpulent Kazakh woman climbed down from the first-class car's door. She was perfumed and fresh, smiling as though she'd just alighted from heaven. In fact, she had: the car was air conditioned, and I felt the cool even standing on the platform.

"He needs a ticket to Aqtöbe, Saida," said the *dezhurnaya*.

Saida smiled at me. "Five thousand tenge [forty dollars]. Can you pay that?"

"Yes."

"Then be here tomorrow morning at nine and I'll seat you in first class, with a TV correspondent. You'll have the cabin to yourselves."

She kept her word. The next evening I arrived rested and happy in Aqtöbe.

IN CENTURIES PAST, on the clement, lightly wooded steppes around the Kargala and Ilek rivers, Kazakh tribes repelled Dzungar incursions, and the turmoil threatened the caravan route connecting Orenburg with Central Asia. It was up to the colonizing Russians to secure the area, so in 1869 they built the fort of Aktyubinsk (Aqtöbe, or White Hill, in Kazakh), in the environs of which Cossacks settled and farmed. These days foreign and Kazakh companies are busy pumping oil and gas out of the land nearby, but Aqtöbe remains untouched, quaintly Soviet, a grid of nondescript streets lined by boxy, shambling Brezhnev hovels. Nevertheless, the town boasts a modern-era saint, a daughter of the steppes canonized in Russian and Kazakh literature and film: Aliya Moldagulova—one of the most lethal Soviet snipers of World War II.

A simple brick museum dedicated to Aliya sits near the center. My guide there was a twenty-year-old woman named Akmara who was diffident about her shaky Russian. The exhibits were scant—few of Aliya's personal effects have survived, and hardly anyone ever thought to photograph her at the time.

Placards and pictures hanging along the walls told her story. Aliya was born in 1925 in the village of Bulak, north of Aqtöbe, to a modestly prosperous Kazakh family. During Stalin's 1929–33 campaign to collectivize agriculture, their "spare" cows and "excess" sheep drew the wrath of the Communists, who branded Aliya's father a *bey* (a "lord," a putatively wealthy exploiter of the poor, the Central Asian equivalent of the kulak) and dispossessed the family. Her mother and brother died soon after, possibly of disease brought on by the immiseration and famine collectivization provoked. Aliya's grandmother adopted her and sent her to school in Moscow and Leningrad. The few photographs on display show a camera-shy girl whose impassive flat adolescent face nevertheless conveys something of a survivor's mettle.

When the war broke out Aliya enlisted and discovered her forte: sniping. Akmara timidly pointed to Aliya's pride, a tattered red "Scorebook of Military Vengeance" inscribed with the number of Germans she had gunned down by the age of nineteen: seventy-eight—a Soviet record.

A bleak Socialist-Realist mural depicts Aliya's last moments. Somewhere outside the snowbound steppe village of Kazachikha, in January of 1944, the Nazis fought her advancing battalion to a standstill. Aliya, at least as the official version has it, arose and rallied her dispirited comrades with cries of *"Za Rodinu!"* (For the motherland!) and, doubtless, though the exhibit did not say so, *"Za Stalina!"* (For Stalin!"). The painting shows a dead-eyed, blocky-cheeked Kazakh girl bundled in khaki, leading the charge into the German trenches, just before being cut down and martyred.

After the Soviet Union fell, a number of "war heroes" turned out to be fakes, their biographies trumped up for propaganda purposes. But not Aliya. In 2005 the Kazakh government celebrated her eightieth birthday, spending millions of tenge on the fête and hailing her as a Hero of the Kazakhs.

Stalin's various campaigns of violence almost wiped the Kazakhs off the map in the 1930s, yet Aliya had given her life to defend his regime. The obvious paradox left me dumbstruck. I turned to Akmara.

"How could a girl who lost her father and mother to a tyrant, a tyrant who had vast numbers of her people murdered, have fought to the death for his survival?"

"We have many such heroes," Akmara said flatly, and then rattled off a few statistics to prove it. "When World War Two broke out, the Aktyubinsk oblast sent one hundred and twenty thousand citizens to the front. Thirty-eight thousand of them died, and twenty-eight thousand went missing in action."

"I understand the numbers. But think beyond them. Just try to imagine the government throwing *you* out of your home, stealing *your* land, killing *your* family, and yet you rush off to fight to defend that government in a war brought on, in part, by your leader's miscalculations."

She winced. Her eyes darted about.

"It is beyond our understanding. I cannot imagine it."

Aliya represented an ideal the Soviets famously loved to tout: the selfless, unquestioning killer for the state, the *Homo Sovieticus* (and, in her case, the *Femina Sovietica*) devoted to the dictatorship of workers and peasants, espousing all the "correct" party-sanctioned political views, seething (on command) with ire at the capitalists abroad and enemies at home scheming to destroy the Bolshevik Paradise, and ever ready to make the Ultimate Sacrifice. Leninist-Stalinist social engineering—the obliteration of social classes, the use of mass terror, the state takeover of the economy, education, and the media—did work, at least for a number of decades, and created people who, in their majority, proved both obedient to their oppressors and victorious in World War II. The Soviet regime, in effect, orphaned the country and took advantage of the disoriented, grief-stricken survivors to defend itself when the Nazis attacked. These days post-Soviet rulers exploit their citizens' entrenched apathy and cynicism to make off with the resource wealth that should, for the first time in history, be allowing them a decent—or even better than decent—standard of living.

Nevertheless, such social engineering, now almost two decades discontinued, produced a New Soviet Human possessing traits favoring survival under direst duress: ingrained distrust of the government and the media (always perceived as serving the state); disbelief in justice as embodied in laws (written, of course, to serve the elite), and, consequently, a willingness to flout the law to get ahead; cynicism toward government officials (regarded as ever on the take); the spurning of piety, probity, and honesty as the attributes of naifs; and, finally, the exaltation of deceit, the lionization of crooks, for only through cleverness could one succeed. The Soviet system, in sum, created a populace of survivors who would excel in stealth and criminality and yet be unwilling to confront their governments and demand what is owed them.

I returned to Aliya's photographs and studied her eyes. They were less impassive than inured, dead blank, the eyes of one who would do whatever it took to survive.

ON A WONDERFULLY COOL MORNING a couple of days later (the northern latitude gave this corner of Kazakhstan a pleasantly Russian feel), I climbed aboard the Moscow-Bishkek Express for the ten-hour ride southeast to Aralsk, Kazakhstan's outpost on the blighted Aral Sea.

Wised up this time, for a ticket I directly approached the conductor, a sloppy, overfed Russian woman with doughy skin and bovine eyes. She understood straightaway what I was after. Lisping thickly, she asked, "Where to and how much? Ah. Deal!"

I liked the train immediately; the windows opened and it was clean. She showed me to my compartment.

"I can take any bunk?"

"No, this one." She tapped the upper berth, pocketed my tenge, and walked out.

I grabbed the rail and began to climb into my berth. But a shaven-head Slav with Neanderthal brows pushed grunting past me and hoisted himself into my spot.

"Excuse me, but that's my seat," I said.

He grunted again and turned to face the wall, falling asleep immediately.

The conductor stuck her head in. "Oh, he's not taking your spot. He's a conductor from another car and just needs a nap. Will you be so kind?"

"Sure."

The train inched out of the station. I sat down on the lower bunk opposite him. He looked like a thug, and a pathetic one. He wore too-tight gym shorts and a shrunken T-shirt that rode up, disclosing a mass of pink-yellow belly flesh. His bare, corn-toed feet smelled. His almost hairless legs were dotted with mosquito-bite sores. Eyes closed, he rolled over to face me and dozed baby-style, with his cheek resting on his pressed-together hands in such a way that his mouth opened and his tongue lolled out; with all his subsequent sleepy yawns, he expelled fetid breath that filled the compartment.

Every few minutes the conductor returned with new ticketless passengers. There was a bashful young Kazakh woman with an entirely gilt smile. ("I work in Mordvinia but am going to Bishkek," she would tell me. "I've never seen a camel and want to on this trip.") An elderly Kazakh with droopy eyes and excellent Russian. A Russian engineer from Samara named Gennady. Three Kazakh teens, all well groomed, clear-skinned, and polite, took the last places, but the conductor still managed to squeeze in an obese woman and her obese husband and their wailing jumbo-size baby.

We coasted south through sun-showered steppe and open woodlands. But gradually the trees disappeared, the grass dried up, desert crept in, and the burnt sienna ridges of the Mugadzhar Mountains rumpled the eastern horizon. Most assuredly, we were heading back into Central Asia.

Gennady and the old Kazakh carried on a casual conversation that touched on all the post-Soviet themes: the *mafiya* runs everything; officials steal; and life goes on, with no cause for alarm.

But Gennady turned to me.

"One thing does bother me, though. It's a crime, a shame, a disgrace."

"What is?"

"My grandpa was born ninety years ago in Shymkent, where I'm going now. He'll die there, in his own hometown, the only place he's ever lived, but in *exile,* as an unwanted Russian, a minority in his own land." Gennady's pale blue eyes were stark and set deep above prematurely aged cheeks; his clothes were threadbare, flea market purchases. He was probably earning a pittance in Samara as an engineer—a job he'd be well remunerated for in the West. "What did Grandpa do to deserve it?"

"He didn't want to move to Russia when independence came? So many did."

"What, move at age seventy-five? Start all over again, in a country he'd never even been to? He loves Shymkent. But he's Russian, so no one wants him there now. He's a foreigner in his own land."

Eyes dropped to the floor all around. Except for me, everyone was Kazakh.

Gennady frowned hard. "America stirred up ethnic brawls all over the Soviet Union to bring it crashing down. We lived like brothers until the Americans messed with us. And look at what kind of state we got as a result. In Russia companies make billions in oil profits, but does that money go to the people? Does the government use it to raise the wages of doctors and nurses? No, it goes to the West, to banks in the West, to Western companies, or to offshore zones. See any connection? It was all a plot against us, to get our resources and cash transferred to the West."

He was expressing a well-worn conspiracy theory now believed here more often than not, a theory seemingly supported by everyday life and news stories that cast the United States as Villain Number One and absolved former Soviet citizens of responsibility for their continued misery. The new Great Game for him, as for so many Russians, had begun in 1991 with the death of the Soviet Union, and the West had thought out all its moves in advance. But then he surprised me. "We can't seem to get it together like the Kazakhs. Just from this trip I can see the Kazakh government is really doing something for the people."

I myself couldn't see this, and wondered if one of the Kazakhs might respond. None did.

"We're regressing, they're progressing," he said. "Where're you from, by the way?"

I told him.

"Oh-ho!"

Displaying no embarrassment about his remarks, he leaned over to shake my hand and said he was so pleased to meet me. He invited me out into the corridor, where he asked me about the Iraq war and President Bush, and why Americans had twice elected "such a cretin." Our talk then ranged over gas and oil, the United States' dependence on foreign oil, and Russia's oil- and gas-based stature in the world. How fatiguing was all this talk of energy!

But there was no escaping it. Dominating desert steppes rendered increasingly indistinct by the fading light were oil derricks, gas flare-offs, and pipelines, the view of which passing trains of tanker cars at times obscured. Station stops, preceded by tumbledown Kazakh cemeteries ("*Nekropoli,*" said Gennady, and how apt the Russian word sounded!) ransacked by dust devils, grew bleaker, becoming little more than haphazard formations of concrete bunkers huddled on a dimming plain. Against this apocalyptic backdrop of surging gas flares grazed Bactrian camels, gaunt and shaggy, tended by Kazakh women in red robes, their long red scarves tied tight around their bony skulls. On a telephone pole a golden eagle perched defiantly, his wings half spread, his beak open, as if daring us to alight, an avian Cerberus guarding his preserve of the damned.

As the sun's orange orb slipped beneath the desert horizon we pulled in to shacks lost in half-light. Aralsk. I grabbed my bag.

Gennady jumped up. "You're not getting off here?"

"Yes, I am."

"Forgive me, but there're only Kazakhs here. They're not civilized. How can animal herders who never lived in cities be civilized? It's probably not safe for an American. You should just stay on board."

"I'll manage. I've enjoyed talking to you." I shook his hand, wished him well, and jumped off.

Silence, save for the wind, which was now picking up, driving dust clouds and tumbleweed through the shacks. I hired the one taxi in the lot—a scrapheap Zhiguli with some windows tinted, others not, piloted by a Kazakh whose face I couldn't see. We set off in a sandstorm, bouncing down sandy streets, passing pedestrians in surgical masks, and arrived a few minutes later at the Aral Hotel—a grit-blasted hovel with a front door banging in the wind. Just beyond, fishing boats stood stranded and listing in a sand basin—Aralsk's port. Not a drop of water was to be seen.

Taking the key from a kind but astonished receptionist, I went upstairs to turn in. I fell asleep to the echoing quarrels of drunks outside on the street, to the susurrus of sand blowing against my window, blowing over the stranded boats in the waterless harbor and the shacks and the drunks.

IN THE LENGTHY CHRONICLES of Soviet environmental calamities, the Aral Sea disaster stands out—in fact, it ranks as one of the world's worst ecological catastrophes. A century ago Aralsk was a thriving port. In 1905, from the Aral Sea (a giant saltwater lake, really, then the world's fourth-largest body of landlocked water) Kazakh fishermen pulled in an annual catch of 660 tons of bream, carp, roach, perch, and prize, caviar-bloated sturgeon. During the years of civil war and famine following the Bolshevik Revolution, these catches grew, filling ever-longer supply trains to Moscow; by 1925, yields had risen threefold. In that year the Soviets established Aralgosrybtrest (Aral State Fish Enterprise)—a rare example of a successful Soviet state business. By the 1950s three thousand fishermen manning boats around the clock were shipping twenty thousand tons of fish—fresh, frozen, and salted—through Aralsk to destinations across the Soviet Union.

The bounty was not to last. As far back as the 1880s the Russians had been discussing how to use the Aral's "excess" water for irrigation, but disaster would stem from a Stalin-era scheme, initiated in 1946, that aimed to boost cotton production in Central Asia (to achieve national self-sufficiency in the crop). The plan called for the augmented planting of the fibrous plant in Kazakhstan and, especially, in Uzbekistan, along the two legendary rivers that watered the Aral: the Amu Darya and the Syr Darya. Increased cotton production required mass irrigation, so the authorities tapped the Daryas. Within twenty years Soviet farmers were harvesting four times more cotton, but water flow into the Aral had dropped tenfold; sea levels plummeted by two-thirds, reducing its surface area by half; and the Aral had divided into three basins, leaving fishing villages, among them Aralsk, far from shore. Accelerated evaporation raised the proportion of salt and minerals in the water, which poisoned and killed off most of the fish, rendering extinct four native species, including sturgeon. The Soviet centrally planned economy being what it was, Aralrybprom was still operating in 1975 (the first year without any catch at all), processing fish dispatched by train from the Baltic and even the Pacific. But the Aral's own fishing industry was dead and its Kazakh practitioners moving away, leaving behind ghost villages. Irrigation, however, continued. By the 1980s, during the almost rainless Central Asian summers, the Daryas themselves were drying up.

As freezers from Vladivostok to Vilnius brimmed with fish processed in Aralsk, the Soviet military was using the island of Vozrozhdeniye (which ironically translates as "Renaissance") to test biological weapons, including those containing bubonic plague and anthrax. Once the water drained away, Vozrozhdeniye's formerly seabound mammals began ambling across the sands, posing a theoretical threat to people. The threat became real in 1999, with the discovery of live anthrax spores (since detoxified with U.S. aid). The region's perpetual winds proved efficient carriers of toxins, blowing poison-, pesticide-, and salt-laden grit across much of Central Asia, causing cancers, anemia, renal and respiratory diseases, kidney failures, and miscarriages—plagues that continue. Without the Aral's tempering influence, the already severe climate worsened, becoming hotter in summer, colder in winter, and drier.

One fact seemed as irrefutable as it was irremediable: the Communists had killed the Aral Sea. After the Soviet collapse, the disaster received a good deal of media attention, but the partial, fledgling, yet potentially momentous, return of the water and revival of the fishing industry has not. In the mid-1990s a Danish scientist named Kurt B. Christensen visited the sea and, shocked by the sight of boats marooned in Aralsk's waterless port, began considering how to resuscitate the fishing industry using the salt-hardy Azov flounder, a species introduced to the Aral by the Soviets in 1979 but uncatchable with local gear. (Traditional nets couldn't snare bottom dwellers.) In 1994 he and other concerned scientists arranged to ship special Danish tackle and flounder nets to the Aral, and counseled the Kazakh to organize themselves into private, agile "brigades" of ten fishermen each. The Kazakhs divided the sea into ten zones and set to work. The World Bank and the Kazakh government then agreed to finance the construction of a dam (finished in 2005) across a narrow stretch of the Aral that would allow the Syr Darya's waters to accumulate more effectively and flow back into their original domains.

I had not heard how the Aral Sea was faring, but I was determined to find out.

THE NEXT MORNING, with the sun in nova but the wind in abeyance, I stopped by the local NGO, Aral Tenizi ("Aral Sea" in Kazakh), and hired its stolid driver, Batyrbeg, to take me in his Land Rover a hundred miles south across the desert, out to the Kok-Aral Dam between the Aral's northernmost two basins, where fishermen gather to sail into the rising sea.

With Batyrbeg I immediately sensed that I had left the Russified west of Kazakhstan and entered the realm of the country's most traditional *juz* (one of three Kazakh tribal groupings), which had never adopted the Slavic tongue of its occupiers. Batyrbeg at first seemed close-mouthed and glowering, and with his shaved skull and angular jaw he reminded me of a Buryat *mafiyozo*.

"We must buy camel milk and bread," he said in thick, Kazakh-accented syllables. "For journey. Steppe, danger."

"Fine with me."

We climbed aboard his Rover. He thwacked the dashboard with a rag, displacing a cloud of dust; I took a seat and more dust puffed out. He yanked his gears and we backed out onto the sandy road and then turned and headed for the center.

We trundled around the settlement as the wind picked up. Quickly our expedition took on a doomed air. We were driving through a sandstorm, and the swells and troughs of the road bounced me about the cabin. Pedestrians trudged by in surgical masks, going about their business. We stopped at a couple of bare-shelved grocers and stepped out into the stench of sewage to look for camel's milk, but in vain. Nearby, disheveled barbers staffed a puzzlingly large number of hair salons releasing customers who might have coiffed themselves with garden shears. Toilets were common but rarely flushed; pipes for running water existed but were dry. Aralsk had just enough trappings of modernity to make everyone miserable.

"Market, market," said Batyrbeg in Russian.

We then went to the market, a sandlot strewn with tables and plastic sheeting, on which merchants had spread canned wares and piles of green melons but also bottles of raw camel milk, sold in used mineral water bottles. Everywhere resounded the guttural clucks and umlauted vowels of the Kazakh language; many people here resembled my driver, with blocky brows and spiky hair. There were no Russians anywhere, and no one was even speaking Russian.

We picked up a piste leading straight out onto the steppe—a table-land of sand and scrub and rock.

"Why go dam?" asked Batyrbeg.

I explained. He couldn't understand my answer.

We turned to simpler topics. I tried to decipher his Kazakh using Turkish, which was not always possible. I learned that he was twenty-six years old and had received his education in Kazakh, with only a minimal exposure to Russian. He told me he owned this Land Rover, had a wife and three children, and supported eight people, all of whom were living under the roof of the house he had built with his own hands. I asked him about Islam, whether he believed or practiced, but I couldn't convey my meaning.

At first his deficient Russian frustrated me—how could he not know the language? But this was an absurd imperialist question on my part: he was a Kazakh in Kazakhstan, and with the fall of the Soviet Union Russian was no longer obligatory here. Akmaral Ötemisova, Aral Tenizi's manager, had explained the situation to me. "We no longer study Russian in schools here, for the most part; we have eight schools, and only one of them is Russian. In Kazakhstan we have now two mentalities: the mentality of the village, where people say, 'Why should we speak Russian?' and the mentality of the big city, where people see no need for Kazakh at all." More and more, citizens of northern, Russophone Kazakhstan find themselves unable to communicate with their compatriots in the south.

The steppe began undulating. We spotted camels and herds of horses grazing on the thinnest of grass. As we drew near them, the camels raised their heads and, keeping one eye on us, loped away; horses stampeded to escape. Sheep clogged our piste, clearing only with Batyrbeg's persistent honking. We were rolling out into the middle of an empty infinity, and I wondered how the Russians felt crossing it.

Two hours later we slammed clanking down a steep embankment and bounced over a green pontoon bridge spanning the Syr Darya

—hardly more than a stream—and pulled up near a trailer-size refrigerator van by the Kok-Aral Dam. There was quiet save for the brush of sand blowing against the van, the scream of a fish hawk, and the thrashing of the shallow sea, green and choppy.

A middle-aged Russian with a heavy belly and mussed-up hair hopped down from the van's rear, swearing and wiping fish goo from his hands, and asked, with some suspicion in his gravelly voice, what we wanted.

"I thought I'd see for myself if fishing is really picking up out here."

"Well," he said, "life is beginning here again with this dam, that much I can say. I represent my son's firm. I sit out here and take in the catch, which is now around four or five tons a day, sometimes ten, and mostly carp, pike, perch, snakehead, and some sturgeon. We thought all these fish had died off before we started looking for them. The catch we pull from the Little Aral is best of all, not too salty but very flavorful. Our firm is building its own fish-processing plant back in town."

The waters, with the dam's completion, have surged back, covering anew almost a thousand square miles. Flounder catches have jumped from zero in 1995 to a thousand tons in 2002—still little compared to early Soviet yields, but catches are growing. One cooperative I later spoke to, Kambala-Balyk ("Flounder Fish"), processes three hundred tons a year, but it has to export its produce to Russia and Ukraine. The Kazakh government still doesn't afford fishermen tax privileges that would make it profitable for them to sell domestically.

"Are you from here?" I asked.

"Yeah, but so what?" he asked, the wind ruffling his gray locks. "I mean, it doesn't matter where you're from, if you're Soviet. Fucking thieves and bandits cut apart the Soviet Union, my dear country. Anyway, we'll drive away any competitors who show up here, wherever they're from."

Was that a hint? The Kazakh men who jumped down from the van looked like thugs. Maybe he took me for a spy scouting out fishing grounds for a competitor. I got the sense we were not welcome, so we said goodbye and drove back to Aralsk.

AKMARAL HAD INFORMED ME that I had to register with the police. I was only to be in town a few days and so saw no reason to waste my time on such bureaucracy, but having unaccounted-for days on my visa could create problems for me at the border. She graciously provided me with a letter, adorned with her organization's stamps and seals, requesting authorization for my stay. Armed with her missive, I set off for the police station.

The protracted, inept inspection of my passport on entering the country had already shown me that Kazakhstan has retained much Soviet-style suspicion toward foreigners, as well as the red tape used to keep track of them. This really reflects the government's fear of its own people, who suffer far more from meddling bureaucracy than do travelers; legislative strictures of all sorts keep citizens submissive to a state to which, its leaders know, they could owe no genuine allegiance. The strictures also offer their enforcers opportunities for graft that undercut their purpose — control. But they nevertheless serve as stifling reminders of the System, in which what counts is a bureaucrat's signature, not personal initiative or individual rights, for which a regime based on oil and gas revenues has, anyway, no use.

Aralsk's police station was just another gray brick building on a nondescript sandy street. A tall young Kazakh guard in light blue stood out by the gate with his arms crossed. Carrying a Walkman loaded with a Chinese-language study tape, I approached him, pulling out my earphones and readying my passport.

"*Zdravstvuyte!*" I said. "I'm—"

"Give it here!" he barked.

I offered my passport.

"No, the tape player! Give it here!"

I handed it to him.

"You're not playing anything forbidden, are you?"

"Please listen for yourself."

He put in the earphones and flicked the button, landing on a dialogue in Mandarin about train tickets and Tang dynasty poetry. He listened, frowned, scrunched up his face, and blurted out, "Yo-yan-yo-yang ya-ya!," mimicking the speaker. He laughed, "Yo-yang-yang!" kept the tape on, repeated his imbecilic gibberish some more, and called over another guard, who found the Chinese equally hilarious.

"I suppose you don't see many Chinese in Aralsk," I said.

"We had a few. As soon as they showed up, all our dogs and frogs disappeared! Ate 'em all up, you know." He guffawed, and they took me inside to meet the chief.

A beetle-browed, pudgy fellow in a much darker uniform sat behind his desk in a corner office. When I walked in he looked shocked to see me. I mentioned Akmaral's name and handed him her letter and my passport.

He sniffled, set aside her letter, and sighed. He slowly, *slowly,* flicked through my passport, sniffling more and restraining belches from an undigested breakfast. I stood before him as one accused, the two officers flanking me, sober, all hint of their puerile joviality having vanished.

After ten minutes of scrutinizing my document, adorned with the bald eagle and my country's name, he looked up at me. "You German?"

"No."

He seemed unconvinced.

"Actually, I've got a U.S. passport, as you see there."

"*That's* not what I meant." Without further explanation he went back to flicking through the pages. I could think of nothing else to say. He belched, rubbed his nose, and broke the awkward silence. "Tayler's a German name."

"Actually it's British, or British-Canadian, in my case."

"It sounds German to me," he said harshly, as though he had caught me in an incriminating contradiction. He fixed me with his stern brown eyes.

I shrugged. "Well, I'm sorry, but I'm not German."

He sighed, reached for one of his registers, opened it, shut it, and then reached for another. He paused in midmove, sniffled, and reopened my passport. He examined my photo and compared it with my face. He grabbed a pen and began to indite, but then he halted, as if engaged in an activity of momentous gravity. He stood up, leaned over his desk, riffled through more notebooks, and came up with one that had a map of the world in the back.

"Where's Vasheengton?" he asked, his fingers running over Brazil toward Paraguay.

"In the United States."

His fingers wandered north, stopping in Guatemala. "Still don't see it."

I reached over and pointed out the city.

"Ah. Of course. Well, hmm, yes . . ." He sniffled and began, once again, to write slowly, *slowly,* pausing to reexamine my photo and compare it with my face.

There were footsteps in the corridor. In walked a hulking, potbellied man in a beige safari suit and sunglasses. He was in his early sixties; he had a vaguely menacing hauteur about him. The guards snapped to attention; the passport officer stood up, saluted, and shook his hand. As did I.

Taking a seat, the hulking man rubbed his globular nose and exhaled voluminously, reeking of unbrushed teeth and *peregar*—the morning-after stench of vodka-soured breath.

"Where's he from?" he asked the officer with my passport.

"Vasheengton." He pointed to Guatemala.

The Boss slowly turned toward me. "Got a smoke?"

I said no. His request jolted into action the guard at my side, who loped about the station, creaking all the floorboards, until he found someone with a cigarette. The Boss took it, struck a match, and inhaled, held his breath, and then exhaled an effluvium of smoke and *peregar*. He flicked the still lit match toward the ashtray, but missed. It burned a puddle in the desk's lacquer.

"He's studying Chinese," said the guard.

"Chinese?" said the passport officer. "We had a few of them here. As soon as they showed up, all our dogs and frogs—"

"Disappeared," I said. "So I've heard."

Everyone laughed except the Boss, who stared ahead through his dark glasses at points unbeknownst to us mortals.

An hour later, I retrieved my passport, accepted wishes of bon voyage, and left for my hotel to pack.

11

An airy, open-windowed bus rocked and jolted me from Aralsk 280 miles down a ruined highway that paralleled the depleted, soupy green waters of the Syr Darya, to the town of Kyzylorda, on its banks. Once the northernmost outpost of a Kokand-based khanate, and briefly the capital of Soviet Kazakhstan, Kyzylorda, standing at the edge of a terrible wilderness, would only be my point of departure across that same wilderness. From Kyzylorda I needed to reach the former gulag outpost of Karaganda (a byword for remoteness in Russian), six hundred miles to the northeast, over the least inhabited, most desolate and perilous swath of Kazakhstan, the Betpaqdala Desert. (Karaganda was one place no player in the Great Game, past or present, ever reached, but it was a necessary stopover on the way to Astana, Kazakhstan's capital.) The Betpaqdala covers twenty-nine thousand square miles of terrain too parched to support farming (rainfall there averages 75 percent less than elsewhere on Kazakhstan's generally dry steppes) or animal husbandry. Its prickle-thorn-scattered wastes are so blighted by sandstorms, drought, and salt deposits that not even the harebrained Khrushchev, enamored of planting crops where they could never grow, would touch it at the peak of his enthusiasm for transformative agriculture.

I asked my hotel receptionist how I could get from Kyzylorda to Karaganda. A soft-spoken Russian with melancholy hazel eyes, she warned me, "The road, if you can call it that, is terrible and no one drives from here. There's only one bus, and it hardly ever runs. Try the trains."

I took her advice. At the railway station I learned that trains did go to Karaganda, but they circumvented the Betpaqdala, which no tracks cross, and so took a minimum of thirty-one hours—too long. Taxi drivers in the station lot refused the trip, saying, "The steppe has no water! . . . The bad road will break apart my car! . . . There're only steppe rats out in the Betpaqdala! . . . They grow drugs out there and bandits rob people . . . You can't make it through!" Finally, one burly Ukrainian who had watched me suffer refusal after refusal said, snickering, in his elliptical native tongue, *"Ne mae durakov?"* (No idiots available to take you?). The sole edifying commentary ("You need to go to Karaganda by way of Zhezqazghan. That's two hundred and sixty miles from here, and it's a bad trip. But from Zhezqazghan on the road is okay") came from the fellow who ended up taking me to the bus station. There I learned that in the morning a bus—a dusty white crate standing out in the lot—might go to Zhezqazghan, or might not, depending on whether there were enough passengers.

I was wondering what to do when I noticed, on the bus station lot, a dented white Mazda with tinted windows—surely a taxi waiting for customers. I went up and knocked on the window. Out jumped a spry old Kazakh, grinning and wizened, with a spiky crewcut.

I shook his hand. "Can you take me to Zhezqazghan?"

"Can *I* take *you* to Zhezqazghan? I used to drive the *bus* to Zhezqazghan!" he shouted in a raspy voice, waving his free wiry arm. "A driver out on the Betpaqdala is not just a driver, you know. He's the captain of a ship sailing through a sand sea! I'm just the person to get you there!"

"Can your car handle the road?" I asked. He had still not let go of my hand.

"Road is bad out there, dangerous. However, come . . ." My hand locked in his sandpapery paw, he pulled me around to the rear bumper, on which a dealership logo was pasted. "See, it says 'Norden.' That means north. It's German. This car is much better than a Soviet car. It won't break down."

Zheksin was his name. He would be the Charon who would ferry me into hell, though for a bit more than an obol. We settled on a fare of two hundred dollars' worth of tenge—a strangely small sum considering the risk to his vehicle. Another Kazakh later explained to me, "Kazakhs only settled recently, so we don't really value money as much as Russians or even the other Central Asians. We have no commercial instinct."

I found Zheksin's élan uplifting, and appreciated the pride he took in his work, something common among old Soviet salt-of-the-earth types but rare in these parts now. We would set out early the next morning.

JUST AFTER DAWN I got dressed and took my bag down to the lobby. The sun was already firing the air, and the heat hit me as soon as I stepped outside. Zheksin was waiting and eager.

"Your captain is ready to sail!" he announced hoarsely, shaking my hand. "We need to stop by my house so I can pick up water and some food, and also, if you don't mind, my brother-in-law. He can help out if we run into trouble."

I threw my bag in the trunk and hopped in. Hanging from his rearview mirror was a dust-caked plastic pendant showing the Kaaba in Mecca. The call to prayer drifted from a nearby minaret through the hot still air.

"Good luck for us," he said, pointing to the Kaaba.

We would need it. The Kaaba talisman reminded me that we were about to cross part of a desert larger than Saudi Arabia's Empty Quarter, if one that lacked a Thesiger to romanticize its wastes in prose.

We took off down Ayteke Bi Boulevard and soon left it for a maze of dirt roads—about all there was, away from Kyzylorda's center. Soon we found ourselves deep in a neighborhood of whitewashed homes and wobbly weathered fences and guard dogs baying and rattling their chains.

We stopped by his house. His wife, chubby, fretting, and antsy, ten years younger than he, came out in a robe and pressed on him a plastic bag stuffed with warm meat and onion pies; the brother-in-law, half his age and silent but muscular, followed her. Grim, carrying a muskmelon on his shoulder and a footlong knife to cut it with, he looked like an Al Qaeda assassin. After a flurry of farewells in Kazakh we pulled away, picking up a pack of barking rat-faced strays. We lost them when we hit a smooth tarmac and drove out of town due north under a heraldic blue sky, bisecting tawny steppe sprinkled with dead grass and prickle thorn that looked not frightening at all.

A sign read ZHEZQAZGHAN 419 K. *What bad road?*

Zheksin hit the gas and we flew along at seventy, seventy-five miles an hour—too fast for the local fauna. Every quarter-mile sparrows or plovers of some sort were congregating on the highway, but our speedy approach left them no time to escape. We blasted through them, tiny bird corpses bouncing off our windshield and rolling to a halt behind us.

I felt sorry for these birds and asked Zheksin to slow down.

"I can't now," he said, "or who knows when we'll arrive. We shouldn't drive at night. We can get lost."

Now and then his brother-in-law shoved a pie over the seat and Zheksin took it. Chewing loudly and open-mouthed, he told me about his life after losing his job as a bus driver. "In our country no one hires anyone older than fifty. So what was I to do? Roll over and die? I used my savings to buy this car. It's foreign-made, so it can take anything . . . Back in Soviet times, we drivers were *respected*. Now you have to fight to stay alive and earn a living."

The engine roared with occasional (and inexplicable) jarring clanks. As steppe changed to out-and-out desert, the wind gusted through my open window and then began howling, growing shriller and hotter, drowning out his banter. Within an hour we were shooting across sun-cauterized wastes the color of cigarette ash, scarred with salt patches, spiked with camel bones, with sticks and rock shards and prickly shrubs.

"*Verblyuzhaya kolyuchka*" (camel thorn), said Zheksin, looking at the shrub. "There's nothing else out here."

Kazakhstan's 1.6 million square miles are home to only fifteen million people, and most of those live in the southeast. The Betpaqdala was all baking wastes that were baking wastes and no more, geographic incarnations of death too ugly to merit the attention of literary-minded explorers, so uncomely that they conjured up notions of after-the-blast desolation (though no nuclear weapons had been tested here) and industrial despoilment (despite the absence of man's footprint).

The tarmac cracked up and degenerated into a cratered piste. We vaulted onto it and skidded, dust flooding through our windows, which we rolled up. Clouds of cement gray sand were now blowing over the carcasses of trucks overturned at roadside, long abandoned, their crushed cabins evoking mangled drivers. I found myself almost yearning for oil derricks and gas flares, for signs that we were not alone.

The heat and dryness mounted; my lips were chapped, my throat itched. Zheksin snapped his fingers. His brother-in-law, bouncing about in the back with his melon and pies, lit a cigarette, puffed it once or twice, and passed it over the seatback. Zheksin inhaled deeply and coughed, inhaled and coughed, and puffed and puffed. Soon the sand-storm mixed with cigarette smoke to fill the cabin. I rolled down the window, got a lungful of dust, and rolled it back up. When the dust cloudbanks dwindled, dust devils came upon us, wandering west, some no higher than a man, others the size of whirling lighthouses.

I closed my eyes to the glare.

In the early evening, ten hours after we set out, smokestacks trailing plumes of rusty-hued gas peeked above a faraway strip of green, slightly higher steppe: Zhezqazghan, north of the desert, south of Siberia, quite in the middle of nowhere. As we drew near, the air grew moister and the land came alive with grass and even tiny flowers. COPPER IS OUR WEALTH! shouted red wind-whipped banners. In 1938 Soviet planners founded Zhezqazghan, really an agglomeration of smelting plants, to exploit the mineral during Stalin's industrialization campaign.

We finally drove back onto a tarmac that forked, with one branch heading north toward Kurgan, in Siberia, and the other east into town. Not knowing the way to the center, Zheksin left me on the outskirts, where I picked up a gypsy cab to the Samsung Hotel, a comfortable modern inn built on the grounds of a hospital.

The hotel was paradise. There I recovered, rinsing off Betpaqdala's grit with hot water before feasting on steak and potatoes. Later I lay gazing through my window at plumes of smelting smoke gilt and then pinkened by the late-evening sun, smoke drifting over surprisingly green neighborhoods, and a breeze-rippled azure reservoir, an inno-cent eye reflecting a sky of protean pastels. My room was a domain of peace and cool, and soon I dozed off.

The next morning a four-hour taxi trip took me 320 miles northeast. Toward the end, the steppe began rolling and turning grassy; trees popped up along the banks of brooks. Then from behind a rise, fore-told only by the tops of telephone poles, erupted Karaganda. A railway track paralleled us; leafy districts of *izbas* appeared, weather-beaten, blue and green, and soon traffic jams and multistoried buildings mot-tled with exhaust grit and steppe dust. Crowds of Russians thronged on crumbling pavement, hurrying about their business. Karaganda was rough-hewed, but *alive.*

12

Equidistant from the Pacific and Atlantic oceans, Karaganda (population 446,200) lies at the very heart of Eurasia. The Great Game never reached this far north. Covering three hundred square miles and comprising twenty settlements, a spread-out array of industrial parks as much as a metropolis, Karaganda ranks as Kazakhstan's second-largest city, and owes its oversize dimensions to commensurately large deposits of coal, waves of political repression, and misplaced élan from the bumptious premier Khrushchev, who won his "harebrained" moniker partly through his doings to its environs.

Things began auspiciously in tsarist times. In the midnineteenth century, as Russian entrepreneurs reconnoitered in Central Asia, a clever merchant named Nikon Ushakov arrived on the then almost empty steppes here. Intrigued by bituminous "burning rocks" he heard of from Kazakh nomads, Ushakov bought a plot of land from a "Kirgiz" (according to the bill of sale) tribal leader, Baydzhana Taktamyshev, for a mere 250 rubles. The coal-mining settlement born on the plot in 1856 took its name from one of the steppe's few living things—the lean caragana bush. Karaganda's mines, remote even by Russian standards, did well enough for a while, but they had slipped into eclipse by the time the Bolsheviks seized power, recovering only when Stalin's industrialization drive of the 1930s mandated their full-scale exploitation to support factories in the Urals.

But there was one problem. Like so many resource-rich yet far-flung hellholes of the Soviet Union, Karaganda lacked manpower. Stalin solved the problem in his characteristic way. The 1934 "assassination"—most likely a Kremlin-ordered hit—of a popular Leningrad Communist Party leader, Sergey Kirov, provided the dictator with a pretext for launching the Great Terror, an all-out assault on potential rivals as well as entire segments of Soviet society that might one day resist his rule. Many of the Communist Party's highest officials were charged with treason, espionage, and "counter-revolutionary activity" and subjected to show trials that ended with their execution. Conveniently for the cash-strapped state, the secret police "uncovered" traitors, wreckers, and anti-Soviet agitators everywhere, and kangaroo courts sentenced millions of innocents to hard labor in regions that just happened to need rock breakers and loggers, construction workers and miners.

Karaganda was one such place. Two million people were condemned to *vechnoye poseleniye* (eternal domestic exile) in the Karaganda Correctional Labor Camp, a sprawling complex of some two hundred prison settlements known by its short and nasty nickname, Karlag. After the Nazis seized the mineral-rich eastern Ukraine, the coal mined in Karlag would prove vital to Soviet victory in World War II; and Karaganda's metallurgy would evolve into a pillar of national industry. Among the condemned were hapless representatives of the fifty minority peoples (totaling 3.5 million, mostly from the Caucasus) whom Stalin deported en masse on suspicion of disloyalty, which made Karaganda one of the most ethnically variegated cities in the Soviet Union, a true melting pot of misery.

After Stalin's death in 1953, Khrushchev ordered the liberation of millions of his former boss's victims. As a condition for release, however, the state compelled Karlag's inmates to sign pledges of silence about their prison time and denied many residency in their hometowns, effectively stranding them for life in Karaganda. Throughout the Soviet decades, the government restricted access to Karaganda, labeling it a city "closed" to foreigners.

Karaganda was still to undergo one more period of pell-mell expansion. Khrushchev devised a plan to put the barrens of Siberia and Central Asia at the service of the Soviet State: the Virgin Lands project, which mandated the tilling of seventy million fallow acres of steppe to boost ever-deficient national crop yields. In 1954, responding to his call, millions of Russians and Ukrainians moved to Kazakhstan to start farming. Yet within a few years, they found themselves beleaguered by the harsh climate, their soil and seed blowing away in the perennial winds or poisoned through overfertilization. The Virgin Lands project was called off (and later, after Khrushchev's dismissal, derided as *pro-zhektyorsvto*, "harebrained scheming"). The Slavic migrants remained, however, and, together with other minority peoples, outnumbered the Kazakhs, setting the stage for a short-lived pro-Russian secessionist movement in the north after the collapse of the Soviet Union.

KARAGANDA IS UNREMITTINGLY UGLY, a gargantuan phantasmagoria of steel-, iron-, and cement-plant horrors that nevertheless contains a university, a Palace of Culture, a few theaters, and various industrial institutes in its crumbling haphazard center. Few have studied its tortured gulag past. Yevgeniya Gavrilova, an art historian, is one who has. She has devoted a decade to documenting Karlag and the fates of its victims, a disproportionate number of whom were artists and writers. I got in touch with her through Karaganda's municipal museum, and she agreed to show me the labor-camp settlement out on the nearby steppe, where, to this day, former inmates and their descendants still live.

At nine the next morning I stood waiting for Yevgeniya (I would recognize her by her white hat, she said) on the cracked pavement outside my hotel. As usual, the day was sunny, but not nearly as hot as it had been down south. A patina of grime caked the faces of passersby; grit nestled in wrinkled brows, between corn-studded toes, under fingernails. The dust blowing in from the steppe, I had read, was toxic, still containing trace elements of fertilizers spread indiscriminately during the Khrushchev years.

A white-hatted woman soon disembarked from a bus, carrying copies of a Russian-language book, *A Memorial to Karaganda: Karlag, Culture, and Artists*. Chubby, impish, and middle-aged, with darting eyes, Yevgeniya greeted me with a kiss on the cheeks. We agreed to take a taxi out to Karlag's principal settlement, Dolinka, twenty-five miles southwest of town. But she then shot me a worried look.

"Wait, you want to go dressed like that out into the steppe?" she said, stuffing her notebook, a messy tome of sketches and scribbled names and addresses, into a plastic sack filled with sausages, bread slices, and bottled water.

"I think I'll manage. We'll only be out there a day."

"You never know. I've brought my steppe hat"—a floppy straw affair to protect her from the sun—"and spare shoes. The weather can change and it can be dangerous." Like so many Russians, she reveled in the severity of her town's climate.

She pulled me toward a taxi stand and began talking nonstop. Only in 1997, when Nazarbayev designated a day of remembrance for Stalin's Kazakhstan victims, did she start researching Karlag. "Before that, we didn't know whether it was safe to study it or not. Even in Gorbachev's day, the government found Karlag too dangerous a subject. I wanted to write my dissertation on Karlag, but the university here was afraid of the subject and wouldn't let me. No one wanted to hear about the prison conditions, the daily executions. After all, Karaganda was one big *zona* [labor camp] all the way until 1958"—five years after Stalin's death, when Khrushchev's liberalizing Thaw was well under way elsewhere, and the same year the premier awarded the city the Order of Lenin, for its "major successes" in his corn-growing *prozhektyorstvo*. "Such official achievements, but we were a closed city and no one could leave!"

We bartered with a taxi driver and set off for Dolinka. Dolinka was founded in 1931, when the Soviet government was dekulakizing, arresting and exiling millions, and needed laborers for its crash industrialization campaign. I learned to my surprise that most inmates were not locked up in cells. Karlag, as Yevgeniya described it, was a *zona* within the larger *zona* of the USSR, so remote, so lost out on the steppes, that the authorities knew few would ever try to escape.

"Until recently, only those with special passes could visit Dolinka," she said. "A lot of its residents, who are descendants of inmates, still can't find anywhere else to go. Most of them were from elsewhere, you see. They used to call our region the 'oblast of a hundred ethnic groups.'"

Low-hanging clouds mercifully moved in and obscured the sun; a dull heat radiated earthward nonetheless. Our taxi creaked over bad roads into Dolinka, which, exposed under a gloomy gray sky, resembled any impoverished former Soviet village, with its tumbledown shacks, litter-strewn yards, and weed-clogged hedges. But then we passed walls crowned with rolls of barbed wire. From guard towers silhouetted, rifle-toting sentries peered down on us through binoculars.

"What," I asked, "there's still a prison here?"

"Oh, yes. But it just holds regular inmates, not politicals. All the same, we have to present ourselves to the *akimat* [local administrator's office] or we could arouse some suspicion. Driver, ask this man where it is!"

A slavering old drunk teetered along ahead of us, his uncertain steps raising an ashen trail of dust. We pulled up to him. He responded with a spray of spittle and gibberish, gesturing so wildly that he almost fell through the window and into the driver's lap. The driver shoved him away in disgust. Next Yevgeniya ordered him to seek directions from a bony-browed, snarling youth covered with tattoos and scars. But this fellow turned away, refusing to talk to us.

"You think it's a good idea, asking these drunks for help?" I said.

"I'm an optimist," she answered. "You need to be out here or it's all too much."

"Well, why don't we ask a woman?" I suggested.

"You're not an optimist," she said, wagging her finger at me.

In short order we found a woman (young and sober) who directed us to the *akimat*. After stopping in there, we released our driver and began our tour. We walked down the dirt road, our steps raising pulverized dust as fine as volcanic ash, to the Technical House—the name, for some reason, given to the prison camp's theater.

"Karlag had a theater?"

"Of course. You see, in our gulag of a country, the rulers saw that Karaganda was becoming a major coal-producing center, so it needed culture to go with industry. Even in the labor camps. And don't forget, a large number of our inmates were the best of artists and intellectuals and actors. The guards, who fancied themselves barons of a sort, considered the actors and dancers their serfs and forced them to perform. We also had some of the greatest thinkers in history doing time out here."

"Really? Like who?"

"Chizhevsky."

"Chizhevsky?"

"The scientist who discovered that the sun's radiation incites people to revolt in regular cycles. That pretty much would have made the Communist Revolution nothing special. So they had to punish him."

"I've never heard of him or his theory."

"Of course not! Because they sent him here."

A few marble columns reigning over weeds were all that remained of the Technical House.

"As the Soviet era was ending the authorities set about destroying everything, including records and files, as fast as they could, so no one would know what they'd done here," Yevgeniya said. She still found the ruins moving, and she described how inmates would put on shows inside, creating their own aesthetic solace in a hell few expected to depart in this life.

We walked on, kicking up dust that the breeze wafted along with us. Kestrels disported themselves over overgrown bushes, and beyond the village, the steppe swept away, incalculably vast—a peaceful sight that stilled the heart and induced reflection.

Yevgeniya continued talking. "And over there, those are women's barracks, eight in all, for the 'wives of traitors to the motherland.' This was a very serious charge back then; if you were married to someone found guilty you were guilty too. And once you were out here, sentenced to eternal exile, your children suffered. You see, even after Stalin died and the kids could leave, they had to fill out forms when applying for jobs and tell who their parents were, whether they had ever been imprisoned. If they said yes, no job."

"Couldn't people lie on these forms?"

"*Lie?* We believed in our system, just like children. We thought we were serving the motherland! We were serving Stalin and the cause of world socialism! How could we lie to the Soviet authorities, the most progressive government on earth?"

"With all the killing and imprisoning, you believed this?"

"We were under something like universal hypnosis. We thought we were showing the world how to live in justice and equality and liberty." She laughed. "The reality is barbed wire and barking dogs! Barbed wire is our culture out here!"

We reached the headquarters of the NKVD (the KGB's predecessor), a stately shell of a palace built in Stalinist neoclassical style, with faux-Grecian pillars and marble steps. No door was left so we walked in. It had not been maintained, but everywhere was evidence of tsarist-era talent long lost—sculpted cornices and engraved ceilings, splendidly carved pilasters.

"*Zeki* [slang for prisoners] designed and built it," said Yevgeniya. "Some of the *zeki* were the best of our architects."

Past the next fence we found *zemlyanki*, earthen-walled, steel-roofed hovels half sunk in the ground for insulation against winter's forty-below frosts. "The *zeki* themselves lived in these *zemlyanki*. And they were happy because they had no prison boss. In this way the Soviet system widened our concept of happiness, and we should thank them. Foreigners need a diamond ring to be happy, we—just a *zemlyanka*!"

We halted by a rotting fence and peeked through missing slats at a *zemlyanka* ensconced in a mess of creepers, yellow and blue flowers, and thornbushes.

"Say, would you like to meet my friend Lidia Leier? She can tell you all about Karlag. She's a German who was born and grew up here."

I said yes. Yevgeniya rattled the fence, provoking dogs inside to a frenzy of growls and chain-rattling. The gate creaked open. A tall, handsome woman in a frumpy dress peered out. Her hair was silvered and fluffy-clean, her eyes arrestingly blue, her fair face ruddy in spots from the sun. Large-boned in a way uncommon among Russian women, she exchanged greetings with Yevgeniya and invited us in, smiling at me. "Wait," she said, "let me just tie the dogs up a bit tighter."

We were soon seated on a sofa in her *zemlyanka,* drinking tea. The tan linoleum floor had warped; the windows were caked in ash; but the walls were newly papered in orange and the furniture was clean and sturdy, much of it handmade. On shelves and tabletops all around a pantheon of relatives stared at us from yellowing black-and-white photos set in ancient frames.

From the kitchen emerged her husband, wiry, sun-bronzed, with reddish brown hair. He was bare-chested and hale, the skin around his eyes intricately wrinkled from a life of labor outdoors. His cheeks were shaved to leave a trim beard rimming his lower jaw, which gave him the look of a young Solzhenitsyn.

He sat down with us. Lidia began telling her story.

"I was born in the barracks over there, across the road, and educated as an accountant. Father was an ethnic German from Samara, along the Volga, a descendant of those Germans Peter the Great had invited to settle the river region. Father was a Catholic. The Soviets charged him with being an 'enemy of the people' and sentenced him to eternal exile out here in 'forty-one."

"What was his alleged crime?" I asked.

"They said he was trying to convince people not to hand their grain harvest over to the state. Which wasn't true, of course. He met my mother—may she rest in the kingdom of heaven!—out here in Karlag, and they married in 1950. They . . . they . . ." Her voice broke and her eyes watered. She turned to face the yellowed photographs. Her father, pictured in an ill-fitting jacket and tie, had a broad nose and a wide forehead, a Germanic dourness to his features; Mother was masculine, heavy-jowled, and equally serious. "Anyway, her name was Maria Yurasova. She wasn't a German. She was from an orphanage." She took a deep breath and suppressed a sob. Involuntarily I did the same; her grief put me in mind of my own mother. "So, my father's dying wish was that we carry on our German bloodline. I've done my best to honor him. My daughter is a German teacher."

"Why haven't you emigrated to Germany," I asked, "as have most of Kazakhstan's Germans since 1991?"

"Oh, we've tried, but the authorities there always find some reason to refuse our application. Anyway, we're staying here. We're at home here."

"How did your mother end up out here?"

"She was denounced by one of her girlfriends for saying that German sewing machines were better than Soviet ones. She died in 1973." She wiped away tears. "We've raised five children out here, my husband and I."

Holding an armful of books, one of her daughters entered and sat down. She was smiling if bashful, and dressed in well-pressed slacks and a fresh blouse—a sartorial achievement out here amid all the dust and decay.

"We've denied ourselves everything to give our children an education," Lidia said. "But I never get depressed about how tough things are. I'm just like my father in that way. He refused to let anyone call him a fascist just because he was German, and said we were sent here because we were loyal to Russia. Our ancestors came trying to *help* the Russians, after all. Well, in World War Two, all his relatives—all of them!—were conscripted into the Soviet Labor Army and died. Father was exiled out here. He told me he'd often wake up between two cold corpses; people were dying all the time in Karlag."

"Karaganda is built on bones," Yevgeniya said. All nodded in agreement.

"Father spoke High German. But he loved the Russian song '*Brodyaga*' ['Hobo'] and used to say, 'That song tells of my fate!'"

She raised her head and began to sing, her voice clear but trembling.

Po dikim stepyam Zabaykal'ya
Gde zoloto royut v gorakh
Brodyaga, sud'bu proklinaya,
Tashchilsya s sumoy na plechakh . . .

Ostavil zhenu moloduyu
I malykh ostavil detey
Teper' ya idu naudachu
Bog znayet, uvizhus' li s ney!

Otets tvoy davno uzh v mogile,
Syroyu zemlyoyu zakryt.
A brat tvoy davno uzh v Sibiri,
Davno kandalami gremit . . .

Through the wild steppes of Zabaikal'ye,
Where they dig for gold in the mountains,
I, a hobo, cursing my fate,
Dragged my feet, a sack on my back.

I've left my young wife,
I've left my little children.
Now I wander at random.
God knows if I'll ever see her again!

Your father's long in the grave,
Covered by damp earth.
Your brother's long in Siberia,
Rattling his shackles.

Your father's . . . your father's . . .

Her voice broke. Tears were streaming down her cheeks as she gazed into his photograph. We sat heads lowered, as at a wake. Her husband reached over and held her hand.

Once we were back outside, Yevgeniya suggested we pay a visit to a *zemlyanka* a few dirt lanes away. "I just want to check in on my friend there, Ludmila Dembovskaya. She's getting on in years."

Old she may have been, but her smooth skin, long gray hair, and spry gait bespoke rude health. She invited us in and offered us tea. Yevgeniya asked her to tell me about herself.

"Father was from Kalinin, near Moscow," said Ludmila. "He was an agricultural consultant. He went everywhere telling people how to improve their crops. Then, in 1937"—at the height of the Great Terror—"all the pigs died in this kolkhoz he'd just left. They blamed him for it, and he was sentenced to exile in Komi. But he was guiltless! He was such a loyal Communist, he named his son Vil"—for Vladimir Il'yich Lenin.

"We were under mass hypnosis back then," interjected Yevgeniya. "We believed."

Ludmila continued. "They say he asked to look in on me through the hospital window, before they took him off to prison, so I know he at least saw me. Then the state grabbed his children, my brothers, and sent them to an orphanage. That's . . . that's all I know. I've been trying to find them for years. I've even gone on this TV show, *Zhdi Menya* [*Wait for Me*], and pleaded for them to contact me. But no one's answered."

"You really think they're still alive?" I asked.

"The authorities say they died in Leningrad during the blockade, but then they told everyone that. You see, no one wanted people snooping around and making trouble." Tears welled up and spilled over her grayed eyelashes as she stroked her kitten. "Mother was exiled out here that same terrible year. Oh, how we starved out here! We had bread and macaroni at best, and so often, nothing, nothing to eat at all! We'd go walking through the fields in summer, just to find bugs to eat. We even ate cockroaches!" She chuckled, oddly enough.

"I also ate bugs," said Yevgeniya.

"Well, Mother worked in the laundry. She died back in 1969. She—"

She stifled a sob, tried to speak, and choked up again. I felt awful; my presence was compelling people to relive their grief. But she regained her composure.

"All this, and I . . . I had a family here of my own. I . . . I had two sons. But . . . but . . . I've lost both of them. They got heavy doses of radiation out in the nuclear testing zone near Semipalatinsk. Both my dear sons, my dearest sons! Gone forever!" Her lips trembled, her eyes watered again, and she broke out sobbing, hiding her face in her wrinkled hands, her breast heaving.

"Karlag is built on bones," said Yevgeniya to me, patting Ludmila's arm.

Yevgeniya had not teared up once listening to these stories, which certainly she had heard before. She possessed the discipline of a researcher, determined to get at the truth.

YEVGENIYA AND I WALKED toward the main road to catch a bus to Karaganda. Dogs howled from every gate; flies buzzed; sterile ashen earth powdered my shoes and caked on my sunglasses; the sky was a low sheet of hot steel.

"Now you've seen our culture here in Karlag," said Yevgeniya cheerfully. The two interviews had unsettled me; I didn't want to talk. "Upset? Well, you've got to be an optimist in our country, or it's all too much."

This optimism (enforced good spirits, she meant) seemed the only defense against alcoholism, suicidal urges, or murderous desires. No one has done jail time for Stalin's crimes. But would punishment — legitimized vengeance, that is — restore lost loved ones and sundered lives? Or would it just set the stage for a new round of slaughter?

13

On the morning I left Karaganda, clouds crept in from the north, louring and leaden, bathing the city in luxurious cool and auguring a change of seasons; the tenuous incunabula of autumn were finally at hand. In the bus station's gravel lot, I climbed aboard a *marshrutka* marked ASTANA (Kazakhstan's capital, 120 miles to the northwest) and took a seat in the back, where I could stretch out. There were only a couple of other passengers.

Once we were under way I grew drowsy, soothed by the darkening clouds, and then by wonderful thrumming washes of rain on the windows. The two-hour ride down a fine divided highway cut through the so-called *Sary Arka,* or Yellow Steppe, but it was green and entrancing. Now and then I glanced at the horizon, awaiting my first glimpse of Astana.

The Russians founded Astana in 1824 as a military outpost. They called it Akmolinsk, having slavicized the local Kazakh name for the region, *ak mola* ("white plenty," in honor of the bountiful dairy products yielded by animals raised on the steppe thereabouts). Khrushchev renamed it Tselinograd (City of the Virgin Lands) in 1961, and it served as the local headquarters for his doomed agricultural campaign. But in 1992, after independence, Tselinograd reverted to Akmola. It would probably still be called that today, but in 1997 Nazarbayev transferred the capital here from Almaty. He rechristened the city with an appellation endowed with all the creative panache one might expect of a life-time party boss. Astana means "capital" in Kazakh.

In switching Kazakhstan's capital to Astana, deep amid steppe that was once populated by Kazakh herders but was by the 1990s home mostly to Slavic settlers, Nazarbayev, analysts opined at the time, hoped to thwart separatist aspirations held by ethnic Russians. (Stalin's collectivization campaign and the resulting famine had killed off large numbers of the region's Kazakhs in a little-known episode of Soviet-era genocide.) His political opponents lambasted him, punning *ak mola* to its other possible meaning, "white grave," for who would want to move from sunny, blossoming Almaty, with its inspiring view of the Tian Shan, to gale-swept steppes associated with "harebrained schemes"? Why, Kazakhs, of course—not Slavs. And not Western diplomats, not Western employees of multinationals, who preferred Almaty's creature comforts. Nazarbayev persisted, launching one of the grandest construction projects on earth, with the intention of transforming an agricultural backwater into a metropolis brimming with all the optimism and wealth that Kazakhstan's energy resources promised.

Comforted by the cool, I fell asleep as we approached the city. I awoke at the bus station—in what looked to be a new world.

MY GUIDE TO ASTANA would be a friend of a friend named Azat, a real estate agent in his midthirties. Azat and his driver pulled up to my hotel off Abay Avenue in a shiny silver Lada. I jumped in the back, quickly closing the door against the gusting dust clouds and thunderheads over the flat cityscape; Astana seemed exposed, the sky low and menacing.

We began talking. The diminished number of Azat's blackened teeth gave him a speech defect, but he was articulate and plainspoken. He took an almost visceral pride in the severity of Astana's climate.

"How do you like our weather? Rough, isn't it! In the winter it blows like this too, when temperatures stay around forty below for weeks and weeks! Imagine!"

By Kazakh standards Astana is large, with some 600,000 people. It was the evening rush hour, but traffic was light and pedestrians few—oddly few, I thought.

"So you're from here?" I asked.

"Certainly not. I'm a Kazakh, but I was born in Omsk, and Russia is my homeland. But how could I resist the call of Astana? Think about it. The West, Europe, the United States—what can they offer us? Everything's been tried and developed there and there're few opportunities left. Only Kazakhstan remains, it's the final frontier, the land of tomorrow. It's a country for *energetic* people willing to *work.*"

"Well, if you're connected with oil and gas, I suppose you're right," I said.

"There's more to it than that. I'm in real estate and doing well. Our property prices are skyrocketing. A square meter here costs twelve hundred dollars. Not like the thirty-seven hundred a meter in Moscow, but we're getting there." (Moscow ranks as one of the most expensive—most outlandishly overpriced, that is—cities in the world.) "It's incredible. Hennessey cognac here costs forty-eight dollars a shot, French wine, eighty dollars a bottle. Amazing, isn't it?"

It wasn't; such were the predictable side effects of energy-based bubble booms. Azat accepted inflated prices as harbingers of a lasting bonanza. I could only think of Mobutu's Zaire. In the 1970s world market prices for its copper rose so high that the almost roadless African country became, for a time, the world's largest importer of Mercedes. The eventual collapse of that country's economy (and society in general) is well known.

We shot along smooth, empty lanes heading downtown, where glass and steel and copper-colored towers rose amid a rusty skeletal forest of cranes. Kazakh municipal workers in orange suits were almost the only people about.

Azat rambled on. "You should see Duman"—the Dream. "It's the most inland oceanarium in the world. You can learn a lot about the world there. And especially, you've got to see the sharks they have! They're incredible fish, you see. Educated people need to know about them. We won't go there today, but put it on your list. Look over there—what does that look like?"

We were passing a landmark, a wedding-cake building just as ugly as the ones Stalin had built all over Moscow.

"Looks like a Stalin skyscraper," I replied.

"Yes, but it's *here,* in *Astana!* We call it 'the Triumph of Astana.'"

We swerved around a corner and confronted an assemblage of glinting coppery Lego block towers, some embellished with globes on coppery spires. "Our *akimat!*" said Azat. "And look over there. It's Kazmonaigaz, our national oil and gas company. It's built in a half-circle just like the Russian oil company headquarters in Moscow, Rosneft."

Further turns led us into a complex of bland brick cottages with gabled roofs, all freshly built, if covered in steppe dust. No one was out and about; the buildings looked abandoned. "Our *dipgorodok*"—diplomatic residence quarter. "You can find a lot of your compatriots here. Luxurious, isn't it?"

On and on went the tour. A repetitive array of humongous glistening cylinders and sky-high tubes and jumbo glass boxes and earthbound spaceships flashed by, and Azat expounded on each. "We're building *forty-story* skyscrapers here, and it's going to be like Manhattan!"

"Well, at least it gives your people work."

"Oh, no, no. Turks and Yugoslavs do the construction—it's all going to be top-quality. Look, there's our Islamic center, built with Kuwaiti donations. Of course, you heard about the Congress of World Religions that we recently held."

"No."

"It met right there."

"What did it accomplish?"

"I'm not quite sure, but it met right there. And over there's the Palace of Peace and Social Accord."

"Sounds like the Ministry of Truth in *1984*."

"Ours is probably built even better than that, because it's newer. The Palace means a lot to us—because Kazakhstan is a multiethnic country, with thirty-four percent Slavs, fifty-three percent Kazakhs."

"What does the Palace do?"

"That I can't tell you. Now, look over there on the horizon. That's our cigarette lighter—doesn't it look like a giant metal lighter? It's the tallest building in the CIS! Astonishing, isn't it!"

I nodded reflexively, trying to differentiate between all the eye-numbing conglomerations of steel and glass. Soon pyramids appeared, the crystal sides of which reflected the thunderclouds—a singular pleasing aesthetic effect amid the endless modernistic architectonics.

"Those pyramids are going to house some of the most advanced apartment buildings on earth," Azat said. "And in the lobbies there'll be artificial lakes and beaches, so people will be able to hang out on shore all year and go swimming, even when it's forty below outside and snowing."

But what would happen in a power outage here? How would it feel inside these skyscrapers if the electricity failed in summer, or the heating in winter? How much energy, in fact, would it take to make these buildings inhabitable?

"We have so much energy, we don't worry about that," Azat said.

We finally halted on a gigantic concrete square ringed by multilaned (but empty) roads, and got out. Flower beds ranged in geometrically patterned profusion across its central expanses. A good half-mile away stood a rectangular beige monolith topped with an azure dome and a brass globe. The wind stirred the flowers into subtle wavering dances and drove dust our way, and we shielded our eyes. Beyond the monolith was nothing, the edge of the world; it seemed this was the highest part of Astana.

"This will be our Red Square. Look at all the lanes! And that, that building with the blue dome, is our Kremlin, the Ak Orda, the president's residence."

Rosneft, Red Square, the Kremlin, Stalin skyscrapers—all the references here were Russian, not Western. The buildings themselves resembled those being tossed up all over China, soulless and glitzy. We climbed back into the car as one of the few vehicles about—a police car—drove our way. Possibly the officers inside wondered what we were doing pointing at Nazarbayev's house.

"Impressive, huh?"

"Well, yes. But where are all the people? And all these are government and oil and gas buildings. Is there anything else? Anything for regular people?"

"According to the State Housing Plan for 2005 to 2007, the government will build three to five million square meters of housing for the people. They live in other parts of town. What I'm showing you here, in effect, is the future, is *Kazakhstan—the final frontier*. Our economy is growing at eight percent a year, and has been for a long time now. Can't you see, you're looking at the *future* here!"

"You're proud of it."

"Of course I am. You see, I believe we have immortal souls. Our souls want to be devoted to something greater than the here and now, to live on through something *grander* than they are—like Astana. Here we devote our souls to the *future*—to history, from another perspective."

"I suppose you didn't find anything so grand in Russia."

"Things are so much better here than in Russia, where the birthrate is falling and people are disillusioned and embittered. The government there is trying to force individualistic capitalism on them, when they were used to living communally. It will never work, and so people are angry and don't have kids. In Kazakhstan, however, we have a baby boom crisis, with two or three kids being born to each family. This is because we Kazakhs have maintained our traditions and respect our elders. You won't see drunks out on the streets here, like in Russia."

In Russia the population growth rate is negative, at -0.37 percent; in Kazakhstan it is 0.33 percent—not exactly a population explosion, but he did have a point. And I hadn't seen a single drunk in public since arriving in Atyrau. "Well," I said, "I suppose you have reasons for optimism, at least as long as energy prices are so high."

"We Kazakhs are steppe people, and so we're optimists. You can't be a pessimist and live out on the steppe, where you depend on rain and nature to survive. Look: for instance, the Kazakh government found it had to cut off social benefits. It did so with no problems. In other countries, there would have been protests, but not here. Kazakhs are optimists and knew they'd get by."

We drove on and arrived at one of the many look-alike cement-block cafés on Beibitshilik Square, which was at least at some remove from all the construction, in a low-rise neighborhood. Trees had been planted on the adjoining square, but overall, the sky's kaleidoscopic mélange of grays and blues dominated the scene.

We found a red plastic awning and sat on white plastic chairs. We ordered beers from the many foreign labels on tap.

"But is history," I asked, "or the future, or whatever Astana is, all just about oil and gas?"

"Our government is investing in its citizens. Nazarbayev is seeing to it that energy revenues are wisely invested, putting aside some to establish the ten-billion-dollar offshore fund for the future, the Bolashak [Future] Fund. The state sends kids abroad to study, on the condition that they return and work five years for the government."

Past us strolled people coming off work. None of the women wore anything resembling Islamic or traditional Kazakh dress; and men, like Azat, sported jeans and T-shirts, with the usual designer logos—Western prêt-à-porter. Everything had been imported.

This was fine with Azat.

"We welcome Western culture here. Islam was imposed on us in the fifteenth century, you know, but Kazakhs, being nomads, didn't take it too seriously; we're moderate by nature, like all nomads. And remember, if it weren't for the Russians, who protected us from the Dzungars and the Chinese, we might have ceased to exist as a people. It's not black and white, of course, but let's say we find more good than bad in being loyal to the Russians."

I would hear this repeatedly during my stay in Kazakhstan. But Kazakhs were definitely not Russian, so I often asked what being Kazakh means now. The answer was usually "It means living in a yurt on the steppe and tending animals and drinking *kumys* [fermented mare's milk]"—things people no longer wanted to do.

Notably absent from Azat's discourse was any mention of the human rights and political freedoms that the West widely regards as deficient here.

"Nazarbayev is a dictator," I said. "Doesn't that bother you?"

"We need his guiding hand to maintain order. Kazakhs have given up their freedoms to prosper in stability. We see what happened to Russia when Yeltsin was in power and everyone was free: mass impoverishment, the *mafiya,* anarchy. But in general smart people here don't get involved with politics, because it's dangerous and all closed off to them. Our president won elections with ninety-one percent of the vote, as you might know. However, I can say that people here don't *value* their vote, because it was *imposed* on them. They *had* to vote. So, you see, we could have no Kiev-style Orange Revolution here, because people don't care about their rights and don't mind having no freedoms. That's the problem with imposing democracy—people won't value it. What matters to us is prosperity."

Other Kazakhs I spoke to credited Nazarbayev with keeping them safe from the ethnic conflicts and border disputes that in the early 1990s took so many lives elsewhere in the former Soviet Union, and with sparing them from the chaos that afflicted Russia in the Yeltsin years. Facing Nazarbayev's track record of stability, and hindered by state-controlled media, opposition parties could hardly garner support. A popular uprising similar to those that shook Ukraine, Georgia, and Kyrgyzstan (the latter two extremely impoverished) would thus probably not succeed in Kazakhstan. Prosperity, or a modicum of it plus stability, substituted for political freedoms.

We drank our beer and watched the dust eddy around cars as they sped by. The struggle between autocracy and democracy, the staple of debates here and across the former Soviet Union in the 1990s, and once a key Western ideological weapon in the new Great Game, hardly figured in Azat's thoughts. Still, if the Kazakhs are not "free" in the Western sense, they are at least freer than at any time under the Soviets. This suffices to keep them in peace—at least for now.

THERE WAS NOTHING overtly disagreeable about Astana. But it was alienating. Kazakhstan-born Russian friends of mine in Moscow described its building projects as a huge boondoggle, a mammoth scheme for money laundering and kickbacks.

I wanted a closer look. Taking Azat's advice, the next morning I went for a stroll in the construction district we had toured by car. I started at Bayterek Tower, hoping to enjoy from its top floor the synoptic view that Azat had praised. It was strangely deserted. I found the concrete walkway leading to its entrance fractured and sprouting weeds; up close, its glass showed cracks, its metal looked crude and cheap, and steppe dust and exhaust fumes had dulled the sheen visible from afar. I tried to open the front door, but a crew of foreign laborers shouted and waved me away in annoyance: it was closed for repairs already. Everywhere else I wandered beneath the cement and wide-open sky, dump trucks growled, wind blustered, and gyrating cranes creaked and beeped warnings. On a grid of streets haunted by black Mercedes and Audis I was almost the only person afoot.

Azat also had urged me to "sample Kazakh cuisine" at a restaurant called Farkhi, one of Astana's best, by the Ishim River. Implicitly, the "Kazakh" was something to be experienced as distinct from the Western, Russian, and Soviet flavors on prevailing menus. Farkhi's name sounded Middle Eastern, but the food turned out to be both East and West, or, more accurately, neither. In the "Western" inside section, diners read *Sezon,* a Kazakh fashion magazine, or the Russian edition of *Elle,* attended by waiters standing stiff and bored in black suits, with ironed white napkins hanging on their forearms. Outside and around back, almost as if hidden away, was the "ethnic" part, called Ali Baba. (The name has nothing to do with Kazakhstan but comes from *A Thousand and One Nights.*) There, every waiter wore a jaunty skullcap with a swinging gold tassel and a brocaded vest, and every Kazakh waitress clicked about the patio on stiletto heels. A brick oven stood behind the bar, promising home-baked *besparmak,* but the cooking was actually done in a gleaming white kitchen, the door of which banged open and shut as staff carried dishes out to the diners. The effect here was more Uzbek casino than herdsman's lair, and I wasn't aware that Kazakh shepherdesses wore high heels as they tended their flocks.

Everything there and elsewhere in town had seemed bland, numbingly modern, resolutely non-Soviet. Needing to change money, I headed down the glitzy Avenue of the Republic under a waning twilight sky and ended up in Ramstore, a Turkish department store where diplomats and well-off Kazakhs browsed through all kinds of Western goods on the shelves.

Off to one side I found the exchange bureau. A young Kazakh woman stood at the booth's double-paned window. "I'll be here for ten more minutes," she warned me.

"No problem," I said.

A glimpse of a document in the woman's hand revealed that she worked for a holding company. Her business, like so many across the former Soviet Union, ran on cash. The cashier, a Russian redhead of about fifty, was busy stamping her client's receipts, scribbling in a ledger, batting out numbers on a calculator, adding up more numbers, and grabbing fresh reams of receipts.

Half an hour passed before she finished. I stepped up to the window. Just as I presented my dollars for exchange, a little Kazakh woman rushed up and pushed me aside.

"I'm sorry," I said, "but I've been waiting here a long time."

"Oh, I was really here before you, but I had to do some shopping."

She was clutching her own little bag of bills and chits; if I let her pass, I'd be there forever. "I'm sorry," I repeated, holding my place by the window. "I'll just be a minute."

She frowned and got in line behind me. But the cashier was still occupied with paperwork from the previous customer. Ten more minutes passed, fifteen.

"Excuse me," I asked, "how much longer will you be?"

She ignored me.

The Kazakh woman pushed past me and shouted. "What you doing in there? Why you taking so long!"

"Please be quiet," said the cashier, her eyes on her papers.

"*You* be quiet! Just do your work and keep your trap shut! Work and no talk! Work! Work! I'd like to know *what* work too!"

The cashier looked up. "Please be quiet and let me finish!"

"Shut up, bitch!"

"You shut up!"

"Go back to Russia, whore!"

"Woman, I'm going to sue you for insulting me!"

"Oh yah? Go to hell on your way back to Russia!" She pounded on the glass; as she raised her elbow, I caught a whiff of sweat. "You Russians go around with upturned noses!"

"Give me your coordinates. I'm suing you!"

"Oh, right, I'll give you my number and address. What a laugh!"

I gently edged the obstreperous woman away from the window. "Please, just let her finish so we can both get served and leave."

"She a bitch in there, taking so long!"

"Sasha, quiet down this woman!" the cashier ordered.

A guard in a black army outfit stepped out of the booth, and the Kazakh woman fell silent, her little black eyes afire. I changed my money and headed back to the hotel.

Whatever Astana was, it was still at heart Soviet.

"I'M GOING to the Duman Oceanarium," I told a taxi driver the next day.

"The what *where?*"

"Duman. The new sea amusement park."

"Oh, the *UFO*, you mean. Hop in."

The planet's farthest-inland aquarium did look like a flying saucer awaiting takeoff on a cosmic Lego launch pad. But inside it turned out to be even more: a shopping mall, a food court, a historical and cultural theme park.

I fell in with a crowd of goggle-eyed Kazakh mothers dragging about bandy-legged children licking Baskin-Robbins softies, and ambling Kazakh grannies in faded print dresses, sampling their first hot dogs. Greeting us all was a statue of a jovial turbaned Kazakh mounted on a pony-size locust and flourishing a knout—the folk hero "Tazsha Baba." Just beyond him was a pile of bricks labeled "A Piece of the Great Wall of China." About to storm it was a life-size, noble-visaged wax Mongol barbarian clad in a tunic and brandishing a sword. Mongol and Turkic tribes had long besieged China, prompting the construction of the wall; the hero here was the assailant. Across from him, and of the same height, stood the Statue of Liberty, beneath which teens in rented sumo wrestler fat suits squared off in a cushioned ring, lunging at each other, bouncing bellies first. Toddlers climbed all over a nearby wigwam and pounded the bulging eyes of a totem pole; beside it was a padded "corral" where young men took turns riding a mechanical bucking bronco. There was no Lenin effigy or Stalin bust, no fake Kremlin or Red Square corner; nor were there any other signs of Russia and the Soviet Union —the defining influences in Kazakhstan's modern life and times. Perhaps people didn't want to be reminded of this in their leisure time but preferred a mishmash of relics of Western "soft power."

The pinging and zinging of a video arcade, plus the soundtrack from a 3-D movie theater upstairs, invaded every corner. Off to one side was the entrance to the oceanarium. A clock-based sliding price scale assured that almost anyone could afford a visit. I bought my ticket and entered a glass-enclosed passage into an underwater world of quivering blue-green aquatic light, brimming with aquatic plants and rocks set in sand. The exhibit actually began with a freshwater jungle tank. Caiman crocs basked on rocks in tropical light, observing piranhas, described on the window's label as "a very aggressive shoaling fish that can eat a victim immediately, leaving only a skeleton."

The "ocean" began thereafter. Entering it with me was a chattering crowd of squat Kazakh peasant men and women and their broods of children, plus shaved-skulled Russians with their beauty-queen dates done up in Chinese counterfeit designer threads. *"Akula! Akula!"* (Shark! Shark!), all murmured. An introductory placard listed maritime Duman's impressive stats: three thousand species of aquatic life from all oceans and seas swam in three million liters of water, salinated with Red Sea salt and contained by a three-inch-thick acrylic glass tank. The blue light and mock depths effectively recreated an open-sea ambiance. Along mock reefs drifted Indian boxfish, sullen and spiky, with poison-finned stonefish and lionfish, giant grouper and swift, glistening bonito.

Then a leopard shark appeared, provoking raised fingers and a chorus of *Akula! Akula!,* and then, all around, as if swarming to attack, swam black-tipped reef sharks and zebra sharks, graceful and velvet-hided.

Adults crowded around an explanatory sign in English and Russian: "The shark is a very serious fish . . . an extremely voracious and dangerous predator . . . a fierce and invulnerable creature . . . It isn't difficult for some sharks to cut a man in half immediately, outrun a motor torpedo boat and even make a yacht wreck." Finally came the "Mystery of 1960" plaque, in reference, of course, to the "terrible events" off the coast of Mozambique when passengers began swimming ashore from a stranded ferry and were "attacked by a shoal of sharks . . . Malicious predators tore to piece 46 people during several minutes, only three people survived." What could possibly protect you from such beasts? "It looks like a spear, charged with a cartridge of carbonic gas. When it gets into the body [of the shark] it explodes and compressed gas starts puffing up the body. The shark is thrown out onto the water surface where it swims blankly."

Phew!

Kids cavorted up and down the underwater corridors, waving at the sharks. Few Kazakhs here would make it to an ocean; even the Caspian Sea is distant, ill served by transport, and lacks resorts. Culture as amusement-park paraphernalia, history as comic book fodder, wildlife as horror flick villains — Duman had all the flimflam trappings of Western fun. And the crowd loved it.

14

On one of those endlessly waning summer evenings of the northern latitudes, when the set sun lingers beneath the horizon, suffusing the empty sky with a dreamy golden pallor, I mounted the railway station steps, for once looking forward to the ride ahead. I had bought a ticket for the Talgo, the Spanish-built high-speed train that, according to the schedule, would cover the 1,200 miles from Astana south to Almaty in just twelve hours (as opposed to the twenty-four or more taken by the usual rolling Kazakh crates). The Talgo glided into the station on time, blue and white and sleek in a generic modern way, promising generic modern comforts I would dearly appreciate. No scramble to board ensued. Ticket prices were high enough to keep the passengers few, upscale, and polite. Attractive conductors checked tickets and showed us to our seats.

Once aboard, I might as well have been in Europe. This was not entirely positive: the train was cramped in a way more European than Kazakh. (In the former USSR, tracks are wider and cars roomier than in the West.) Futuristic bulging white metallic walls narrowed the corridor so that two could not pass at once. I settled into a bunk in one of the four-person compartments, which, it turned out, I would share with a thirty-something Kazakh woman. We sat down, facing each other in our bulkily upholstered blue seats, and our knees almost knocked.

"Oh, this train is fine for Europe, where the distances are small," she said in smooth Russian, brushing an auburn-tinted bang away from her pleasantly oval face. "But it's too cramped for Kazakhstan, where every journey takes forever!"

"You're right," I said.

"Trains take seven days to get from Moscow to Vladivostok," she added, pushing at the cushions as if to shove them into retreat. "You'd never want to make that trip on a train like this."

She picked up a glossy Russian fashion magazine and, with manicured fingers, started leafing through it. I stole glances at her. Her hair was tousled sensuously; her bones were delicate but ensconced in a comfy embonpoint; and her eyes, brown and wide, were almost smiling, as though she'd just remembered a funny scene from a favorite film.

The train inched into motion. At that moment we heard sneezes and sniffles in the hallway, as well as a child's whining, coming our way. Simultaneously we raised our eyes and looked at the empty berths in our compartment, and the same thought crossed our minds.

We were right. Two young Kazakh women, one with an agitated toddler, stopped at our door and checked their tickets; they had the top berths. They nodded hello and began hustling their bags past us. One asked me to help them pull down their bunks (stored flat against the wall) so they could turn in early. They were slender and dressed in designer garb, but red-eyed, sneezing, clearing their throats, ever yanking at Kleenex tissues from a box they shared and blowing their noses. Once settled in, they poured syrup into little plastic cups, which they gurgled and swallowed and followed with hoarse, phlegmy coughs; nasal spray came next, and pills, and then the child began to cry . . .

"Let's go to the dining car," I suggested to the woman across from me.

"Good idea."

As we were sidling down the corridor she told me her name was Sabina, and asked mine. We reached the dining car, which was well lit and airy, with high windows bringing in the steppe and a moonless sky now turning violet and glinting with stars.

We took seats at a table and stared out the window.

"Should we drink beer?" she asked, as moved as I was by the view. Sure.

We toasted to our meeting. I straightaway anticipated the earthy, soul-baring conviviality that comes here with long train rides and drinking, ever the preferred way to pass the hours. Her Russian brimmed with educated turns of phrase; both her parents had been professors of Russian philology.

Sabina said that at nineteen she had hastily married an older man who cheated on her constantly, so she divorced him. She now owned and managed her own travel agency. As a financially independent woman she had chosen her second husband according to his character, and, for now, her family life was fine. She had no children and wanted none, which was rare in these parts. Her father had recently died in her arms of cancer, at age sixty-one.

"How did you come to start your own business?" I asked.

"Well, after my divorce I ended up on my own. I couldn't turn to my parents for financial help, since they had been against my marriage, and I certainly didn't want to live at home, like so many Kazakh girls do. But I found myself really at a loss, with no experience, since I had gone from my parents' home to my husband's. I spent some time being sorry for myself; women in our society usually depend on the man for guidance, and I had no man. Eventually, though, I pulled myself together and I looked into forming a travel agency. I studied all the laws and learned the business and how to deal with clients, all on my own. It really took off. Here's my card."

She presented me with an artfully designed chit, printed in Russian and English, with a logo of a seagull circling a globe. She downed the last of her beer surprisingly quickly. She looked toward the waitress and squinted at her nameplate. "Ayna! Another round of beers." Ayna obliged. "And so, I travel myself a lot and get to see the world. It's part of my job. Just last year I visited Israel and Spain." We toasted again. "You don't find it tough, living in Russia?"

"No, not at all."

"Well, Russia's a mess compared to China."

She admired China, with its measured reforms and authoritarian system, a combination that, she said, allowed the country both prosperity and order. Nazarbayev had followed the Chinese model, she said, and it was working; certainly, she didn't fear the *mafiya*, as she might if she were running a company in Russia. She regretted that Kazakhs tended to dislike, even fear, the Chinese.

"I think," she said, "that what counts is what people intend on doing for society, if they can work for the common good. I wouldn't mind if millions of Chinese came here to farm our steppes, as long as they worked for the common good; maybe historically they've been our enemies but history can be just history. We have enough resources here in Kazakhstan, and on the planet in general, for all of us. Aynochka, another round!"

Calling a waitress by name was almost unheard of here, a very American thing to do. Had she read Dale Carnegie? Anyway, Russia furnished an example of what could go wrong, and, as she upended her new beer, Sabina offered cogent analysis.

"The Kremlin is using the skinhead movement to get rid of the Caucasians, and the skinheads are too stupid to understand that they'll be next, once the government has no use for them. The *muzhik* [common man, peasant] out in the village is drunk, embittered, and unpaid, so soon you can imagine another situation developing like the 1917 revolution. The masses will rise up again, but they'll just bring to power some *bydlo*"—uncultured brute. "History is repeating itself in Russia. I'm so happy we're now independent!"

"So you're afraid of Russians?"

"I don't fear them, but facts are facts. During Soviet times, the Communists wouldn't let Kazakhs have their own history. We were supposed to supply Russia with natural resources and keep quiet, so they didn't want us thinking we were our own people with rights and so on. But thousands and thousands of Kazakhs died in rebellions, or they starved to death when Stalin forced them to settle and join state farms . . . Aynochka, more beer!"

Perhaps a bit too rapidly, and to the surprise of the waitress, she downed the contents of her half-liter bottles. But creating and running her own company, all on her own, inclined her to do just as she pleased.

"You know," she said, "I don't really want to say a lot of bad things about the Russians; we have a shared history and we've learned a lot from them. Russians are physically very beautiful. Just look at the women. But they're so angry, so aggressive, and still have so many imperial ambitions. We Kazakhs could never be this way. Most Kazakhs are just simple people from the steppe, without pretensions. I myself was born in Moscow and educated in Russia. Russians have done a lot for me, for all us Kazakhs. They brought us the modern world."

Before the Soviets so rudely interrupted it, Kazakh life on the steppes had been tribal, nomadic, and mostly illiterate. One way or another, it was destined to disappear as the Great Powers, including China, divided up Eurasia and imposed their systems of governance. Here Russia had won the first Great Game (and, from what I saw, was dominating the second round), of course, and under both the tsars and the Soviets had done much good for its "minority peoples," the Kazakhs included, bringing them literacy, the (partial) liberation of women, universal secular schooling, exposure to and a chance to participate in the fine arts, and an internationalist way of thinking (even if its slogan was "Workers of the World, Unite!"). Though clearly seeing themselves as older brothers, Russians established no apartheid vis-à-vis their colonized peoples. Intermarriage was common, and, at least in Soviet times, career progress depended not on ethnic background but on hard work, education, and, in some positions, loyalty to the party—qualities that by and large left the former Soviet peoples with what they need to find their way in the world of markets and globalization.

Sabina knew all that. So I told her that I could not have imagined my own life without Russia, without the bruising education it had given me, without Tolstoy and Turgenev, Chekhov and Nabokov. These, not Kazakhs, were her favorite writers too, it turned out; her culture was Russian, not Kazakh. We drank to Russia—not to the Russian government, but to all-embracing *Matushka Rossiya* (Mother Russia), to the worldly, welcoming, infinitely rich legacy she passed on to her children, even her adopted children, like me. We also drank to the Russian language—without it, how could Sabina and I communicate? How could I talk to so many people, whose native (minority) tongues I would never learn, from Moscow to Kabardino-Balkaria to the Chinese border?

Sabina sat back and let the beer work its magic.

"You know," she said, "I go to the mosque and pray, but I believe that God is one, whether he's Allah or God or Jehova. God is love. It's what's inside us that counts, not our ethnic group. It's what's inside us that lets us help others. Helping others is all that counts."

"Is that a conclusion you've reached from your reading?"

"Oh, no! My mother taught it to me. It's really a Kazakh view, a view from the simple ways of the steppes." She cleared her throat. "Aynochka!"

If views like hers spread here, and it seemed they would, as long as the oil boom prosperity lasts and the middle class grows, then their espousers no doubt would one day, of their own accord, come to reject authoritarianism and find their own path to more democratic and egalitarian governance. If they succeeded, they would certainly reject vassalage — either to Russia or to the West.

The world outside was now murky steppe, a black firmament faintly dimpled with stars. We finished off another beer and returned to our cabins to sleep through the final hours left to Almaty.

15

Marching in from Siberia, in 1855 the Cossacks reached Almaty (the "Father of Apples"), a river-watered oasis named for its fruit trees, which once sheltered a settlement the Mongols had obliterated five centuries earlier. Few places on earth were at the time remoter than Almaty, south of the Betpaqdala Desert, along a forgotten branch of the Silk Road, beyond the outer realms of Manchu China, and within sight of the Alatau Mountains (a spur of the Tian Shan). To halt Chinese expansion westward and stake out territory for their sovereign, the Cossacks established the fortress Zaliyskoye. Slavic peasants and Tatar merchants soon joined them. By 1867 the Russian presence had increased across the region, and Zaliyskoye became Verny ("Faithful"), the capital of the Semirech'ye province of tsarist Turkistan. Verny was still, however, remote enough to serve as an abode of exile; Trotsky found himself banished here for a while. The Soviets changed the name back to Almaty, but throughout the Communist decades the town remained isolated, the site of industries evacuated east during World War II, and achieved a flash of international prominence only in 1991, when the leaders of the moribund Soviet republics met in it to announce the death of the USSR.

After independence the Cossacks of Almaty found themselves stalwarts of a twice-deceased Russian-led empire, and the government mistrusted them, even harassed them as potential separatists. Almaty is nevertheless culturally a Russian city, peopled by equal numbers of

Slavs and Kazakhs whose first language is mostly Russian. It is still the economic capital of the country, home to the Kazakh Academy of Sciences, the national library, educational institutes, and opera and theaters. In other words, it bests Astana on every civilized count.

As I walked down Gogol Street to Panfilov Park, toward the gilt onion domes of Saint Nicholas Cathedral, I luxuriated in the shade of Russian-planted poplars even as I squinted against blasts of leaden exhaust huffed out by patched-up Russian Ladas in traffic jams clogging the center from dawn till dusk. I had hoped to see the peaks of the Alatau, which rise to the south, across the border in Kyrgyzstan, but smog and heat haze obscured them. Still, the lived-in feel of Almaty's ramshackle fin-de-siècle homes and Brezhnev-era apartment blocks, its crowded outdoor cafés and burgeoning markets, invigorated me. The city had roots, and, in contrast to Tselinograd-Astana, its future would not depend on the whims of politicians but on trade and proximity to other Central Asian capitals and China.

I wanted to learn how the Cossacks were faring, so I arranged to meet Vladimir Ovsyannikov, ataman of the Union of Semirech'ye Cossacks. Ovsyannikov, portly and pale, hurried between tables at a Gogol Street café to greet me, a worn leather folder under his left arm, his driver-bodyguard standing grimly nearby. He asked me several suspicious questions, the gist of which was *What would an American be doing in these parts, asking after his reputedly seditious people?* As I had with Dmitry the museum keeper back in Vladikavkaz, I managed to calm his concerns by telling him about my recent recreation of a Cossack exploratory expedition on Siberia's Lena River. Cossacks were a passion of mine, and that's why I wanted to talk to him.

We sat down under an awning and ordered mineral water; it was 95 degrees and humid. Nodding, he absorbed my biography and raised his eyebrows.

"Well, as you must know, then, Queen Victoria called the Cossacks 'the last knights on earth.' The Kazakhs, however, call us colonizing troops, but how could we colonize a people of nomads who owned no land? We founded this city on land we drove the Chinese from during a twenty-year war in the nineteenth century. We're not foreigners here. And then, when the Communists came to power, what did they do? In 1919 Trotsky signed a genocidal order to wipe us out. The Communists knew they had to eliminate us. We were the most militarily inclined, able-bodied men in Russia, and all of us, all twelve Cossack hosts, opposed the Bolsheviks. A lot of Cossacks ended up fleeing to China to escape *raskazachivaniye*"—the Soviet campaign to dispossess and destroy the Cossacks—"shooting entire families, killing even those who professed loyalty to them. To merit execution, it was enough to have a Cossack uniform in your closet."

I asked him how the Cossacks had done since independence.

"We just don't understand. The Communists executed us, and now, after independence, we're still repressed. The worst time was the mid-1990s. The authorities still keep the pressure on us. They searched my house for twelve hours, looking for something, anything, incriminating. They subject us to beatings, fake criminal trials, and even murder. Recently, they forbade us from holding a meeting in Astana, and made us move it a hundred kilometers out of town." He sighed and sat back in his chair. "Putin has proposed to take us back into Russia—it would be in Russia's interest if we agreed, since so many of us are able-bodied, and you know how unhealthy Russian men are. Many of us are considering his offer. The federal government here says it doesn't want us to leave, but on the local level they do all they can to push us out."

"If you're as strong and organized as you say, you can imagine their concern."

"Actually, they *need* us. The Kazakhs should remember that just across the border, there're all these Chinese who say, 'You kicked us out of our land! Almaty is Chinese!' One Chinese division has one hundred and twenty thousand men, but the entire Kazakh army only has eighty thousand soldiers! Just look at all the empty land in this country. How could the Chinese resist taking over if we left? But as long as we're here—and we're half a million altogether—they're afraid to attack."

"Do you really think the Cossacks could beat the Chinese, given the numbers against you?"

He chuckled. "We have a saying about that: 'The more wood, the brighter the bonfire!' But the danger is actually subtler than that. The Chinese are expanding into our land stealthily. They plop a hundred dollars on a Kazakh bureaucrat's desk and buy their way in. Now look around you. The Chinese feed us and dress us, and what do they do with all the profits? They take them back to China. There are eight Chinese banks in Almaty alone."

Ovsyannikov soon had to leave to attend a meeting, but he arranged to have his secretary prepare a selection of clippings for me from the Cossack newspaper, *Kazachi Kur'yer* (the Cossack Courier). The next day I picked them up at the Cossack Cultural Center, grand words for a fenced-off hodgepodge of old wooden buildings served by an outhouse, in a neighborhood of pleasant if weather-worn Russian homes. However moderate he had sounded, his group's flagship publication resembled a ranting Bolshevik rag, if one with (surprising) touches of sycophancy toward Nazarbayev. Headlines shouted, "ACCORDING TO THE U.S.A.'S PLAN, RUSSIA WILL BE DEFEATED," "THE U.S.A. IS PLANNING TO STRIKE RUSSIA," "WHO BENEFITS WHEN RUSSIA IS ACCUSED?" and "US AND THEM: WHY THE WEST HATES RUSSIA." There was nothing remotely seditious anywhere. The paper celebrated the Day of the Republic (October 25) with a glowing account of the state-orchestrated festivities in Astana and pictures of crowds carrying banners inscribed with NAZARBAYEV IS OUR LEADER!

As they were back in Russia, here in Almaty the Cossacks, instead of looking ahead, were consumed by old hatreds, reveling in anti-Western ire, allying themselves with the Kremlin (and their host country's autocrat) in the new Great Game. Broken by decades of Soviet repression, they could do nothing more than propound an extreme, but pointless, nationalism. I stuffed the papers into my bag and tried to forget about them.

NOTWITHSTANDING the cordial nature of Russian-Kazakh relations today, the Russians', or more specifically, the Soviets', crimes in Kazakhstan stand out as some of the worst in a history dense with state-orchestrated bloodshed and rapine. Given that Nazarbayev was Kazakhstan's Communist Party boss during the last years of the ancien régime, the laconic truthfulness of the words on the first placard of Almaty's Museum of Repression came as a shock to me: "The entirety of Soviet history is replete with many violations of national rights and acts of genocide. [During the Soviet years] the number of Kazakhs was reduced by half."

Reduced by half?

The museum, which I toured the next morning, sits in a prematurely pockmarked concrete building off lively Nauryzbay Batyr Street. Displaying mostly copies of Soviet documents and photographs, it well documents these "acts of genocide" and what led up to them. From 1897 to 1916 Russia expropriated hundreds of thousands of acres of land from the *Kirgiz* (as Kazakhs were erroneously labeled in tsarist decrees) and settled thereon millions of Russian peasants. The *Pereselennoye Upravleniye* (Directorate of Resettlement) was in charge of all this, assisted by Kazakhs serving on local administrative counsels. Black-and-white photos showed bearded, caftan-clad *muzhiki* arriving in horse-drawn carts loaded with their wives and numerous children and all their belongings. When World War I broke out, the tsar tried to mobilize the Kazakhs (officially termed *inorodcheskiye,* or "people of foreign blood," though they were of course the indigenes) to build defensive walls, but this sparked a mass uprising and spurred the creation of a movement for national liberation across Kazakhstan. As the embattled Russian Empire foundered and collapsed under the weight of war and inept leadership, with the abdication of the tsar and the Bolshevik seizure of power in 1917, Kazakhs began forming an opposition government. The Whites, including the Cossacks, refused to recognize it, desiring neither dismemberment of the Russian Empire nor indigenous rule. The Soviets, of course, smashed the resistance and liquidated the Kazakh government in 1920, the members of which they hunted down and shot.

The first "all-*Kirgiz* Soviet" trumpeted the end of the tsarist "policy of distrust and lies, hounding and provocation." Lenin minced no words, ordering the "merciless suppression of the uprising"—that is, of the independent Kazakh government. "Hang and definitely HANG the kulaks, so that the people may see them, and seize their bread." The Soviets promulgated posters declaring, "Glory to the Muslim population filled with revolutionary spirit!" During the civil war that followed the revolution, *prodotryady* (food-confiscation battalions) seized all "excess provisions" from the hapless Kazakhs. Those who refused to hand over food (there was no "excess," of course) were "dekulakized"—dispossessed on charges of being "exploitive rich peasants." In 1921–22 famine resulted, killing 2.3 million Kazakhs.

Almost two and a half million dead, yet their sufferings were to continue! In 1928 the Soviets, to solidify their control over the Kazakh countryside, designated marginally better-off Kazakhs *beys* (big land-owners) and seized their property, noting down every spoon, fork, and broken bracelet they confiscated, and handed the loot over to *bednyaki,* the designated "poor peasants." The Soviets thus set one segment of society against the other, winning support from the poor as they began eliminating the potentially rebellious middle class.

They finished the job in Stalin's collectivization campaign, executing thousands more and dispossessing the remaining "*beys*" of hundreds of thousands of heads of livestock. In 1930 Moscow issued secret instructions to local party committees to "strengthen the socialist reconstruction of agriculture," boilerplate Soviet verbiage that ordained mass executions and banishment. Now the Soviets sicced the poor on the less poor, allowing the *bednyaki* to designate *beys* for destitution and death, thereby decimating a further 3.5 percent of the Kazakhs. The instructions also mandated the expropriation of the *beys'* "cattle, work and residential structures, enterprises of production, food, grain, and seed stocks, excess property and cash," ordering families be left only with "a minimum of household items and food." More than a million Kazakhs fled their homesteads; others launched uprisings (as did dispossessed peasants in Ukraine and the Northern Caucasus), but they were poorly armed, badly regimented, and easily suppressed.

Much more blood remained to be shed. In the early 1930s Stalin launched his industrialization campaign, hunting down and executing opponents, real and imagined. By 1933, 600,000 more Kazakhs had fled their republic, 100,000 had been imprisoned, 25,000 more were executed, 10,000 were dispatched to Siberia. All in all, of the 6 million people living in Kazakhstan in 1926, a decade later 2.5 million had died, of whom 2.3 million were Kazakh. This was still not enough blood for Stalin. The party then announced that it was "cleansing the cultural front of the remnants of defeated nationalism." Members of the intelligentsia who escaped the firing squad were often shipped to Karlag to mine coal and starve to death.

The museum's statistics and photocopied decrees adumbrate cruelty, injustice, theft, and murder on scales too vast to be grasped. Of course, more than fifteen years have passed since the fall of the Soviet Union, and no one has been punished for all this killing, looting, starving, and torturing, neither here nor in Russia nor in the other parts of an empire that covered one-sixth of the globe's land surface. That much of the population collaborated blurs notions of justice. By now, the dead have been dead a long time, as have most of those who knew them. Their tribulations survive, if at all, as part of family narratives. As former Soviets say, casually, Grandpa suffered this, Grandma that, but it's all behind us now, and there's no point in opening old wounds. They are right.

I walked back out into the heat and sunshine, and, just barely, managed to descry the peaks of the Alatau, snow-covered even now, rising above the hectic traffic and grimy housing blocks like a cooling vision of paradise.

THE NEXT EVENING, at the palatial restaurant Jeti Kazyna, I was to have dinner with Sergey, manager of a Russian supermarket chain with branches in Almaty, and his friends. Jeti Kazyna was a mansion of many chambers and patios serving Chinese, Japanese, Kazakh, and Russian cuisine, and was as sophisticated as any such establishment in the West. Recognizable as a native of Saint Petersburg by his pale complexion and dishwater hair, Sergey surprised me by showing up dressed in a tracksuit (if a silken one) and a baseball cap, but many of the other diners were similarly attired. Among the affluent of Almaty, the 1990s' over-the-top mania for flashy fashion had clearly passed.

We sat down to examine a complex, trilingual menu. His friends, all also in their twenties, soon joined us. Tayir was a perky, markedly Chinese-looking Kazakh dressed in a chicly wrinkled T-shirt; his sylphic, exquisitely featured wife, Aykirim, was twenty at most, nicely decked out in jeans and a baggy green jacket. Marina was many months pregnant, yet otherwise svelte; her hair was bobbed, and her large eyes peered out warmly from behind Annie Liebowitz horn-rims. Her husband, Aydar, was the only one, apart from me, whose shirt (black, DKNY) had a collar. All said they were involved in "various types of business, import and export," and hinted that they had not come to talk shop. Their native language was Russian. (In fact, no one around us was speaking Kazakh.)

Soon the feast arrived and the cognac and wine started flowing. After the usual rounds of toasting, they asked me what I was doing in Almaty. I told them I was on my way to China.

"Really?" said Sergey. "*Tao Te Ching* is my table book of reference."

"It's hard to find a decent translation," said Tayir. "In fact, Eastern religion is one thing, but I have the utmost respect for Christianity."

I hoped this last remark was not intended to curry favor with me, whom they might have assumed to be Christian. "Apart from the Sermon on the Mount and Ecclesiastes and Proverbs and some of the Psalms, I find very little in Christianity that suits me," I replied.

"Well, you should rethink your position," said Tayir. "Christianity—that very Sermon on the Mount—is the only religion that changed the world, that *improved* it. Think of Roman society before the Christians. You wouldn't have wanted to live in it, with all its slaves and cruelty. The same with ancient Greece. What changed everything was Christianity; before it, Europeans were barbarians. But Christianity taught them mercy and told them they had to free the slaves. We Kazakhs are Muslim, but I have no trouble in admitting how much Christianity has done to better the world. It made the West what it is."

We toasted to the West. I sipped my cognac, finding that its acrid bouquet burned my eyes.

Aydar said, "He who doesn't want to think just grabs the Bible and points to the Ten Commandments and makes observing them the point of his life. That's really limited. I don't see much in it for me."

"You don't understand," answered Tayir. "The point is, we now have these Ten Commandments, and they're better than barbarism and worshiping Zeus or Achilles or whatever. The whole point of the Commandments is mercy. That's what Christianity taught us."

In fact, the Ten Commandments belong to the Old Testament, hardly a treatise on forgiveness. But I didn't want to quibble. However, Marina disagreed. "Humanity should forget about holy books and worship nature. We won't destroy our environment if we worship it."

Aydar added, "But we do destroy each other when we follow organized religion. It's just a justification for bloodshed."

Ten or even five years ago, it would have been rare to find rich former Soviets expounding on such subjects; then, fashion and money-making and trips abroad were the rage. At least some of those who had done well had moved beyond that.

Our talk shifted to Confucius and Mencius and other Chinese sages, whose impact, we agreed, had been great on China but less significant abroad, which was not the case with Christianity, Tayir pointed out. Tayir advocated a utilitarian approach to religion: the religion that deserved the most allegiance was that which had most improved the lives of its followers. We cited other faiths and mused about their merits and demerits. Islam never came up. This at first surprised me, but then I remembered that all had been schooled in the atheist Soviet days. Religion now was elective, and they were ready to choose what, if anything, in it suited them.

Sergey added, "If you want to follow an incredible ancient religion, then why not Kabbala? Now, *there's* wisdom. And it's part of the Judeo-Christian tradition."

"And Madonna believes in it," said Aydar.

"She certainly does," said Tayir. They all agreed that if someone as successful as Madonna followed Kabbala, there must be something to it.

We kept drinking, but at a civilized pace. Absent also were Russian-style vodka-bash themes: conspiracy theories about who won the cold war and why, or how the CIA had suborned Gorbachev, or how Russia would rise again and confront the West. Kazakhs seemed an innately modest people, aware of the ethnic divisions in their society, divisions that precluded development of imperial ambitions similar to Russia's. If there was a Kazakh brand of nationalism, neither here nor elsewhere had I encountered it. The Soviet slaughter of Kazakhs belonged to the past and never came up.

My dinner partners had absorbed superlatively not just "Western" culture but an eclectic *world* culture, and they felt passionately about it. We agreed that for all its faults, the Soviet secular Weltanschauung was better than the nationalism, often tainted with religious chauvinism, that divides peoples of the former Russian Empire these days. In their opinion, all nationalism did was provide local elites with cover to steal. I noted that my dinner partners did not honor me, on the basis of my passport, as a "Westerner," as they might have a decade ago. "Western" has come to denote open-mindedness, an espousal of choice and welcoming attitude toward diversity.

Our talk turned to Mamelukes and eunuchs and the fall of the Ottoman Empire. Sergey interrupted and suggested we move on to a nightclub. We paid the bill and piled into Tayir's Cherokee, and Aykirim, who had drunk very little, if at all, jumped behind the wheel. Though tiny, she ably forded traffic jams and maneuvered at high speed down crowded lanes as we kept up our historical banter.

The venue they had selected was Sweet and Spice—a striptease club with an unremarkable cavernous black interior and a bilevel stage with steel poles. Female dancers, Russians or at least Slavs all, emerged in body-painted pairs and performed well-choreographed moves reminiscent of ballet; their nakedness seemed incidental. All around us sat not vodka-guzzling thugs but sippers of Bacardi, connoisseurs of Hennessy and Absolut.

Tayir and his wife snuggled on the sofa next to me, watching the show, and Marina commented on the salient aspects of the dancers' physiques. A shower act followed, then an Andalusian number, and finally a masked girl in black leather pounced into the spotlight brandishing whips and chains . . .

After she had disciplined her partner and left the stage, the lights dimmed and the disc jockey played "Hotel California." We all looked up, paused in our talk, and observed something like a moment of enraptured silence.

"No one has written a better song," Sergey said, his voice breaking. We all agreed, and raised our glasses for a toast. The American tune from so long ago had marked their lives as much as it had mine; it was as much theirs as mine, and I was glad of that.

16

From Almaty I took a taxi through grassy golden hills, dry in the strong sun and empty in a haunting way that hinted at my progress east, toward the deserts of western China. After a three-hour ride I found myself before a complex of brick and aluminum buildings—the frontier post with Kyrgyzstan. As on my arrival from Russia, the Kazakh agent took forever examining my passport and visa and seemed determined to find me guilty of some infraction. He didn't, of course. The Kyrgyz official down the road stamped my papers right away, smiling and wishing me welcome.

Huge snowcapped mountains, the Alatau, towered beyond Bishkek (population 1.1 million), the messy outer districts of which began just after the border. Within no time we pulled in to a parking space at the Dostuk Hotel, the Brezhnev-era, eerily vacant cement high-rise where I would stay.

I HAD FIRST VISITED BISHKEK in October of 2001. It was then much as it is now, a shabby, primitive, and flat city of low buildings serviced by bumpy roads and strewn with flyblown cafés and kebab stands, yet still sporting a modest selection of Western and Turkish restaurants catering mostly to expat businessmen, foreign aid workers, and diplomats. Rare was the nightclub resembling the gangster lairs of Moscow; no homes recalled the palatial digs of Russian oligarchs. In short, nothing suggested that Bishkek was anything more than what it had been in

Communist days—a backwater town, capital of a mountain republic with few natural resources. What wealth there was in Kyrgyzstan, Kyrgyz told me not without envy, lay in the hands of ethnic Uzbek businessmen residing in the Fergana Valley down south, where cotton and tobacco were grown and narcotics transited. With the Uzbeks' long history as a settled people of trade and agriculture, all evidence indicated—and still does—that they outperform the Kyrgyz economically, even in the Kyrgyz homeland.

Kyrgyzstan had its problems, thus, but its affable and balding president, Askar Akayev, in office then since 1991, had largely managed to run his country smoothly (or so the Western press had it), enacting reforms that supposedly derived their legitimacy from an innate Kyrgyz love of liberty. The Kyrgyz style themselves as Central Asia's aristocrats, denizens of the Tian Shan (Celestial Mountains) who long maintained pure nomadic ways and would never submit to tyranny. The prevailing myth abroad was that, as a soft-spoken physicist and chairman of the Kyrgyz Academy of Sciences, Akayev governed as a scholar-democrat in a region infamous for Stalinist personality cults, clan-based rule, xenophobia, and corruption. Crucially for his image in the West, Akayev professed faith in American political values (in his office he kept a bust of Thomas Jefferson), encouraged tourism, and welcomed foreign investment, maintaining an open-door policy toward foreign businesspersons. Already a star player on the Western team of the new Great Game, after 9/11 he also became a stalwart in President Bush's "war on terror" by allowing the United States to base troops at an airfield outside Bishkek, from which coalition forces flew round-the-clock combat and supply missions to nearby Afghanistan.

Yet within hours of my arrival in town in 2001 I sensed things here were not all so sweet. Russians derided Akayev as just another Central Asian Big Man who had pulled the wool over American eyes; Kyrgyz spewed insults at him for his alleged corruption and ruinous economic policies. I started my stay by visiting the closest thing Bishkek had to an amusement park—a gated city block in the southern suburbs covered in metal twistings, cracked concrete statues, and chipped marble oddments. Hens rooting about in weed-choked flower beds cackled at me, and stray dogs growled and bared yellow teeth. I rapped at the gate-booth window. A gloomy young Kyrgyz in a camouflage uniform stepped out, tucking in his shirt and wiping the sleep out of his eyes, and asked me what I wanted. Admission, I told him. After driving away the dogs, he rudely demanded I pay the five-som entrance fee (about ten cents). I gave him the money and walked in.

After much staring, in crescents of aluminum on cement pedestals I discerned rams' horns, and in what looked like decrepit birdcages large enough for pterodactyls I made out medieval helmets. Only atop a platform at the far end of the deserted complex, in soot-stained yurts draped with grimy plastic sheeting, did I find intelligible evidence of what this junkyard was: *Epic of Manas* City, a theme park erected three years earlier by the Kyrgyz government to introduce children to the glories of their founding father, the warrior Manas.

Manas City was Akayev's showpiece project. He had proclaimed the oral poem the *Epic of Manas* (twenty times longer than the *Odyssey*) to be the country's "spiritual foundation . . . our pride, our strength, and our hope," and prevailed on UNESCO to declare 1995 the "Year of the *Manas*," the celebration of which cost the cash-strapped Kyrgyz government eight million dollars. When Kremlin rule ended in 1991, Akayev, to endow his people with a past that, at least culturally, would justify the new Kyrgyzstan's existence, followed banana-republic traditions of state hagiography in reviving the *Manas* epic, which had been suppressed during Soviet days. The poem recounts how Manas summons his Muslim people to return from their wanderings along the Yenisey River in Siberia and liberate their mountainous homeland from infidel Mongol and Chinese invaders. In the ensuing battles, a Cyclops is defeated, the yurts of the enemy are laid waste, noble steeds trample treacherous khans, and prophetic dreams augur a splendid future for the Kyrgyz. The epic concludes with the sacking of Beijing and the birth of Kyrgyzstan.

The one problem with all this versified derring-do is that it never happened. The epic is fiction, Manas never lived, and the Kyrgyz people know it; they refer to Manas as their "imaginary hero" when they refer to him at all, which is rarely. Moreover, the epic has both Kazakh and Kyrgyz origins, so *Manas* could not embody the quintessence of Kyrgyz nationhood. Its dual origin should not surprise: a couple of centuries ago, the two Turkic peoples were one, with the Kazakhs preferring the steppes, the Kyrgyz, the mountains. (Russia annexed the territory in 1864.) Both peoples were wandering herders whom the Soviets later forced to settle; neither possessed their own written culture.

But even if Manas had lived, he could not symbolize the unity of all Kyrgyzstan's five million citizens, who include, besides ethnic Kyrgyz

(64.9 percent), Uzbeks (13.8 percent) and Russians (12.5 percent), among others. They found themselves thrown in together thanks to Stalin, who had the borders of the Kyrgyz Soviet Socialist Republic drawn in 1936 to embrace antagonists who would look to him to keep the peace. To an extent he succeeded: within Kyrgyzstan are controversial enclaves belonging to Tajikistan and Uzbekistan, with which Kyrgyzstan still has not demarcated its borders.

DECAY IN KYRGYZSTAN pervades much more than *Epic of Manas* City. President Akayev presided over "reforms" that saw Kyrgyzstan slip from being a poor, relatively modern republic at independence (modern in the Soviet sense of the word, which meant, if nothing else, with functioning industry and basic infrastructure) into a wasteland of political repression, anger, and despair. Kyrgyz government statistics for the year 2001 indicated a GNP growth rate of 5.3 percent (which would have made the Kyrgyz economy one of the best-performing in the world), but growth by 2006 had slowed to 2 percent; 40 percent of the population still lives below the poverty level; and industrial production remains far below Soviet levels. One thing Kyrgyzstan did do effectively after independence was borrow money: financial assistance from abroad played a significant role in the Kyrgyz federal budget, and its external debt now amounts to $2.5 billion, which exceeds the country's gross domestic product by more than $200 million. In all the former Soviet Union, only Tajikistan is poorer.

Kyrgyzstan differs from many other formerly Soviet republics in one respect: it lacks natural resources that could serve as poles around which a viable, even if inequitable, new social order could coalesce, as has happened in Turkmenistan, Kazakhstan, and Uzbekistan. Monthly income in Bishkek has averaged around fifty dollars, and half that elsewhere in the country—far too little for stability. In 2005, the population, enraged over corruption in Akayev's government, rose up and ousted him. That summer, the opposition leader Kurmanbek Bakiyev won presidential elections. At the time of my visit, in late August of 2006, violent protests against the new government were erupting.

Would the country stay its pro-Western course, or slip back into the Russian orbit? I hoped to find out.

THE DAY AFTER MY ARRIVAL turned out to be August 31, the anniversary of Kyrgyzstan's 1991 independence from the Soviet Union. Marching bands and chattering crowds thronged down the potholed streets. (Though almost half of Bishkek's population is Slavic, almost none had turned out for the celebrations.) A high-ranking official of Russian origin in a state-run company met me at the Dostuk and invited me home. I'll refer to him as Victor. Victor was in his fifties and well built, carrying an imitation leather briefcase, with a sad, wearied cast to his intelligent eyes. We set out for the half-hour walk across town.

Victor told me that gold sales provide 10 percent of the country's budget. He went on to add, "The masses kicked out Akayev because he was stealing too much. The new president, Bakiyev, is no genius, so he surrounds himself with second-raters. Our politicians profess democracy, but really they're just out for themselves. Bureaucrats here pass laws to enrich themselves. They get rich mostly on illegal trade—underground vodka, contraband of all sorts."

We crossed parks, unkempt but green and refreshing nonetheless, and reached Victor's building. As we stepped into its dingy entrance, two Kyrgyz women seated in the dark on a bench startled us, greeting us in Russian.

"*S prazdnikom Vas!*" (Happy holiday!) answered Victor.

"It will be happy if you give us a bottle!" said one.

They laughed, and we mounted the stairs to his flat, a capacious spread of rooms decorated with careworn but comfortable Soviet furniture. Bookcases stood stocked with translations of the Soviet-era mainstays, Cervantes, Turgenev, Tolstoy, and Dreiser; breezes ruffled white lace curtains. Victor invited me to the dining room, where a table was spread with vodka, wine, sausages, and all sorts of cold cuts and marinated vegetables.

"You're celebrating Independence Day?" I asked.

He grimaced. "What, are you *kidding!* This is all for you! I would *never* celebrate this holiday!"

His wife, tall and redheaded, hurried past us with a tray of pilaf.

"He thinks we're celebrating independence here!" Victor said. We took our seats. "Look, with Kyrgyzstan becoming independent, I've lost all sense of motherland. You Americans would run to the aid of your government if you were attacked. But what would I be defending here? You'd never find me manning the barricades. The funny thing is, these Kyrgyz consider themselves the elite of Central Asia. But they didn't even have *writing* before the Russians came."

"Well, they must have resented being colonized," I said.

"If you ask me, I think the Russians gave them an awful lot," he answered. "During the Second World War the Kremlin moved a lot of big factories down here, and they even tested submarines in Issyk Kul Lake, so we've brought them a lot of work and industry. [To say nothing of still lethal radiation.] And you know, so many scientists and artists moved down here. We've got the most universities per capita here of any place in the former Soviet Union. Not a bad record for exploitative colonizers, is it?"

"You're a Russian and able to work in a high-level government job. So they must want you here."

"Oh, I have a specialized degree, so they need me, that's all. Otherwise they'd have replaced me with a Kyrgyz long ago. My salary is high by local standards—two hundred and fifty dollars a month. But my children are seeking their futures abroad. There's no hope for Russians here."

Only his age kept him in Bishkek; were he younger, he would have left. Victor went on to recount his family history, the Bishkek part of which began when his great-grandfather arrived during tsarist times to build the railroad. "The most advanced and enterprising Russians came down here. We still maintain old Russian traditions. We drink less than they do in Russia now"—in fact, we hardly touched our vodka—"we swear less, we still respect the elderly. I travel to Russia and I'm shocked by the poverty and alcoholism I see in the villages. We're better off here. This has a lot to do with Muslim culture, which doesn't approve of drinking."

We dug in to our pilaf and lamb; Russians in Central Asia took well to local cuisine. Breeze kept ruffling the curtains, cooling the room. Victor was volubly melancholy, lost-sounding at times.

"In Soviet days I felt I belonged to a real society. I felt solidarity with workers abroad, I felt *international,* just like the government taught us. We had our values back then, humane values, values taken from the Bible, even if Communist ones. Even living out here, I dreamed of seeing the Hermitage, I read the classics, as we all did. We were all more or less equals, and we were taught to believe we could perfect ourselves, that we should do more than just *exist.* I'm not saying the Soviet system wasn't rotten and that we didn't have propaganda. But since independence all I've been able to do is slave away to feed my family, and I never have time for reading."

His recollection of Soviet days was selective, tinged with nostalgia for youthful times, but one thing was sure: the modern states of Central Asia had come up with nothing as inspiring or unifying as Soviet mythology, which glorified ideas of equality, progress, culture, and solidarity with working classes abroad.

Victor walked me back through the center to my hotel. It was evening, and the streets still swarmed with Independence Day merrymakers, scarcely a Slavic face among them. At Victory Square we parted. I stood for a minute and watched my host head home. He was quickly lost in the crowd.

IN A TIDY BASEMENT OFFICE in a Bishkek suburb the next day I met a prominent Kyrgyz publisher and asked him to tell me about the current political situation, under the reformer Bakiyev. He was in his forties; his Russian was clear, reflective of a solid Soviet education. He, tellingly, requested anonymity.

He described Kyrgyzstan's virtual disintegration while the American ally Akayev was in power.

"When a ruler here has no money to buy loyalty with, he survives by giving out freedoms," he said. "So it was with our former president, Akayev. But Akayev was losing control and everyone was demanding bribes—you had to pay bribes to do just about anything here. The people eventually didn't even know whom to give them to, there were so many bribe takers, so the system of corruption overwhelmed itself and broke down. You Americans might call this democracy, but we called it democratization of corruption."

"Can you explain what you mean?"

"I mean that without the controls of the Soviet police state, everyone here had the freedom to be corrupt, fearlessly corrupt. Call it chaos. Now, with Bakiyev, order has been reestablished and the system of bribery functions again; you can actually call the police after, say, a robbery, and they respond. They love catching crooks, because it gives them an opportunity to extort bribes from them. But the police need a certain order to be able to feel in control and demand their bribes. With gangs ruling in the street, who would pay attention to them? The police here hide during riots. That's why disorders spread and get so out of control."

"Was that how it was during the uprising that ousted Akayev?"

"Yes. The police hid. Youths and grandpas and entire families came running out to loot the stores belonging to Akayev and his cronies and his Turkish friends; they just smashed the windows and stole everything. The second night citizens banded together and, armed with hunting rifles, reestablished order. They did their own patrolling, since the police were hiding."

"In general, though, it seems like there's a measure of democracy here, at least compared to other Central Asian states."

"Well, we can say this: Bakiyev controls thirty percent of society. His allies control another fifteen percent, and the rest is split up between competing interests—the parliament, the prime minister, and NGOs. This isn't democracy, it's the *weakness* of the president. Kyrgyzstan is no monolith, in any case. We're divided into northern and southern clans. We've never had a tsar, only elected tribal leaders. We don't submit to other tribes. Why should we submit to just another bunch of nomads like us? We'd laugh at a would-be dictator and say, 'But you're from the same mountains as we are!' If anyone tries to take away our freedoms, we rise up.

"So, President Bakiyev is reinstating power and stability is returning. We've got a growing tourist industry, mostly Kazakhs and Russians, around Lake Issyk Kul, and Russians are buying up land out there. Bakiyev is ceding to demands that various *siloviki*"—officials in the military and police—"be replaced. Also, the government has hunted down and killed a number of big *mafiozy* here; this country isn't big enough for two *mafiyas.*"

"How's that?"

"You see, Kyrgyzstan is what we call a red country, where the police are behind the *mafiya,* as in Kazakhstan, Uzbekistan, and Russia. Our police shelters the *mafiya.* Our government officials patronize the *mafiya*'s casinos with their easy money; the *mafiya* owns parts of our largest markets. Drug trafficking from Afghanistan is another big business, as is trafficking women."

"So there's really only one *mafiya*? In Russia there are several—the Chechens, the Armenians, the Azerbaijanis, to name some."

"The problem is that we all know each other or are related. We're a tiny country. With our blood ties we'd just laugh if a relative came up and tried to extort us. What, me give to you? We're relatives! But by contrast, a Kyrgyz in Kazakhstan or Russia is completely defenseless, because he needs blood relatives to back him up."

"Were people upset with the United States for supporting Akayev, since he let the *mafiya* rule and allowed such corruption?"

"I'm not sure, but the United States, we see, lost big when Akayev was overthrown. Russia's position has grown much stronger. This makes sense. We have a half-million Kyrgyz working in Russia, who remit a half-billion dollars a year, so we need good relations with Russia. Russian businesses follow the Russian state's lead. Russian businessmen arrive with suitcases full of bribe money. They use business for political ends; the more oil they sell, the more influence they buy. The Americans, who say their businesses won't follow state interests, can't compete with the Russians. The Chinese are expanding here too, but they don't hurry, they go step by step. But strongest of all are the Russians, who are buying up our gas stations."

"Bakiyev has said the United States will have to leave the Bishkek air base it set up after September eleventh once Afghanistan stabilizes. What do you think?"

"Well, America is paying thirty to forty million dollars a year in rent, in overflight rights, and for fuel; and most here think that refueling supply contracts went to Bakiyev's people. We have a Russian base here too, you know. But we think it's in our interest that Russia is here, to protect us from terrorists, so we don't take rent from them. The Shanghai Cooperation Organization includes Kyrgyzstan, so that's their legal basis for being here."

"But are people negative about the U.S. presence?"

"No. We know that one thousand American troops could defeat ten thousand Taliban. In other words, if the United States weren't here, the Taliban would be. We had Islamic guerrillas attacking us in our southern mountains, but since the Americans arrived in 2001, they've disappeared. During the Yeltsin years, the 1990s, Russia was bankrupt. Yeltsin had no spirit for the fight against the Taliban and wouldn't do anything about the problem. I mean to say that we're grateful to the Americans."

"Is the United States a model for Kyrgyzstan?"

"No, Russia is, as it is for the whole former USSR. All former Soviet leaders will do what Putin does. Putin sets the rules."

His last remark was off-mark, at least in part. With their recent revolutions, the Ukrainians and Georgians had shown as much; and the Baltic countries had broken decisively from the Kremlin in 1991. But he went on to express admiration for the "order" Putin was reestablishing. He was vague about whether such "order" would suit Kyrgyzstan. Only the alarm that flashed in his eyes when I asked him if I could print his name in these pages told me how he really felt. Whether Akayev and

Bakiyev enjoyed American support or not, Kyrgyzstan remains in Russia's historical and current sphere of influence, and Putin's rules, not Western rules, could be counted on to apply.

WHILE OUT WALKING AROUND BISHKEK I met Erlan, a lanky Kyrgyz in his twenties with a slender face and buoyant demeanor. He had the look of promise about him—clean-cut, clear-skinned, dressed in freshly laundered threads that might have come from the Gap or Diesel. There was something refined about his Russian, which he attributed to his erudite father, a television reporter. We agreed to meet later that evening so he could show me how he spends a typical Saturday night. He had a car, which would make things easier.

"Nightlife's quite exciting here in Bishkek now," he said. "Your memories are out of date."

We started out at his favorite café, the Shoola, which was decorated in familiar Russian provincial style. It was packed. Most of the Kyrgyz were drinking vodka or beer, but none were drunk. A live Kyrgyz band played Russian *popsa*. Save for the atmosphere of sobriety and the Kyrgyz faces, we might have been in any small Russian town.

"So," Erlan said, after refusing my offer of a beer ("Thanks, but I don't like alcohol"), "are you going to ask a girl to dance?"

"You go ahead."

"I will if you will."

"Really, be my guest."

"But look at that one! Isn't she pretty? Or that one? Wouldn't you like to meet her?"

"I'm at least twenty years older than they are."

"That doesn't matter at all! You can still get one!"

In fact, it did matter, and not just because I was happily married. I tried to envision making conversation with them and found myself fatigued at the thought, which took me back to the dating scene and all its banalities, ennuis, discomforts.

I explained this to Erlan. He was unfazed. "We must be in the wrong place, then." He paused. A randy eagerness widened his eyes. "Hey, let's go to a sauna!"—in post-Soviet parlance, a brothel.

"No, that's okay."

"Oh, I don't mean just any sauna. I'm talking about a brothel where girls who can't get enough go." My eyebrows must have arched. "No, they're not there for money, really. There're a lot of girls like that here."

He was, to be sure, availing himself of the opportunity I had presented him with: I had told him I would pay for his evening out.

Still, a change of venue did seem in order. We ended up at the Golden Bull, one of Bishkek's hottest nightclubs, a "cool place kids from all over the countryside come to party in," Erlan said.

The Golden Bull was jammed. I was one of the few non-Kyrgyz faces in the crowd, but no one cared. The club was sprawling and multi-roomed, with a pinewood Californian interior lit in blue neon.

We looked for seats but there were none. Then the music stopped and a slender MC in black, apparently half Russian, half Kyrgyz, with gelled spiky hair, strode out onto the dance floor, gripping a wireless microphone. He addressed us in Russian, the language of chic in Bishkek even now.

"I need four volunteer couples for a sex competition!" he shouted, his mike screeching.

"Go on!" prodded Erlan. "Get out there!"

"Are you mad? You go!"

"You can do it! Go!"

Go I did not. Anyway, four couples, all Kyrgyz in their teens or early twenties, all dressed in something like Manhattan hip-hop attire, answered his call and took places beside him. One of the girls, a saucy Turkic belle in a pink blouse and tight white slacks, was a little *too* enthusiastic in her strut and "Who, me?" bashfulness. She must be, I thought, the club's *podstava*.

Erlan nudged me. "Watch! Watch!"

"Now, couple number one," said the MC, "show us how you have sex!"

Techno beat blasted through the speakers. Couple number one danced out onto the stage, grinning idiotically, and closed in on each other but pulled back, repeatedly. The MC hollered at them to copulate. They fumbled through some fake caresses, but the song ended with no salty simulacrum. They skittered back onto the podium.

"That's not how you have sex!" shouted the MC. "Come on, couple two!"

"Oh, now they'll *really* do it!" said Erlan. But they didn't.

Only couple three got into it: he pushed her to the floor and "mounted" her from behind, then pantomimed a canine hump.

"*Rakom! Rakom!*" (Crab-style!), shouted the MC. "Now have sex! More realistically!"

They shuffled themselves around but then they lost nerve and, laughing, jumped up.

"More! More!" shouted the crowd. She began a handstand. He grabbed her upside-down hips, pulling her off the floor; wobbling, trying to keep balance, and almost at times falling over, she "performed" fellatio, he cunnilingus.

"Wow!" said Erlan, poking me in the ribs. "It sure makes you want to go to that brothel, doesn't it? Come on! Look at them! *Wow!*"

Everyone was laughing and pointing; their act was the hit of the night. Couple number four, which included the pink-bloused *podstava* phony, was up next. She played the vamp, stalking toward him, pushing him to the parquet, and rode him as Debra Winger did the mechanical bull in *Urban Cowboy.* Then she dismounted and pulled him over onto herself for the missionary number, her legs on his shoulders, her head waggling.

Podstava! I could only think. But, judging by the ebullient grins and raunchy shouts around me, I was alone in my cynicism. Erlan's hormones had him beside himself, squirming in place, ever nudging me to keep watching.

At his age, maybe I would have been just as excited. But here, now, in Kyrgyzstan, as in Almaty, I was witnessing a banal, if in some sense saving, truth: even as corruption putrefies, as natural resources are spirited abroad, as the word *democracy* shields a puppet ruler supported by a foreign power and liberty comes to mean the chance to loot fearlessly, the people, once restricted by a prudish state but now free, will *get down*—and in doing so release a lot of energy that might have flowed into political activism. The system here was bearable, and for now, few found reasons to seek more.

Disappointed with my aversion to his brothel, Erlan took me back to the hotel, but offered to drive me out of Bishkek and into the mountains the next morning, to my next destination.

Oh, to the mountains!

17

The next morning low bulky clouds shielded Bishkek from the sun. Erlan, who was to drive me to Kochkor, up in the Alatau, to the southeast, pulled in to my hotel's lot in his red Lada, still cheery despite my abstention the previous night.

"I have an errand to run before we leave town," he said. "Got to pick up some goods for my mom's store." His mother ran a kiosk in Bishkek's outskirts, and he had to fill her order with a wholesale merchant in Alamedin Bazaar, somewhere in the city's north. This was fine with me.

The name "Alamedin Bazaar" and its entranceway sign, inscribed in Arabesque Cyrillic, reeked of Ali Baba allure and Sinbad exotica, but the market turned out to be no more than a noxious prefab assemblage of slapdash shacks tossed up around a giant humdrum hangar of steel and concrete, impressive only for its sheer Soviet junkiness. Whatever the Soviets had done for literacy in Central Asia, however infamous had been their assorted political purges and campaigns of terror, their most visible and lasting legacy here consists of the standardized ugliness of almost everything they built—a curse on all the former Soviet lands that no one has the money, time, or energy to lift. From Grodno, in Belarus, to Magadan on the Sea of Okhotsk, I had seen hundreds of such markets (without the Arabesque), yet I could remember nothing save that I chose to forget them.

Still, elements in the chaos environing the bazaar were distinctly, if not romantically, Central Asian. Beneath the exhaust-caked boughs of stunted willows, patched-up pickups and carburetor-less minivans wheeled about, coughing through their tailpipes and disgorging three-somes and foursomes of traders clutching their wizardlike *ak kalpaks* (traditional white felt Kyrgyz hats). These were hurried men in dark hand-me-down jackets and trousers who shouted in agglutinated Turkic, peppering their speech with *Allah-Allah!* and *Salam-alaykum!* Toting plastic suitcases, most had the sunburned brows and callused knuckles of rustics; they would haul their purchases back to their mountain villages and resell them there, for such were the supply net-works. Food on sale was all local: men in white skullcaps stood over steaming vats and ladled meat-filled samosas and *manty* dumplings into little plastic serving bags; youths in ornate Uzbek *tyubeteykas* lined up to sip tepid *kvas* dispensed from rusty tanker-trailers into commu-nal tin cups on chains.

"Villagers!" said Erlan. "Look at them! This city has been ruined by all these villagers!"

"But you're not from here, either. You come from Osh, right?"

"Yes, but I grew up *here*. All the Bishkekis complain about these vil-lagers coming more and more and spoiling everything. There's no work in the countryside so they move to the cities. But we can't live a civi-lized life with people like them around."

We plunged into the crowd, dodging men shouldering sacks leaking grain, dragging carts of cotton bolts, or ferrying beams, shoving and shouting to make way, as if such wares would self-destruct unless spir-ited out of the market in breakneck haste. Hopping over rills of sewage, we found the store. Erlan unfolded his list and shouted out its contents (varieties of vodka, matches and cigarettes, plastic-bottled beer, Mars bars and Snickers—the staples at corner kiosks) as the owner's sons tossed the goods down from the shelves and relayed them rapidly to cardboard boxes. This speedy service was Central Asian too, and con-trasted with the glum, lackadaisical treatment we would have received in a Slavic market up north.

In short order we had delivered these supplies to his mother's shop and were off. We picked up the highway leading out of town through fir forests and clusters of stovepiped dachas, and in no time confronted a vision from a new world: the Alatau, stony and sere, its peaks and crags ranging away under massing clouds. The landscape, as we ascended, opened into a forbidding tableau of chasms guarded by solitary sentry cedars, of blue frothy streams rushing down dark slopes to churn through gullies by the road, of hovering hawks and darting falcons. This was not European scenery but neither was it Siberian; it was sui generis Central Asia. These were the outer limits of mountains running from the Eurasian steppes to what, with each mile traversed, was exciting me more and more now: the *tianxia* (All-Under-Heaven), *Zhongguo* (the Middle Kingdom), the Han imperium; in a word, China.

"You're going to enjoy the mountains," Erlan said as we trundled across the silent land. "The people up in the yurts have a better life than we do, with fewer problems. We Kyrgyz of the south have adopted Uzbek ways, we're civilized. But the Kyrgyz where you're going are pure and innocent."

We entered an iron gray defile streaked with yellow-orange grass — the Boom Gorge, Erlan said. I rolled down the window and inhaled deliciously cool air. I sat back, invigorated.

But just as I started to relax, a gray Zhiguli overtook us, honking, and swerved into the lane ahead of us, nearly shunting us off the road. Erlan maneuvered and slowed, pumping the brakes. The Zhiguli slowed even more, but then swerved into the opposite lane and dropped behind us and overtook us again. Erlan jerked his wheel to the right, this time just barely avoiding collision. The Zhiguli accelerated and skidded to a halt sideways, kicking up a hail of gravel and blocking our way.

"Maybe he's telling us one of our tires is low," suggested Erlan.

"He's sure aggressive about it, if that's the case." In fact, robbery, carjacking even, came to mind. Police were few in Kyrgyzstan outside the towns, and there might be nowhere to turn for help.

"Well, see the license plates? He's a villager. They don't know how to behave, even when they want to help."

Erlan climbed out. The Zhiguli driver stepped out too, clearly disinclined to "help." Snarling, he jabbed a forefinger first at us and then behind us. A black foreign-made car was speeding our way; it nearly ran over Erlan, forcing him to jump aside, and skidded to a stop. Its rear passenger-side window was missing. A pug-faced Kyrgyz of about forty hurled himself out of the driver's seat, his eyes angry slits, his belly thrust forward, his fists clenched, one around a screwdriver. Shouting in guttural Kyrgyz, he pointed at Erlan and his missing window and began gesticulating and jabbing his screwdriver toward Erlan's chest. The other fellow drove off.

I got out. "What's going on?"

Erlan stepped back, bumping into the hood of his car as the madman fulminated. "He says we were speeding a ways back, we shot by him and kicked up a rock that knocked out his window." The man shoved aside Erlan and with his screwdriver took to hacking at our front license plate. "He's trying to take my plates!"

Erlan pulled him gently back. Brandishing his screwdriver, the man yelled in bad Russian, "You speed, you kick up rocks, you break my window break-break! You have no conscience, boy!"

"*Bayke* [sir], with all respect, how do you know we were speeding?" Erlan said. "You have no radar."

"Excuse me," I said calmly, "if you have a complaint, we should go to the GAI in Balykchy"—the town ten miles up the road. "Let them settle it."

At this our accoster turned to me and started spitting out invectives in Kyrgyz, punctuated with oaths in Russian. "He bad boy! Bad! Bad! I want one thousand som [about twenty-five dollars]! I want now, now! Give it!" He shoved Erlan and made a stabbing motion with his screwdriver. Erlan jumped back.

"*Bayke, bayke,* please!" Erlan pleaded, holding his hands up and refusing to be provoked. "*Bayke!* You're uncivilized and don't know how to address people."

I took out my cell phone. "What's the GAI's emergency number?"

Erlan didn't know. Calling on a uniformed band of thieves like the GAI for help might have been a bad idea, but we had to do something, especially since there were several other people in the madman's car who could jump out and overpower us.

"Then I'm calling the American embassy," I said. "I'll tell them to send their mobile armed guards, that this guy is assaulting us." (I didn't have the number, of course, and neither would the embassy have done more than notify the Kyrgyz police. But the driver wouldn't know that.)

"You shouldn't do that," said someone in threatening Russian from inside the car.

"The embassy has an SUV full of guards about five miles back," I replied, pretending to punch a number into my mobile. "Along with a Kyrgyz KGB unit. If you won't settle this calmly, I'll let them deal with you."

I put the phone to my ear. Straightaway the ranting man agreed to drive to the GAI checkpoint up ahead. I put away my phone. We jumped back into our cars.

"Maybe he's just trying to get his window repaired at our expense," Erlan said. "Maybe this is a scam."

Five minutes later, at the edge of Balykchy, we stopped by a row of GAI booths and descended; the madman parked crosswise ahead of us, blocking the road. A stout, stone-faced officer, baton in hand, heard out his plaint and Erlan's defense. But then he said something curt in Kyrgyz, shrugged, and walked off.

Again the driver lunged at Erlan's license plate with his screwdriver and the fracas began anew. His wife joined the fray, fat and shrill and virulent, waving her fists at Erlan. More physically aggressive than her husband, she shoved him again and again, shouting about a thousand som, and even tried to kick him in the shin.

"Please calm down," I said, stepping between them.

"You see him break our car! You see too!" she shouted at me.

"I didn't see anything. The GAI should settle this."

"You unjust too!" She raised her hand as if to strike me, but for some reason she restrained herself.

The *gaishnik,* Erlan said, had refused to settle the dispute, probably because no one had hinted at a bribe. He moved to open his door, but the man jumped in his way, and his wife was kicking at his shins and higher, causing him to double over to protect his groin.

"We won't let you go, hooligan!" they shouted. Another fellow was about to get out of the driver's car.

Things were turning ugly. I ran over to the checkpoint and grabbed the *gaishnik.*

"Look, please, help us out! They're getting wild and making threats! They're going to commit a crime!"

Shaking his head, he reluctantly accompanied me back to the fray. This time he looked annoyed, and everyone quieted down. He heard a few more accusations but then wearily announced, in Russian, "I can't keep track of every rock on this highway. Settle this yourselves." Our assailant shouted something at him in Kyrgyz. The *gaishnik* replied in Kyrgyz, cursed him, and walked off.

Bayke turned and lunged at me, holding out his hand. "You pay my window or give your passport!"

"I'm not giving you anything!"

"You no leave here then! No leaving!" he shouted, with an energetic seconding from his wife.

"Get in the car," Erlan whispered to me. Apparently I had missed something in the *gaishnik*'s response. "Get fifty som ready."

He seemed to know what he was doing, so I obeyed. We got in and locked our doors. The man ran around to the rear of our car and leaned into our trunk, as if to block our departure with his body. (We would have to back out and drive around the other car to escape.)

"I'm warning you, get away!" shouted Erlan through the open window.

"Over my dead body you leave! One thousand som, hooligan!"

"Suit yourself," answered Erlan.

Erlan gunned the motor once, twice, but the man refused to budge. Then he wrangled the gearshift into reverse and hit the gas. As we backed up, the man ran backwards and finally fell away to one side, tumbling onto the pavement, but out of our way (and still alive). Erlan put the car in forward and, spraying gravel, sped ahead to the checkpoint, telling me to slip the officer the fifty som. I did, and he raised the red and white crossbeam.

I looked back. "For some reason, he's not following us!"

"No, because the officer is detaining him. He'll have big problems now. He insulted the officer, who's charging him with disrespecting the police. They might even beat him up."

Still, I kept looking back, but then we hung a sharp right onto a beat-up road and headed south and upward, higher into the mountains. Erlan had acquitted himself well, not ceding to provocation, always addressing the man and his wife respectfully, despite their rage. But all this could have ended in violence, and reminded me of just how unprotected people are in former Soviet realms when "law enforcement officers" sniff no graft and so refuse to do their job. If Erlan was indeed responsible for the broken window, the wild man would have had little reason to trust the (notoriously corrupt) authorities to enforce whatever law governed compensation. Where no culture of legality obtains, everyone is at risk. If the American-backed "democrat" and scholar Akayev had accomplished anything during his fifteen years in office, he had not cleaned up the traffic police—hardly the most daunting of tasks. He clearly had other priorities.

It was late afternoon when we drove into Kochkor, all stone and cement hovels and dusty cattle. A road from there wound away even higher into the mountains, the Tian Shan.

"I wish I could go farther than this," said Erlan, "but my car can't take the track. You're going to have to find a four-wheel-drive vehicle."

"I understand."

He drove me to the CBT (Community-Based Tourism) office, which arranges for stays in yurts up by Lake Song Köl, in the highland pastures of the Tian Shan, where I hoped to pass a couple of days. The friendly woman there arranged a Niva (Soviet jeep) and a driver for me. Erlan and I said a warm goodbye. Once again I was grateful to the stars for having provided me with such a decent companion.

My new helmsman was Yusup, an old gnome with a Fu Manchu goatee, a gray skullcap, and distinctly flatter, non-Kyrgyz features. We first stopped at Kochkor's general store, a sort of stone cave emporium, really, where I bought a small sack of *kurut*—salty dried cheese balls made from cow's milk. As we drove out onto the mountain track, Yusup smiled, displaying black rotted shards of teeth. He looked, all in all, more Chinese than Kyrgyz.

"No, I'm a Dungan," he said in response to my query. "I'm more Arab than Kyrgyz."

The Dungan, more commonly known as Hui, do in fact have Chinese blood. Numbering around ten million and spread out around the region, they descend mostly from Muslim immigrants from Persia and other parts of Central Asia who arrived between the seventh and thirteenth centuries. The majority of Dungan live in China, however, and speak Chinese. They've retained their Islamic faith.

"I didn't know there were Dungan in Kyrgyzstan," I said.

"The Kyrgyz are just cattle herders with no culture." He gripped the wheel and, leaning back expansively, smiled black shards. "But we come from the very bearers of Islam."

Yusup's Russian was limited, but I discovered I could communicate with him by mixing in Turkish. This pleased him immensely, and he opened up about his life. For many years he had driven trucks to China and Kazakhstan. He had never been to Moscow and had no desire to go. His hajj to Mecca, made in 2002, was his grandest venture abroad. ("What a glory to see the holy places!") He asked me if I had children and gave me a pitying look when I said no. "I have three sons and two daughters, plus twenty-two grandchildren!" His voice was rich and deep, with an accent different from any I had heard so far.

Within an hour we were alone on the road, climbing bumpy switch-backs toward Kalmak Ashu Pass, into the dun-colored lunar fastnesses of the Tian Shan. From sparsely grassed acclivities beneath jagged canyon escarpments, shepherds on horseback eyed us, dumbfounded, as did their flocks. Up here, men, Kyrgyz all, wore *ak kalpaks,* and some were cloaked in capes that gave them a Robin Hood flair. Clouds hung over stretches of the road, and we drove through them, up into thinning air, to where snow lay on rocky earth. It was early September and the seasons were changing.

Finally the road leveled out. Among prowling goblins of mist, yaks lay strewn about, shaggy, twice the size of cows, each in a puddle of blood, as if felled in battle. Their throats had been slit.

"Herders just finished them off," said Yusup. "They'll take the meat to market down in Bishkek. But we Dungan don't buy from the market. How do we know if the animal was killed in the proper Muslim way? Maybe the Kyrgyz are just selling you meat from an animal that died on its own. That's forbidden by Islam."

"Do Dungan have their own herds?"

"The Dungan? No! We're farmers."

Two hours later, at Kalmak Ashu Pass (altitude 11,500 feet), we crested a rise and stopped. It was as if we had ascended into an Asian empyrean of light, stone, and cloud. Before us to the east spread an idyllic, if treeless, mossy mountainscape. At the base of canyons nestled *jailoos* (Kyrgyz for pastures), many with eyespots of turquoise lakes. Here and there wavered curtains of sun-splashed drizzle, and rainbows limned into view and faded away, but where we were going, the sky was clear.

I stood unsteady, buffeted by the cool wind, my mind on the high-altitude limbo of rock and snow cutting into the sky to the south: the Tian Shan, the Pamirs, the Karakoram, the Hindu Kush, and the Himalayas—mountains, mapped on foot for the British by pundit-agents of the Great Game, that corrugated the crust of the earth from here to the Indus River, and once separated the Russian Empire from the British domains of southern Asia. Moving due south from where we were, one would cross through Xinjiang (the "New Dominion," as the Chinese had named the province two thousand years ago, after having just acquired it); graze easternmost Tajikistan; and bisect Kashmir and the tribal areas of northern Pakistan. If one kept going, one would eventually depart the mountains and the abode of Islam and reach the Sikh-inhabited plains of the Punjab. Pushing even farther south, one would arrive in sweltering Gujarat, on the Indian Ocean, the homeland of Mahatma Gandhi.

I jumped back in the Niva and we drove on, winding around peaks and snow patches until finally, a couple of miles ahead and a hundred yards lower, the pure waters of Song Köl glimmered, pristine blue, sweeping away to dissolve beneath rainbow-tinctured mists. At lakeside hunkered a dozen yurts of gray wool gilt by oblique rays of evening sun. Horses galloped about the *jailoo,* casting long shadows, pursued by mounted herdsmen flourishing leather whips.

Primordial Kyrgyzstan! The storied highlands of the Manas!

Junkun, a Kyrgyz woman in her forties, welcomed us to her camp, smiling gap-toothed. Rather, she welcomed me. Yusup stayed in his Niva, having declared, "I don't sleep in yurts. Yurts are for Kyrgyz. A Dungan sleeps in his car." She took me to my yurt, the felt floor of which was strewn with *shyrdaks*—the crude blankets that were to be my bedding.

That night, enchanted with the ethereal winds and the tranquil emptiness of the *jailoo,* newly aware of how tired I had grown of the lowlands, I climbed beneath my *shyrdaks.* Listening to the silence, breathing the now frigid air, I luxuriated in the warmth of my woolen cocoon. But then I lifted the edge of the yurt's cloth door to gaze out onto the lake, resplendent with the waxing moon's glinting yellow rays. How could this not be the land of Kyrgyz legend, the stomping ground of their pre-Islamic gods?

An hour later, dewdrops on the horse-nibbled grass around my tent froze into crystals, and I fell asleep.

JUNKUN'S DAUGHTER BRUTYA was an attractive seventeen-year-old with wind-ruddied cheeks and rich black hair billowing out from under the confines of a white scarf. Her aesthetic halo dissipated (for me) at dawn, however, when she began snorting the contents of her sinuses into a steel washpan outside my tent door; Yusup followed suit, inhaling drafts of water and honking them grassward in snotty splashes. Later, he slurped his coffee so loudly that he all but drowned out Junkun's plaintive attempts to ask about my family.

All this phlegmy ruckus reminded me that I was not in paradise but up among earthlings of ancient ways, ways yet untempered by modern, mass-market sensibilities.

The day came on cold and clear. Sheepdogs growled and tussled by the campfire. Men in *ak kalpaks* and knee-high black boots emerged from their yurts, jumped atop their horses, and sallied forth to pasture their herds, shouting, *Chaw! Chaw!,* and snapping their whips. Junkun and Brutya were a hundred yards distant, scouring the *jailoo,* stooping to scoop up something brown and lumpy.

"What are they collecting out there?" I asked Yusup, who was standing outside my tent.

"*Kizyak.*"

"*Kizyak?*"

"You know, manure, in Kyrgyz."

"Ah. What do they do with it?"

"Cook with it. Makes great bread."

"What?"

"They burn it for the cooking fires."

"Well, they've got a lot of horses, so they must have a lot of fuel."

"Oh, no. Obviously a horse is no good for *kizyak.*"

"Why not?"

He smiled condescendingly. "Why, because horse manure is all crumbly. Sheep and cows give the firm *kizyak* needed."

Soon after, Junkun served us semolina porridge, sour cream, jam, and tea — a Russian, not a Kyrgyz, breakfast. Yusup slurped and chomped through his portions with raucous burps and gurgles.

Brutya returned with a sack of dung on her back.

"Lunch," said Junkun. "She will soon make the fire for lunch."

Men were charging around the *jailoo,* lashing their horses, shouting and whistling, singing the serenade of nomadic life. The sun soon mounted and the light flattened. After eating I was still hungry, so I pulled out my *kurut* and munched away gratefully. Then I went for an hour's hike to the nearest hills where, Junkun said, brooks ran down from the mountains, but I found only dry rocks. A bizarre drought had hit, and water, apart from that in the lake, was scarce.

So I returned and lazed around my yurt for a while. In the full light of day the pastel hues of the land washed out into uninspiring duns and tans and flat greens. Junkun called me for lunch — a steel bowl of water, boiled on manure, containing noodles and gobs of fat. A boom box sat in the corner, and her four-year-old son, Nurtemir (Light-Iron, as the name translated), flicked it on. To stereo-blasted "I Like to Move It" he gleefully enacted traditional Kyrgyz dances, stirring medleys of kicks and hops. Then traditional, wailing Kyrgyz songs came on, reminiscent of the *türküs* of eastern Anatolia I so loved. Nurtemir frowned, lost interest, and sat down.

EVENING ARRIVED sooner than I expected, with the sun setting early behind the mountains. This would be the family's last week up here in the *jailoo* until spring.

As we dined on pilaf sprinkled with gristly chunks of lamb, Junkun told me about her yurt. The woolen exterior was fastened to stakes driven into the ground in concentric patterns that converged in a circle at the top, leaving a hole that allowed smoke to escape and light to enter; reed mats placed around the edges broke the wind. Yak-hair and horsehair ropes, so finely wound they looked synthetic, tied everything together. Heavy carpets covered the ground. Yurts were mobile and used for generations. When autumn came, families disassembled them, packed them on a yak's back or tossed them in a pickup truck, and hauled them down to the lowlands, where they would be stored in winter dwellings till the next year. All the yurts' materials came from what the Kyrgyz grew or collected themselves. "This wool is from our sheep; these stakes we cut ourselves; this rope is from our yaks," said Junkun. Apart from salt and matches and whatever amenities they chose to buy in towns, they could live up here, weather permitting, in proud self-sufficiency.

The *jailoo*, Junkun explained, meant freedom, communing with nature as the ancestors had, liberation from the clumsy contrivances of modern life. Children of the *jailoo* grew up running in the sun and bathing in breezes blowing down from the glaciers and peaks. As she spoke, however, melancholy tinged her voice.

"Look at the fog coming over the mountains to the north," she said. "End of summer. Winter is coming. We go back to our village in lowlands."

Cold winds belted down and lasted all night, making the valley feel lost and lonely. As relieved as I had been to arrive, I now wanted nothing more than to depart.

18

Dawn broke over a frigid world sunken in mist. I lay in my *shyrdaks* cocoon listening to the wind flapping the yurt's door; the galloping of horses on the frosted grass; Brutya singing as she walked into camp with buckets of lake water; children of all ages crying; and dogs, ever vigilant, barking at the phantom silhouettes of grazing horses.

The sun rose, prompting me to shed my cocoon and get ready to leave. I emerged to find Yusup dusting off his jeep, shadowy against a backdrop of brightening fog.

"We've got to get going," he said. "The passes ahead can be tough."

"You can find your way in all this fog? We can't see ten feet."

"Yes, I've taken the road before."

I threw my bag in the back and climbed aboard. Our destination was the gold-mining settlement of Kazarman, where I would pass the night before heading to Osh, Kyrgyzstan's second-largest city and my last real stop before China. Perhaps Kazarman was a hundred miles to the southwest, perhaps twice that; the dirt road there, all switchbacks and cliffhanging tracks, was not shown on my map, and it led over passes seen by few save nomads.

With Song Köl hidden in the mists, we set out following a pair of tire ruts wending away over reddish earth. Burial mounds drifted by, deepening the sense of solitude evoked by the creaking wheels and lonely land.

Yusup's baritone voice sounded rich and dreamy. "The drought . . . The drought has killed all the grass. And look, you see no marmots out here. They've already hibernated. It makes no sense. If there are no marmots, it means that wolves will attack people's sheep and goats. So the drought is bad for the herders."

We drove out of the fog bank. Across the empty *jailoo* rose endless tawny mountains, ashen chasms. Soon, near the edge of the pasture, by the last stretch of lakeshore, we saw yurts and many herds of bounding horses and nibbling sheep.

"There still seem to be quite a few nomads up here," I said.

"Yes, there are. Ten years ago they'd almost disappeared. You see, the Communists had forced everyone into kolkhozes. With the end of the Soviet Union, the kolkhozes all fell apart, and people didn't know what to do. So they left for the towns. Now they lease their pastureland from the state and are doing better."

"So at least something has improved here."

"Well, before, everyone feared the law, and no one cared whether you were Kyrgyz or Russian. Now, your ethnic identity means everything. And how much money you have. If you're rich you can commit murder. You spend a day in jail, pay off people, and walk free. If you're poor you steal a turkey and get three or four years."

We reached the base of a mountain. We veered off the *jailoo* on to a dirt track that led up and away in switchbacks. A couple of hours later we hit Moldobel Pass, altitude 13,400 feet. A turn in the road there revealed an alpine panorama of fir-forested slopes and gorges. Some of the trees looked ready to slip off their cliff perches and drop into the abysses.

Trees meant life, and their unexpected presence cheered me. But three hours later we left their shade and ascended to another pass, that of Ak Kyya, and beheld a Saharan wasteland of sandy hills, scrub and thorn, parched streambeds, and whiteout sun—a far drier landscape than anything I had seen since the Betpaqdala, one prefiguring the Taklamakan and Gobi deserts ahead.

Late that afternoon, after trundling through valley villages where sheep crowded the road and every man, squinting in the sun, sported an *ak kalpak* despite the 95-degree heat, we pulled into Kazarman, at four thousand feet. We put up at a guesthouse (Yusup would not leave until morning)—a whitewashed single-story home set in a leafy garden behind a high whitewashed wall. Once the sun set and the air cooled, I set out to see the town, ignoring my host's warning: "No go out after dark! Dogs and thieves on street!"

HUDDLED BENEATH SANDY SLOPES and slate-colored summits, with a nameless, sixteen-thousand-foot peak rising just to the north, Kazarman at first put me in mind of Berber villages I had seen deep in the High Atlas Mountains of Morocco; the colors of the surrounding landscape were all North African. Similarities ended there, however. Stray dogs prowled around corner rubbish heaps; stout Kyrgyz women burdened with shopping bags hurried home as the light diminished; and carousing Kyrgyz youths let loose wild cries from points unseen. The drunkenness, the whiff of fear in the air, and the tawdry hints of modernity all belonged to the former Soviet sphere. Hungry from two days of bland nomad fare, I toured the meager selection of derelict shops and kiosks in search of something to eat, but found nothing appealing.

I ended up sitting at the town watering hole and restaurant, the concrete-block Café Paris. A grim teen in rubber sandals dusted droopy potted plants and even wiped clean posters of Swiss meadows tacked to the chipped walls. A bulb on a wire provided the only illumination; flies clustered on it, casting fearsome twitching shadows. Shreds of red and blue felt hanging on the walls marked an aborted attempt at re-creating the French Tricolor, but if this overheated bunker little resembled a bistro in the City of Light, it was better than my empty room.

I ordered a beer and some nuts. At first I thought the waiter and I were alone. But then through openings in dirty curtains in the rear I noticed a pair of bull-necked toughs drinking vodka with rouged-up whores. Shouts and howls then resounded out on the street and three drunken youths stumbled in, unshaved and dressed in soiled tracksuits. They bumped me as they walked by, and fell into seats by a table in the back. Their loud, hoarse banter soon grew intolerable, and I waved over the waiter so I could pay up and leave.

A minute later one of the youths staggered over and deposited himself in the seat next to me.

"I've been drunk for three days," he said in slurred Russian. "Congratulate me!"

"Congratulations."

He extended his hand for a shake; it was sticky, all sinews.

"Any particular reason?" I asked.

"Of course. We're celebrating the birth of my first child, a daughter. I'll be drunk for as long as I can, and my family has to pay for it. Those are my brothers over there. They have to keep treating me. I've passed out ten times already. I stop only when she comes out of the hospital. Then we have to name the baby. I've got to be sober for that. Of course then we get drunk to celebrate the naming." He belched. "Are you old?"

"I don't think so."

"I'm twenty-four. It's my first baby. Say, don't think I've seen you around here."

"You know everybody in Kazarman?"

"Yeah, I drive the village taxi. My family raises grain here, like most of people."

"What about gold mining, you jerk!" shouted a crude inebriated voice from behind the curtains. Shrieking giggles followed.

"God," he said, unperturbed, "I can't wait to see my child. I love her already." He belched beer and bilious gases, and his head drooped.

His friends came over, slapped him awake, and sat down. They raised their beers and toasted to children, and I joined them. We tried to talk, but we had almost nothing to say, so I suggested various toasts, to parents, to peace, to children again.

After gulping down their beers, they stood up and shook my hand. "Gotta keep getting drunk," they said.

They stumbled out into the moonlight and were gone. The whores shrieked with laughter; a moth circled the bulb. I paid and left for the guesthouse.

THE NEXT MORNING a dented khaki Uazik jeep, piloted by Joken, a hulking Kyrgyz who spoke a strange, tweep-tweepy Russian that befit his cheery disposition, drove me from Kazarman out of the desert and into burnt sienna valleys in places velvety with grass, over Sarykyr Pass and down to Jalalabad, in the fertile lap of the Fergana Valley. This took us six hours. The map told me the distance was sixty miles, but with all the hairpin turns, mountainface meanderings, and sudden dips, it might have been twice that.

Historically, the cultural distance from the pastoral Kyrgyz highlands to the settled Uzbek Fergana was as vast as the differences in landscapes, mostly because the mountains held little of interest to the invaders who brought Central Asia much in the way of both destruction and enlightenment; and *jailoo* Kyrgyz saw little they wanted in the lowlands. The

Arabs introduced Islam to the valley in the eighth century; the Mongols invaded in the thirteenth; and Timur rampaged through a hundred years later. The Russians annexed the Fergana in 1876, and their presence inflamed Muslim fundamentalist sentiment. Much was at stake: the Fergana's soil is rich and loamy, watered by the Syr Darya, and yields abundant crops of cotton and silk, fruit and sunflowers. Stalin knew its large, devoutly Islamic population would not take easily to Soviet rule, so he divided the valley among Tajikistan, Kyrgyzstan, and Uzbekistan. This created tensions that have erupted into massacres. In general, Fergana Uzbeks, with their ancient Islamic civilization, tend to look down on the Kyrgyz as bumpkin nomads.

We rolled down out of the cool mountains and trundled onto hot, sun-washed valley farmland, gold and green with crops and grass, swerving to avoid sunflower seeds that scarf-donning Uzbek girls had spread to dry on the highway. Joken dropped me off at Jalalabad's road station, politely refusing to take me the last seventy-five miles to Osh. He feared that his license plates (which announced his distinctly mountain, and thus Kyrgyz, origins) might rouse the ire of Uzbek *gaishniki* along the way, and he lacked the cash to bribe his way out of trouble.

So, I hired a taxi to get me to Osh. For the first time I rued a well-maintained, four-lane thoroughfare. Its endless smooth stretches incited my driver to speed maniacally, to pound his crazy-tune horn and overtake, dodging donkey carts and playing chicken with friends. Vendors crowded the shoulders, and numerous times our journey almost finished in an explosion of mangled steel, human flesh, and melon pulp.

But soon we slowed for crowds of people, carts, and livestock. Huts and hovels and minarets jumbled together in a way that suggested Damascus again: Osh, population 220,000, home to Uzbeks, Kyrgyz, and Tajiks, a stopover on the Silk Road, one of the most ancient cities of Central Asia, and, as locals like to say, older than Rome.

OLDER THAN ROME it may be, but Osh struck me as a hot, flat city of neighborhoods painfully postdating the 1917 revolution. In 2001 I had stayed at the Soviet-style Hotel Osh, so I decided to lodge there again. The receptionist, a woman with a tanklike build and tired but friendly eyes, plus the usual Central Asian complement of gold teeth, welcomed me in a matronly way.

"Eat in our restaurant, use our Internet café, change money at our hard-currency bureau. You're almost our only guest. We're at your service, young man."

But in the restaurant I found only a sullen guard and a surly bartender, both of whom sneered when I asked for a menu. "Go to the fifth-floor café and eat there," they said. The café was locked. "The café guy is in the downstairs shop," said the floor lady. The shop was closed. I tried my luck at the Internet café, but all four computers were on the blink. The currency exchange office was boarded up, as though it hadn't opened in years.

I returned to the receptionist. "Look, does anything in this place work?"

"Everything works. But since we have no guests, most of the employees are off doing their own things. You'll have to track them down. If you must eat now, try the café on the corner."

The café held a scattering of stained plastic tables and chairs arranged under bland peeling posters showing turquoise lakes and pine forests that might have been anywhere on earth but around Osh. Standing behind the bar was a middle-aged man in horn-rimmed glasses, who, with his almost European face and shock of high dark hair, looked more Turkish than Kyrgyz.

"Vodka, beer, borsht, potatoes," he said when I asked for a menu. "Oh, and I do have cognac. The finest around. Straight from France. I recommend it."

I ordered potatoes and a shot of cognac.

He dished potatoes onto a plate (they rolled around like billiard balls, suspiciously dry) but grabbed the cognac bottle and gave it a frown. "Well, ah, I don't have an opener. I can't open it."

"Then I'll just have some mineral water."

"No mineral water here. I'm sorry." He lowered his eyes, as if ashamed. His contrition calmed my urge to complain.

"Then, please, I'll just eat my potatoes."

I bit into one. It tasted like a gob of sodden papier-mâché, and sucked all of the saliva from my mouth. I chewed and chewed, coughed, and swallowed a mouthful before giving up.

A mean-eyed Kyrgyz woman stomped out of the back room and tossed a bottle opener on the counter. She stomped on out the front door.

He pulled the bottle off the shelf again. "France's finest. Still interested?" The price: 240 som a bottle, or about five dollars.

"That's the price for a whole bottle?"

"It's too expensive, isn't it? On the other hand, look at the label!"

MADE IN MARSEILLE AT THE REQUEST OF ASTANA, read a line in Russian under the brand name.

"Oh," I said, "it's that famously fine French-Kazakh five-dollar cognac."

"Something wrong with that?"

"No, no, pour me a shot."

He did. I put the glass to my mouth, and its benzene bouquet burnt my eyes. I took a sip, blinking, but it was so foul that I spat it back into the glass.

"Something wrong?" he asked.

Wrong? I looked at my papier-mâché potatoes and wiped the cognac tears from my eyes, suppressing another urge to spit. All at once I felt a surge of peevish anger. *Osh is older than Rome, but in all the thousands of years since then, you haven't learned to run a café or cook a potato and nothing works in the hotel here!* I thought.

"Look!" I said. "You serve—"

His cell phone buzzed. He turned away to answer it and began speaking Uzbek, which so resembled Turkish that at times I could understand it. His voice broke. The conversation aggrieved him, and involved something about a hundred dollars and a passport and his son.

He hung up and set down the phone. He put his head between his hands.

"What's wrong?" I asked.

"Oh, oh, God. It's just too much to bear. I gave a relative a hundred dollars so he could bribe an official and get a passport to go get my son in Russia. He paid the bribe, but now at the border they told him the passport is an obvious fake. I've been swindled by a swindler. I'm a pensioner and so a hundred dollars is a lot of money for me. Or it is now. I lost all my savings. You see, my son, my son"—his voice broke again—"he took all my retirement savings and gambled them away in slot machines. He kept coming to me and asking for money, and I didn't know why. Those machines are all over the city, but no one told us how dangerous they could be. I told him he couldn't win, but he wouldn't listen. He lost every cent I had. So I've had to come work here."

"Oh, oh, I'm sorry," I said. He sounded educated, and I imagined his humiliation at having to work in this rotten café at his age.

"That's not really the worst of it," he said. "My son, my son . . . he got into drugs. Gambling and drugs. I had to keep giving him money, didn't I? He *is* my son, after all, and he was begging me. Finally I got him into rehab. He spent a year in the clinic and then left for Saint Petersburg to work. But I think he's gone on drugs and is gambling again. It's been five days since I've been able to reach him. Five days. Tomorrow is my sixtieth birthday, and I should be celebrating my retirement. But it will mean nothing if I can't reach my son."

His eyes teared up. I looked down and began chewing the cardboard blobs. The man was, after all, no automaton—he was a human being in miserable straits, and he deserved sympathy. If nothing else, I didn't want to make his day worse by complaining.

The door swung open and banged against the wall. In sauntered a low-browed thug with a crewcut, in tight-fitting trousers and pointy black shoes, with, on his fat arm, a sloppy-busted, potbellied Kyrgyz woman whose mascara-smeared eyes and ill-painted lips could only be those of a hooker.

"A police officer and his girl," whispered the bartender. He hustled to serve them. But they ordered nothing from his meager offerings and walked back out. "She's a hooker," he said, having for the moment forgotten about his travails. "The manager's a bitch and only lets her in."

No doubt she was a "bitch" for keeping out other working girls, thereby depriving him of a cut in their earnings.

I paid for my meal and walked back to my hotel.

THE NEXT TORRID MORNING, from a walkway on the stony northern slope of Suleyman Mountain, I shielded my eyes and squinted down into the glare over Osh's flat daedal warrens, which were bisected by the silty currents of the Ak Buura River and marked by needle-like minarets. From the city's edge, golden fields spread over the valley to meld, afar, with the heat-hazed sky. Recognized popularly as Kyrgyzstan's Capital of the South, Osh may be three millennia old, or it may be older. Zoroastrians worshiped here, and Buddhism was once the dominant religion. Its name may derive from *kosh* (said to mean "Clear the way!" a command merchants shouted to traders arriving on the Silk Road) or possibly from a tribe called Osh, or from neither. Reliable information about the city was scant. Certainly, though, Osh lay on historic invasion routes, which assured it of a diversity of plunderers.

My guide was Samaara, a Kyrgyz schoolteacher with love handles, short bouncy hair, and an endearing smile. She took pride in Osh and was certain of its exalted planetary stature.

"There's no other city on earth with a mountain in its center," she said as we walked along the path.

"Oh?" I replied. "Urfa, in Turkey, has a hill called Nimrod's Throne where Ibrahim [Abraham in Islam] was supposedly born."

"But we're taught Osh is unique and is the only city in the world with a mountain. Suleyman's Throne is our pride and joy."

"Okay, okay."

"Suleyman came here to pray."

"Which Suleyman was that?"

"The prophet. Don't you know him?"

I was certain that Suleyman, or Solomon (the tenth-century B.C. king of Israel), had never come anywhere near Osh.

"Yes, I know him. But—"

"He prayed in Tamchy Tamar Cave, where we're going now. It's Islam's second Mecca."

It is not: the second-holiest place in Islam is the Dome of the Rock, in Jerusalem. Oshians had also told me that the Prophet Muhammad had prayed in the cave, but this was clearly untrue, for he never left the Middle East.

Outside Tamchy Tamar Cave we found the caretaker, Alisher, a bearded Uzbek, long-faced and bony, of fifty or so, coiffed in a frayed *tyubeteyka*. He was busy with three young Kyrgyz guys, who were sitting in front of him on rock bench, their hands cupped and their lips moving in silent, aggrieved supplication, as he, in his soft voice, recited verses from Ya Sin, a sura in the Qur'an. When he finished they wiped their faces, got up mournfully, and filed away down the path. He turned to us.

"*As-salam alaykum!* Follow me."

We ducked into the cave. In the close hot gloom, on various black rock shelves, Alisher was burning sticks of *archy*, a sort of incense. His Uzbek accent lengthened his vowels and hollowed out his *g*'s and *k*'s. He pointed with a flourish to indents on the stone floor.

"This one is Suleyman's left footprint, that one there is from his right knee. You see, he bent down and prayed just like this." His knee and foot fit clearly into the depressions. "And here is his book, the Zabur."

"The Zabur?" I had never heard of it. But the "book" was just a quadrangle of dictionary-size rock. "It looks like a rock to me," I said.

"It is. God turned it to stone."

"What's all this hair doing here?" I asked, pointing to curly clippings on the ground.

"That's children's hair, from kids born from couples whose infertility this cave has cured. We ask the parents to cut the child's first hair and bring it to us."

A tunnel about two feet high and wide led some fifteen feet into the mountain, and at its end, candles burned, creating the effect of a shrine. Alisher gestured toward me.

"Crawl in."

"Why?"

"It's the same as performing half the hajj."

"I'm not Muslim."

"Half a hajj is better than none. Half a hajj will never hurt anyone. Please!"

"Oh, okay."

I crawled, or rather, slinked in, caterpillaring my way over the warm, slick stone, my pores claustrophobically gushing sweat, my head dizzying from the thickening smoke. I reached the end, took note of the flames and dripping tallow, waited a respectable few seconds so as to obviate exhortations to pray, and then slinked out backwards, soaking in perspiration.

"Congratulations!" both said.

Alisher led us back to the cave's mouth. I tipped him and we left him to deal with a new contingent of the aggrieved and childless.

We walked down the next stretch of path. "You believe all that?" I asked Samaara. "I thought Kyrgyz weren't so religious?"

"Well, we accepted Islam only in the fourteenth century, and we blended it with our nomadic customs. We love our freedom too much to be strict about religion. We even fear the Bearded Ones"—the fundamentalists. "It's really the Uzbeks who're so religious. And to think, Uzbeks aren't even a people. They're just a bunch of tribes. The Uzbeks will tell you Genghis Khan was one of them, Timur was one of them, and so on. But in fact we were all just one Turkic people until the Soviets decided to split us up."

We came across middle-aged men, corpulent villagers squatting on the path and selling blue beads — *köz monchuks,* charms against the Evil Eye. After deriding superstition, Samaara told me that she had in fact taken her daughter to *Bakhshy,* Black Shamans, to cure her of "inexplicable fears," and hung a *köz monchuk* on her neck. Here, even among schoolteachers, superstitions were strong, and with so few other resources available, people acted on them, hoping for the best.

We eventually reached Babur's House, a small and plain brick shrine clinging to a ledge on the mount's eastern end. In 1497 the Fergana-born local ruler Muhammad Zahiruddin Babur, descendant of both Genghis Khan and Timur, erected a tiny mosque here before leading campaigns south to conquer much of India. The current shrine is a restoration; the original collapsed in an earthquake centuries ago.

Babur stepped onto the Central Asian scene when the national identities dominating the region today didn't exist. He was born in 1483. His tribe belonged to the Mongols, but its members adopted Islam, and were, at least linguistically, Turkic. By the age of seventeen he had seized Samarkand; he then crossed the Pamir and took Kabul. In 1519 he stormed into the Punjab and seven years later invaded Delhi, becoming the founder of the Mughals (the word is a corruption of *Mongols*), the Islamic dynasty that would rule northern and central India until it was deposed by the British in 1857. The language of Babur's court was Persian — then the lingua franca of the region's Muslims. Several ethnic groups lay claim to Babur's legacy, and each has some justification.

"Babur would come here to read, write, and reflect," said Samaara. Colorfully robed Uzbek families had gathered around outside, chomping on *kurut* and chatting. They of course claimed him as their own.

We ended up lunching at the edge of the grand Jayma Bazaar, Central Asia's largest market, in an Uzbek hole-in-the-wall serving hot pilaf and lamb, to which I added spoonfuls of *lazy* (from *la zi,* Chinese for "chili pepper") — my first culinary harbinger of the All-Under-Heaven. Running the place were Uzbek women. Their features were almost European; their eyes were deep, dark, melancholy, and almond-shaped; their robes and scarves red and black, flowing voluminously. They spoke to Samaara in Uzbek and she responded in Kyrgyz; no one seemed to mind. Samaara herself ordered *laghman,* yard-long noodles favored by the Uygur, Xinjiang's Turkic people — another herald of the Middle Kingdom's proximity.

Of the Uzbeks she had nothing else particularly bad to say. Over Jayma Bazaar's ceaseless din we talked about the recent killings in Uzbekistan, which occurred in May of 2005, just across the border in Andijan. Hundreds of men, women, and children protesting corruption fell to the machine guns of government troops. The Andijan massacre resulted in a big setback for the United States in the new Great Game: President Bush's criticism of the bloodshed prompted the Uzbek president (and one of Central Asia's worst dictators) Islam Karimov to close U.S. bases in his country and join the Shanghai Cooperation Organization.

She found nothing much to criticize there, and even complimented the blood-soaked Karimov. "He knows his people are arrogant and would rise up if they didn't have an iron-fisted ruler. So he gives them the iron fist. Each ruler knows his people best. We admire Karimov here." For the Russians she harbored only respect. "They got us out of the mountains and into the schools. The revolution of 1917 did a lot for us by giving us education. We have no bad feelings toward the Russians."

We washed our spicy feast down with fresh apple juice. Sated, we set out into the bazaar's mazelike lanes, orienting ourselves by the sun. Stalls overflowed with gaudy Uzbek and Kyrgyz clothing and traditional paraphernalia still widely worn and used: *chepken* felt robes; *köshögö* curtains behind which to hide stolen brides; Kyrgyz string instruments called *komos;* embroidered knickknacks called *jazdiks* and *töshöks.*

"We used to make all these things ourselves, for our families, but nowadays specialists produce them," Samaara said.

Through the crowd glaucoma-eyed beggars led by teenage boys circulated, chanting, their bowls rattling with coins and outstretched for more; blacksmiths clanked away in shadowy smithies; peddlers squatting under umbrellas hawked walnuts ("We gave them to Alexander the Great," said Samaara), apricots, berries, dried tomatoes, raisins, peppers, melons and pumpkins, and *vizhdenan* and *patyrnan* breads—a toothsome cornucopia contrasting in every way with the insipid fare of Kyrgyz nomads. Jayma Bazaar, in short, sheltered all the immemorial bedlam of Central Asia, with only a dash of Soviet modernity visible in the corrugated roofs of the stalls, the Cyrillic alphabet used to write the Turkic languages.

Finally we ended up in the center at the Alymbek Datka Museum—a three-story yurt hung with realist paintings and nomadic tack related to grassland life and horse herding. Like the Manas theme park in Bishkek, the museum seemed to have been assembled to create a much-needed national hero. But Samaara told me that Alymbek Datka had really lived and was much admired.

"Datka founded our state and united the Kyrgyz tribes. We *elected* him leader—we had democracy, even then. The tsar executed him in 1867, in the shadow of Suleyman Mountain, for killing a Russian officer who had offended a Kyrgyz maiden by cutting off her tresses. Datka's wife, Kurmanzhan, became our leader. She wisely knew we couldn't fight the Russians, so she united us with them. Since then, we've stuck with the Russians."

IN 1990 RIOTS BROKE OUT between Uzbeks and Kyrgyz in Özgön, thirty-five miles northeast of Osh (to which they spread), and hundreds died. No cause has ever been officially established. The Özgön massacre numbers among the many savage instances of bloodshed in the former Soviet sphere that left behind a multitude of bereaved without hope of justice.

Samaara and I reached Özgön in a taxi we hired for the day. Our driver was a Russian named Igor, a retired Soviet military officer in his forties who, trim, healthy, and sociable, seemed content with himself and his life in Osh. Neither he nor Samaara had any reservations about visiting this town so famed for slaughter; animosities had long since faded away.

In search of a rice-processing plant that Samaara wanted to show me, Igor drove slowly down off the main road and into the town's circuitous, sandy back alleys. All at once we were in village Uzbekistan. Uzbek mom-and-pop shack shops stood by *aryks,* irrigation canals a yard or two wide that burbled like cool mountain streams. Vine-laced trellises covered the walls of whitewashed houses set amid half-acre plots shaded by blossoming fruit trees. Jumbo melons ripened in kitchen gardens.

We drove round and round, but the rice plant eluded us. Igor slowed to ask directions from an Uzbek strolling along in, of all things, a black pinstriped jacket and pleated trousers—attire that set him apart from all the farmers in sweatsuits. He looked to be in his midthirties and was clearly doing well by local standards.

"I'm going there myself," he said. "If you give me a ride I'll show you."

"Hop in," we said.

The mill, as it happened, was closed for the day, but Nursaid, as he introduced himself, would not let his "guests" leave Özgön unfêted; he invited us home for a traditional Uzbek feast of pilaf. We told him that he had certainly done enough for us already.

"No, no! It's my honor!"

Blossoms red, yellow, white, and blue showered down from vines and trees overgrowing his whitewashed house, which stood on a plot of grassy loam by an *aryk*. A profusion of roses, tulips, and chrysanthemums grew in front of his porch, giving his small estate a Bahaman air.

"I told my wife, 'First we plant the flowers, *then* the crops!'" Nursaid announced as we stepped onto the porch. "Tian Shan glaciers water my garden. Look how cool and clear our *aryk* is!"

We entered his living room, a cool chamber strewn with plump *tüshük* cushions and plush red carpets. High windows let in flower-scented air and leafy-green light bouncing off the foliage. We took off our shoes and reclined around a low table. A woman entered, smiling, an Uzbek beauty, barefoot, black-eyed, and slender, dressed in traditional red and black robes and a (non-Islamic) headscarf.

"This is my wife," Nursaid said. He did not tell us her name, and custom dictated that no one shake her hand, but even introducing her to male guests was progressive in an Islamic country. "We grew up and studied together to be teachers, so it was natural for us to marry."

Nursaid was a schoolteacher. He earned about a thousand som (forty dollars) a month—too little to support a family on, so he spent part of the year in Russia doing manual labor in Samarra, on the Volga. There he made two thousand dollars a month for four or five months at a time.

"Thank God for the Russians!" he exclaimed. "My work up there gives me enough to live on all year, and in style, down here in the Fergana. I'm not saying life up there's easy. The police see a *chorny* [black] guy like me and they rob me. But all in all, the money's great in Russia, and that's what counts."

"You don't want to just move there?" I asked.

"No way. There's nothing like the homeland. I love my village. I won't even build a gate here. We have no thieves."

"Özgön does seem peaceful," I said.

"It is now. But my brother died in the massacre of 1990. You know, we think it was the Soviet bosses who started it all, probably to have an excuse to seize land. They got a drunken Kyrgyz to kill one of us, and we had to respond."

When he stepped out to ask his wife to prepare our meal, Samaara whispered that the Uzbeks had shed the first blood by "decapitating a Kyrgyz girl and putting her head on a stake by the road into town. Really, that's how it began!"

I nodded and let the subject drop.

Nursaid's ten-year-old daughter, Rakhatay (Tranquil-Moon, in Turkic), limped to the door, smiling bashfully. She slipped off her shoes at the entrance and spread a gold and blue cloth on the table. She and her father then laid out warm disks of *nan* bread, strawberry cookies, sesame crackers, and homemade jam. He poured us all green tea.

"She got scared really bad once and so became a cripple," Nursaid said, looking at Rakhatay. (Polio, I thought, had more likely withered her leg.) "Ah, wait one second." He trotted out and reappeared with a bottle and shot glasses. "I offer you vodka. We're becoming more and more Islamic down here, and drinking less of this stuff. But we must toast to our meeting!"

In the next room his wife flicked on an ancient black-and-white television. An Uzbek songstress was performing a melodious *türkü*, a plangent tune filled with anguish and unrequited love; as she sang her hands described flowery oriental movements and her eyes batted languidly.

"Oh, I *love* their songs," said Samaara in a hushed voice, as moved as I was.

She and Nursaid, I noticed, spoke their own languages and understood each other just fine; Uzbek and Kyrgyz were mutually intelligible. (I myself could understand only a little Kyrgyz, though.)

"We have no time or energy for that old enmity now," said Nursaid when I commented on how interesting it was that Kyrgyz and Uzbeks could understand one another. "Everyone has to feed his family. And no matter what people say, there *is* work in Kyrgyzstan, if you look for it. Here, the people are rich and the state is poor, just the opposite of Uzbekistan. We can always get by. We're free and happy here."

The *aryk* burbled, bees buzzed over the blossoms, the scent of pilaf wafted in from the outdoor kitchen, the *türkü* drifted through the warm air. We all leaned back, and our eyes rested on the verdure outside the windows. In Özgön, once infamous for slaughter, a languor stole over us, and we almost drifted off to sleep.

An hour later his wife brought us a huge silver tray piled with brown pilaf laced with chunks of lamb and peppers and squash. She smiled and retreated. Rakhatay crawled from around the corner and snuggled under her father's arm. He urged us to eat.

We dug in to our succulent feast.

Had I seen Nursaid in Moscow, we probably would have never spoken. This gentle, friendly fellow would have been one of numberless migrants doing despised labor all over town, subject to skinhead attacks and police extortion. Yet here, in his home, I was his honored guest, and he comported himself with grace and magnanimity—civilization in excelsis.

19

Again the mountains changed their aspect. The warm, earthy siennas of the Tian Shan gave way to the cold, leaden hues of the Pamir. A couple of days after visiting Özgön, Igor and I had left Osh's southernmost warrens and were ascending a gorge toward tufted cotton clouds reposing on a band of powder blue afternoon sky—the first stage in our 250-mile trip to the border post with the All-Under-Heaven, at the Irkeshtam crossing, deep in the Pamirs. Steering around potholes, he slowed the jeep for herds of livestock flooding onto the tarmac from the slopes.

"Damn, these sheep will hold us up! They're already moving their animals down from the mountains! Summer's really ending."

Sheep and then cattle crowded in on us, all chased by husky slavering dogs that trotted about, nipping laggards back into formation. Herders on horseback rode into view, young men in *ak kalpaks,* with sun-wizened eyes and windburned cheeks, faces aged well beyond their years. I thought to ask why, with all this space around, they chose to drive their herds on the highway, but the answer was obvious: it was easy. Igor had warned me that the journey to the Chinese border would take at least ten or eleven hours and require an overnight stop somewhere near the village of Sary Tash. We had left Osh around noon.

The Pamirs rose around us, lonely and treeless, breaking into chasms that darkened as the sun sank. The herds disappeared, but we banged along on the deteriorating road, still unable to achieve a decent speed.

"Moscow used to consider this highway strategically vital, and you wouldn't find a pothole on it from Osh to Khorog"—450 miles to the south, in Tajikistan. "But now look at it." We swerved hard to avoid a crater. "Say, you know the joke about Kyrgyz and Kazakhs and the roads? A Kyrgyz and a Kazakh road builder meet. The Kazakh, shocked by the mansion the Kyrgyz has, says, 'I don't get it. I earn my money like you do, by cheating, by making the road smaller than I'm supposed to, and pocketing the difference. But I can't afford such a palace. How can you?' The Kyrgyz says, 'Have you seen our roads?' 'No,' the Kazakh says. The Kyrgyz smiles. 'Well, there you have it.'"

DANGER! LANDSLIDES! shouted signs wobbling in dusty gusts. Earthquakes had scarred the valley. Slopes ended in slag, boulders stood alone in improbable places, as if tossed from the heavens by angry gods. The sun slipped behind the ridges, leaving us motoring higher and higher beneath a vaulting violet sky. The sense of solitude deepened around us, the wind turned cold, and I pulled my jacket tighter.

At six we reached an altitude of 8,500 feet, with lifeless Pamir peaks rising around us to eighteen thousand feet, craggy memorials to Cambrian eons of flowing lava and tectonic turmoil. Just off the road we spotted a railway-car trailer home sitting by a stream on cinderblocks beneath silver-leaved willows. We pulled in there behind two old Soviet trucks.

"The owner of this little truckers' stop is a friend of mine," said Igor. "I'll introduce you. We'll be safe passing the night here."

We got out. Immediately a wild-haired Russian stumbled out of the trailer, shouting drunken greetings and slurred verbiage about vodka and beer and opening his arms as if to embrace us. He staggered over, grabbed my hand, and shook it. His palm was sticky and he wouldn't let go. He leaned smiling into my face and his breath stank of vodka.

Igor gently disengaged him. "Jeff, meet the owner!"

The owner then hugged Igor, who invited him to do some fishing.

"There's nothing to do out here but fish and booze," Igor whispered to me as he pulled his friend toward the trailer to pick up some tackle. "Just set yourself up in that yurt over there. You'll have it to yourself, as truckers spend the nights in their cabins and I'll be sleeping in the jeep."

I checked out the yurt. In it a dozen *shyrdaks* and a pile of stained cushions would assure me of, if nothing else, a warm night's sleep. I unrolled a couple and lay down and tried to rest. But darkness thickened, the cold bit my skin, the stream burbled away forlornly outside, and I felt lonely. I could never fall asleep so early, so I walked over to the trailer, now a phantom-like pale box in the gloom, with amber-lit windows.

I peeked inside. A mustachioed man, overweight and swarthy, with a sad cast to his brown eyes, was sitting on a shabby low couch watching a Hollywood horror video involving lesbian lovers who turned into beetles and gobbled each other up. Across from him, over a table spread with sausage, cheese slices, and a half-empty bottle of vodka, was an old Russian, his spider-veined face wrinkled like parchment. They were the drivers of the trucks outside.

"Well, come on in and watch the show," the Russian said resignedly.

The noble fellow, an Uzbek, it turned out, pulled up a stool and patted it, smiling at me. I sat down.

"Naley! Davay-ka naley!" (Pour us a drink! Come on, pour us one!), commanded the Russian in a too-loud voice. "That damned dog out there knocked over three of my vodka bottles and broke 'em all!"

The Uzbek obliged him. He set a shot glass in front of me and filled it too. "You from?"

I explained who I was and where I was going.

"Well, we can all sit here and drink together," he said, "a Russian, an Uzbek, and an American, and no hard feelings and no arguments, because we're all brothers. Let's drink to that."

We did. The vodka warmed my throat.

The Russian leaned back and raised his glass.

"I propose we drink to the time when the Russians took care of everyone, when the government threw criminals in jail, when all of us lived in plenty, knowing we'd get the next paycheck, when we had not a care in the world!"

"Hear, hear!" said the Uzbek. "Those were the days! The Soviet Union was a wonderful country."

"It *was* wonderful," said the Russian to himself quietly. He shook his head, looking down. "A *wonderful* country."

We knocked back more vodka. Their nostalgia well jibed with my loneliness, and I was happy to sit with them.

The door swung open, letting in the cold and the sound of the stream, a glimpse of stars glinting above high black ridges. A slender girl with a messy mane of golden hair walked in, holding a puppy in the folds of her moth-eaten sweater. His inquisitive eyes took in the food and all of us, but mostly the food. Smiling to the puppy, she plopped herself down on the couch, caressing him. Her unkempt clothes and hair had an after-sex sloppiness, her hazel eyes an air of debauched fatigue. We all three, in our own ways, seemed lost.

The film was now all blood and screams. It had been dubbed in the usual post-Soviet way, with voices shouting Russian over the English.

"I like *Soviet* movies," said the old Russian. "You know, the ones about love and friendship and honor. All this Hollywood violence and sex and these stupid plots . . . It's like they make movies for idiots. You'd think Americans would be a developed people, with all the money they have. But in fact, look at them. They're all fat, and judging by their films, they're stupid too. No offense," he said to me, "but we're sick of Hollywood films."

"No offense taken," I said. "But I don't think you should generalize."

"Well, you did right to marry a Russian. Let's drink to the most beautiful and caring and decent women in the world, the Russians!"

We drank.

The girl slipped *Pirates of the Caribbean* into the VCR.

"Oh, now this is *one* American movie I love!" the Russian declared. Suppressing a belch, he turned to me, his head wobbling, his eyes gooey. "You seem like a good guy, a real *muzhik*. I'll give you my address and next year you come and visit me in Osh, okay? You can stay with me. I'll treat you for whatever ails you: impotence, backache, headaches, whatever. I know the best healers Osh has. I go to 'em all the time."

"Sure," I said. It was easiest just to agree. I proposed a toast to him, and we all drank.

How much time had passed since the days when I would not have touched vodka for anything! When I first moved to Moscow, I resisted the Russian fête and I felt uncomfortable around drunks. But eventually I surrendered—it was easier to say yes than no. Still, this sloggered old fellow nattering on about impotence and backaches, even the haggard beauty with the puppy, seemed a manifestation of something corrupt, something that *should* be foreign to me. I felt like returning to childhood. How different would my life have been had I spent the last thirteen years back in the States? I couldn't fathom the answer. The country I grew up in—the America of the 1960s and 1970s—no longer existed, and so many in my family had died. My America was more a time in my life than a place.

The owner, still sloshed, and Igor, who was sober, returned, clattering with their tackle through the door and arguing over the species of their catch, a perchlike fish the size of a wallet.

"You will now drink with me!" the owner said to me, pulling up a stool and falling onto it.

"Okay," I said.

He poured me a shot.

"Just one second. I need to use the outhouse."

"Ah, it's around that way," he said, examining the vodka.

I slipped out.

I would not return. In my yurt I found a fat drunken Kyrgyz trucker snoring raucously, filling the close air with the reek of vodka and his salted-fish lunch.

I grabbed a few *shyrdaks* and stole off to a grassy spot by the stream. I spread them out and climbed in. My eyes slowly adjusted to the dark. The moon's pallor bathed the crags, transforming them into lumps of sugar. The Milky Way washed glittering across the deep black sky. The Milky Way and the cosmos, the eternal voids before and after birth, consoled me. All would pass, including this journey, including my life and whatever pleasure and pain I had known, whatever regrets I had nurtured. There was no reason to fret, every cause to enjoy what I could, while I could, here and now.

I AWOKE to a cold blue-green sky and frosted grass. The sun was still well below the mountaintops. Magpies flapped and cried out from the willows, hidden in the dark. Igor was already up and about. I tossed the *shyrdaks* back into the yurt and jumped aboard the jeep.

Saying nothing, we drove back out onto the road, following switchbacks up into the gray-green Pamirs. With the rising sun came a wind that kicked up dust squalls and gave the scene a wild, dangerous feel.

"Look," Igor said, "I recommend you drink a shot of vodka up at the next café."

"What? At this hour?"

"If you don't, the altitude at Taldyk Pass, which is nineteen switchbacks away, will get to you. Your blood pressure can go haywire without it."

It was pointless arguing with Russians against the curative powers of vodka, but I had no desire to drink, so I took a different approach. "How high is the pass?"

"About twelve thousand feet."

"I've been higher. The Khunjerab Pass is higher than fifteen thousand feet and I had no problems."

"Well, suit yourself."

We nevertheless pulled in to a shack café. He jumped down, and, fording blasts of blowing dust, ran inside. I wondered, *Is he going to drink vodka before this cliffhanging ride?* He seemed too smart for that. Nevertheless, I jumped down too and ran in to see, but found him ordering a tiny cup of Turkish coffee. He downed it in a few sips.

"I'm ready," he announced. We climbed aboard and drove on up the mountain.

As passes go, Taldyk was nothing special. A few hours later we rolled onto a green valley bordered in the south by snowbound peaks. About halfway to them stood a pair of radar dishes, giant and decrepit.

"What are those for?" I asked.

"Beneath them are bunkers with antiaircraft missiles. The Soviets never let any foreigners near here. Somewhere around here there were ICBMs too." We were nearing the former Soviet-Chinese border, once one of the most militarized zones on earth, now the domain of cattle and yaks.

The gravel gave way to a dirt track that wound higher and higher along the edges of cliffs, the valley green and vast below. Trucks—filthy, beat-up steel monsters manned by Kyrgyz youths—were barreling down toward us from the Chinese border, at times forcing us to pull over to the edge of the abyss to let them pass. Many times we barely avoided collision, but Igor's hand was steady on the wheel.

NEAR NOON we pounded off the dirt track and rolled onto a smooth two-lane highway.

"The Chinese built this road for Kyrgyzstan," Igor said. "In return, the Kyrgyz have to pay them eighty percent of the customs duties from the border post. In fact, the Chinese will build this road all the way to Osh. It's in their interests, you see, since their exports to Kyrgyzstan travel through here."

The "erudite" President Akayev never thought to build a decent road from one of his country's main cities to the border with the world's rising superpower! Besides soaking up foreign aid, what had Kyrgyzstan's leaders been *doing* since 1991?

Just beneath ragged flinty ridges we came upon trucks backed up for half a mile. We pulled out and drove around them, roaring ahead, until we hit the village of Nura, altitude 9,200 feet—the border post. The wind blew dust over Kyrgyz mamas sloughing about in sandals, hawking samosas and dickering with truckers, over hovels selling tins of fish and bottles of beer and vodka and cheap Chinese sweets. Ages ago, in the Pamirs somewhere around here, Chinese traders bringing goods on camelback from Xi'an sold them to Central Asian middlemen, who took them on down the Silk Road toward Rome.

A quarreling crowd was pushing and shoving at the entrance of a prefab shack: PASSPORT CONTROL. We drove up to it and stopped. My heartbeat quickened: This was it! China was just ahead!

"Well, God be with you," said Igor. "I've got to start heading back. I think you can handle it from here."

He handed me my bag. We shook hands, and, feeling a rush of excitement, I made for the shack.

A half-hour later I was through with customs. I hitched a ride with a Kyrgyz trucker for the five-mile run across a no man's land of cliffs and crevasses, and waited two hours for the Chinese border guards to finish lunch. Finally, up on a stony, arid shelf enclosed by the Pamirs, I presented myself at the gates to the All-Under-Heaven.

The post was actually a military base made up of spiffy white buildings emblazoned with giant blue Chinese characters. Beyond it was a red-orange massif topped by snowy peaks—the main ridge of the Tian Shan running from here east along the Taklamakan's northern rim. Chinese troops were drilling nearby, marching up and down under a fluttering red flag, shouting at each turn; other soldiers were jogging in formation.

I walked on past the last trucks to the first vehicle in the queue—a sleek white bus marked with the Arabic lettering for Kashgar. (The Muslim Uygurs write their language in modified Arabic script.) There, white-gloved officers were gruffly ordering the Uygur passengers, mostly heavyset women in hijabs and paunchy men in skullcaps, all with blockier, more European facial features than the Kyrgyz, to form a line and show the contents of their bedraggled bags for inspection. The officers searched each purse and every suitcase, rooting around and pulling things out, barking orders, and patting down the men, who stood before them, hands up, as if under arrest. The women they ignored. It seemed the Chinese had never forgiven the Uygurs for siding with the Russians and the British in the last Great Game.

An officer stopped me and pointed mutely to the back of the bus passenger queue.

"But I'm alone," I said in my halting Chinese, surprised that I remembered the words.

"Ah." He smiled broadly and told me to wait right there.

Another officer finished with the Uygurs and came over to me.

"*Nin de huzhao!*" he commanded in a clipped tone. I showed him my passport. "Ever been to China before?"

"This is my third time."

"Ah, so you're a friend of China! Please, open your bag."

I did. He pulled out the *Dhammapada* (a Buddhist text) and a slim volume of David Hume's essays. "*Xiaoshou na?*" (Small talk?), he asked, meaning novels. Poetry in China is regarded as the highest form of literature, novels as frivolous diversions.

"Small talk."

Nevertheless, he thumbed through them, puzzling over notes I had made in the margins. Another officer walked over and said, "Today is September eleventh!"

I had forgotten. Both gave me a sympathetic look. My inspector handed me my books and told me I'd have to catch a truck to the actual passport control complex, a brand-new blue and white assemblage of steel and glass blocks a mile or two ahead, down a smooth, straight road. This was just a pre-inspection inspection. Fine, I said. We all shook hands and wished one another well, and I set out to find another ride with a Kyrgyz trucker.

TWO HOURS LATER I was in a taxi and shooting down a well-surfaced highway to Kashgar, inhaling fresh desert air, marveling at the Chinese-character road signs (which I, having studied only pinyin, couldn't read), exhilarated beyond all expectation. By the road hunched gnarled tamarisks and crooked thornbushes; beyond, the valley was empty, a tableland of tan stones. The Tian Shan, umber in the late-afternoon light and vertically striated, walled off the north; to the south spread the Kunlun, its desolate gray slopes recalling Tibet.

As darkness fell, pyramidal poplars and looming palms coalesced into a single low black mass ahead—the oasis surrounding Kashgar, 2,500 miles west of Beijing, and one of the remotest outposts of all China.

Marco Polo had visited Kashgar in 1273–74 and found it subsisting on "commerce and manufacture, particularly works of cotton," a city with "handsome gardens, orchards, and vineyards." He did not think much of the local Uygurs, who, he noted, were "of the Mahometan religion," speaking a language "peculiar to themselves," and, all in all, "a covetous, sordid race, eating badly and drinking worse." My own feelings of dread and alienation (how dismally well I remembered my stay here in 1998!) dwindled as we drove into the ethnically Chinese part of town. I hardly recognized it. Everything now was new, steel, lit up, painted, and bustling. Through my rolled-down window I watched Chinese girls gliding by on old-fashioned bicycles; pedestrian crowds, mostly young and Chinese, circulated beneath neon billboards. Here and there glum Uygur men wandered along behind flocks of sheep—the only sign, so far, that we were in Kashgar and not Kunming.

The All-Under-Heaven. I had arrived.

20

Once known in the West as Chinese Turkistan, Xinjiang, or, officially, the Xinjiang Uygur Autonomous Region, comprises China's bleakest, most inhospitable terrain—635,900 square miles of desert, mountain, and grassland so remote and sparsely inhabited that Beijing has tested nuclear weapons there and found in its Siberia-like isolation a prime location for prison camps. Xinjiang is poor and traditionally Muslim, yet beneath its dry soil lie huge coal and oil reserves (largely unexploited); the latter, in the Taklamakan Desert, are estimated to be three times the size of those in the United States. Over the centuries the Chinese government, strapped for resources and land and burdened with an ever-expanding population, has expended no small amount of blood and treasure to solidify its hold on a region over which it began exercising intermittent control some two thousand years ago but which, since its more definitive conquest by Beijing in 1762, has nevertheless ranked as the country's most turbulent province. (Historically "ethnic" China ends at the western limits of the Great Wall, some eleven hundred miles to the east of Kashgar, outside the city of Jiayuguan.) In recent years the state has recognized Xinjiang's backwardness and set about trying to rectify it, launching its "Develop the West" program.

Han Chinese first arrived in Kashgar in the second century B.C., assigning a military governor to oversee the town, and profiting from taxes and duties collected from Silk Road traffic. Official versions of Chinese history proclaim Xinjiang a part of China since then, and many of its cities paid tribute to Beijing, though frequently they fell under the domination of local warlords and suffered invasions. The Yeda Huns seized Kashgar in the sixth century; Genghis Khan tore through it in 1219; and Timur sacked it in 1389–90. The Manchu dynasty took over in 1762, but only designated Xinjiang a province in 1884. However, the Muslim Uygurs (pronounced "weegurs"), resenting infidel control from Beijing, then started favoring the Great Game machinations of Russia and Britain. To recap, the British hoped to secure Xinjiang and thereby protect the approaches to India, their prize colony, from Russia; Russia, whether or not it had designs on India, was expanding throughout Central Asia and saw no reason that Xinjiang should not belong to the tsar as did other Central Asian lands to the west.

When the Qing dynasty collapsed in 1911, Xinjiang broke away from China and slipped into the Russian sphere of influence. Stalin continued the policy of the tsars, and sent in troops in the 1930s. The Uygurs looked to Soviet Russia as a counterweight to Beijing; many hoped that Stalin might annex Xinjiang and save them once and for all from the hated Chinese. In 1955 the Mao-led Communist government (then allied with the Soviets) declared the establishment of the Xinjiang Uygur Autonomous Region, and, soon after the Sino-Soviet split following Stalin's death, kicked the Red Army out. Xinjiang then fell totally, and decisively, into Beijing's orbit.

Xinjiang was once China's "least Chinese" province. When the Communists came to power in 1949, the Uygurs, who had sided with Mao against Chiang Kai-shek's nationalists, outnumbered Han Chinese nine to one. Originally from what today is Mongolia, and professing Buddhism until the ninth or tenth century, when they started adopting Islam, the Uygurs today account for only about nine million of Xinjiang's nineteen million inhabitants. Since 1949 Beijing has striven to sinicize the resource-rich province, sponsoring Han migration and urban infrastructure projects that mostly benefit the Chinese, all the while officially celebrating the multiethnic nature of the People's Republic. As a result, a shadowy, much-persecuted Uygur resistance movement arose, which in the 1990s bombed markets in Kashgar and led riots against Chinese rule, militating for the independence of what its activists call East Turkestan (no political entity by this name has ever existed). Islam has buttressed the desire of many Uygurs for independence, as has the continuing, burgeoning influx of Han Chinese, who bring investment and open businesses but hire almost exclusively other Chinese, and speak no Uygur.

Since 9/11 the plight of the Uygur activists has worsened. Once slammed by Beijing as "separatists," they are now termed "terrorists" and "Islamic extremists" and suffer harsher treatment than ever. Beijing has even followed President Bush's lead and launched "preventive" waves of repression. "We need to take the initiative and go on the offensive, crack down on gangs as soon as they surface and strike the first blow," declared a deputy secretary of Xinjiang's Communist Party in 2004. Thousands of Uygurs have been imprisoned in Xinjiang, which, with its resources, gulags, and disfavored minority population, well deserves the epithet of "China's Siberia."

MY GUIDE TO KASHGAR was a Uygur chemistry student in her early twenties whose nickname was Güzel. "Güzel" means "beautiful" in Turkish, and indeed she was, with a correct arching nose, wavy henna-streaked hair, and dreamy almond eyes. Possessed of a languid air and lyrical voice, she intoned, "Oooh!" on hearing of my journey from Moscow. She had never been anywhere except Kashgar and her parents' village nearby.

On the warm, sunny afternoon the day following my arrival, Güzel and I met outside her university, in central Kashgar. She showed up in a flowery blouse, a knee-length green skirt, and leather sandals, looking bright and fresh among the drab Uygur women trudging by in Islamic scarves and raincoats. She had pinned up her hair, but stray curly locks hung sensuously down around her petite ears.

We would speak English.

"What would you like to show me?" I asked.

"Tow."

"Tow?"

"Tow. If you want we can eat *tow*."

"What's that?"

"You don't know *tow*? Oooh! Come, it is Uygur freshment."

Fording crowds about equally Chinese and Uygur (*How many Chinese are here now, compared to my sojourn in 1998!* I thought), we set off walking toward Id Kah Square, in the heart of the Uygur part of town. Signs proclaimed street names in both Chinese characters and Arabic script; the buildings were lower, older, and shabbier than those in Chinese neighborhoods. We were soon approaching the eponymous fifteenth-century mosque, the call to prayer ringing out from its minarets. Stocky Uygur men were shedding their shoes and filing inside for the afternoon *namaz*.

"Can we go in and take a look?" I asked.

"You look, I wait here," Güzel said.

I found the mosque's placid, poplar-lined courtyard filling with worshipers; it was rather nondescript, as Islamic places of worship go. Under such trees the Uygurs, nevertheless, should have found an ideal sanctuary for prayer, but tourists—Han Chinese tourists—outnumbered them, traipsing about in large, noisy groups, clicking cameras and jabbering. I quickly rejoined Güzel.

"There are so many Han tourists inside," I said, "that they can hardly pray."

She turned away abruptly, as if hiding her face.

We walked on.

In the cafés on Id Kah Square there were no Han at all, only Uygurs, mostly dour and middle-aged, in skullcaps and scarves. In the jaundiced shade of yellow tarps sat the lucky ones; the rest stood, crowded, pressing forward, transfixed by gory Bollywood flicks playing at a deafening volume on old VCRs. Between gun battles and tearful professions of love and dramatic orchestral flourishes, screechy Hindi tunes rent the air. At times viewers erupted into cheers resembling war cries. Yet their faces stayed grim.

We picked a café and found seats. Behind a counter in the middle of the shade was, Güzel pointed out, the *tow* maker, a Turkish-looking lad in a white skullcap that rested on his jug ears. Oblivious to swarms of yellow jackets dancing airborne around him, he was hard at work, hacking slivers of ice into a steel bowl with a screwdriver, ladling in watered-down yogurt, and "tossing" the resulting slop—how high could he make the *tow* go?—before slinging it down the counter to gangly adolescent waiters, who distributed it to customers. Everyone was slurping *tow*, chomping *tow*, gurgling *tow*, and jeering, *tow* spittle flying, at the Bollywood villains getting their bloody comeuppance. Now and again men leaned over, inhaled stertorously and snorted, and hawked snotty gobs of *tow*-laced sputum onto the pavement.

Shouting above the Hindi-and-gunfire din, Güzel ordered *tow*. Our waiter promptly delivered us two bowls, each with its angry buzzing complement of yellow jackets, which dived-bombed toward my *tow* as

I raised the bowl to my mouth. I nervously shooed them away from my eyes and tried to sip again, but as the liquid poured in, yellow jackets landed and tickled my lips. Güzel, however, daintily applied a spoon to her serving. The wasps clustered on her bowl but ignored the spoon, so I used my spoon too, but the concoction painfully froze my teeth.

Güzel looked up at me, a *tow* mustache gracing her upper lip. A wasp landed on her left cheek and she brushed it away.

"How is *tow*? You like?" she shouted over the tinny ruckus of screams and machine gun fire.

"Yes, but it's too cold."

"What?"

On screen the villain, or maybe he was the hero, was now prancing about a Swiss meadow, crooning with open arms to his sari-clad and wobble-headed beloved. The crowd started singing along, in squeals and wavering yelps.

I flicked wasps out of my hair. "You're almost the only woman here," I said, noticing that Güzel was also the only woman on the premises in Western dress.

"Uygur women do not usually go to cafés."

"You ever pray in the mosque over there?"

"Never! *Oooh,* it is against our tradition. Never! Women must pray at home *only.* I am believer in Islam, but in Islam women are lower than men. I would never wear that," she said, pointing to the Uygur version of a burka on a woman passing by. "In Christian church it's good that women and men can pray together. You are Christian, right?"

"Well, no. I don't believe in God. If I'm anything, I'm a Buddhist."

Her dreamy eyes narrowed and she leaned back. "But . . . but *Chinese* are Buddhists."

"So?"

"Well, maybe Buddhism is good for women," she said, relaxing somewhat. "Their women are free. But rude. Chinese are rude."

She spooned down her *tow* and ordered another bowl. On the VCR screen now, evil-bearded bandits were battling a clean-shaven hero, who was trying to rescue a maiden from a flaming subterranean hideout. The soundtrack racket and sing-along were almost intolerably loud, but we kept chatting. She told me that she studied in Chinese, which she hated, but there was no university instruction in Uygur. When she faltered and needed a word in English, she pulled out a pocket computer translator, typed in the pinyin letters of a Chinese syllable, and chose from among the Chinese characters that popped up accompanied by English translations. The intricate characters and her ability to rapidly select the appropriate one amazed me, but she shrugged off my compliments.

"We have to study Chinese starting in third grade, and it takes up so much time. There are no Uygur universities. We study all together, with Chinese. I hate them."

"So I suppose there's no intermarriage."

"What? Me, marry a Chinese! My parents would *kill* me!"

"Literally?"

"They would *disown* me. They are one point three billion; we are eight million. We *must not* marry Chinese."

They are *everywhere,* she said. She would not let me forget this. After *tow,* we headed out for a walk, and she commented on the crowds of passing Han as though griping about sidewalk litter. The Chinese thinned out only when we entered the rugged dun alleys of the Uygur medina, where the scent of sewage seeped from doorways, gap-toothed elders limped about on twisted canes, and donkey carts rattled down trash-strewn lanes—evidence of the poverty China's Develop the West program was supposed to eliminate.

"We see my friend here," she said.

We stopped and knocked on an ancient wooden door crisscrossed with medieval bolts. A middle-aged Uygur woman in a headscarf and robes answered warily, but she smiled effusively when she saw Güzel. She invited us in. We stepped into a home that reminded me of my old house in Marrakech: an arabesque-tiled floor and walls, no windows, a courtyard open to the sky and surrounded by red-carpeted rooms. The tiles, I noticed, were cruder than those in Morocco, and the Uygurs (Güzel excepted) looked far less comely than Marrakshis, with heavy bones, thick brows, and a grumpy cast to their brown eyes.

Güzel and her friend finished talking and we returned to our stroll.

"You like that kind of traditional house?" I asked.

"I like . . . I like Uygur traditional house." She paused. "Well, no, I don't like. Kashgar is so poor, so poor. I've never been anywhere but my village and here. But I know these are poor houses."

"What are these plaques over the doorways?" I asked, pointing to metal plates with Chinese characters.

She rolled her eyes. "Oh, the government awards them to households that obey the law. A blue plaque says 'House Is Poor and Getting Aid'; a red plaque means 'House Is Clean.' There are five plaques. If you get all five, the government gives you an award."

"Which is what?"

"The Five Plaque Award plaque to add to your plaques." She smirked. "Your government gives you plaques in America?"

"No. I doubt anyone would care if it did."

"Because Bush is bad?"

"No, not because of that. You think he's bad?"

"Bush loves war," she said resolutely. "The American people are good, but Bush, Bush, well, Bush, he, that Bush . . ." Words failed her, her pretty brow furrowed, and she averted her face.

"I know, I know."

She turned back to me, her eyes widening. "I *love* the Russians. Uygurs *love* the Russian government."

"That's not something one hears often," I said. She expounded on the wonderful pre-Mao days of semi-Soviet rule—sentiments I had heard expressed in Xinjiang before, and that boiled down to "anything is better than the Chinese." For the Kyrgyz she had no affection either, and she disdained the *Manas*. "We have the *Turkdillar Diva*"—a comparative dictionary of Turkic dialects composed by a Uygur. "It's much better than the *Manas*!" She pointed to a sign in Uygur announcing the rules of family planning for the community. "We can have two or three children, but Chinese only one."

Our tour of old Kashgar was proving cheerless. We passed huddled noseless lepers, droopy-eyed beggars moaning, *Allah Allah Allah,* and extending wrinkled palms. Chunky women waddled by, their faces veiled; men, beefy and stern, cast me suspicious looks. Yet when Güzel bumped into her female classmates, all Western-dressed, her face radiated joy and everything was wonderful. They kissed on the cheeks three, four, five times, stroked each other's hair and shoulders as they talked, caressed each other's necks. Their affectionate solidarity seemed to say, no one would ever force *them* into burkas.

Kashgar's Uygur old town, like medinas elsewhere in the Muslim world, was "traditional," genuine in a raw, medieval way, and perhaps a tourist attraction, but it really symbolized poverty in brick and dust and sewery effluents, a backwardness that, along with repressive Chinese policies, has kept Uygurs behind even as the country's economy races ahead. I was relieved to return to the Han neighborhoods.

We reached my hotel. Next to it was a restaurant with tables set in a garden. Güzel had said she was hungry, and I was too, so I suggested we eat there.

"But . . . but it's *Chinese!* No, no, *oooh,* no, I won't go! Uygurs *never* eat Chinese food!"

"Oh, I'm sorry. I didn't mean any offense."

She abruptly averted her eyes, as if I had insulted her. Still, she agreed to meet me the next day.

THE FOLLOWING MORNING Güzel and I were bouncing in a taxi down a poplar-shaded road, through wheat fields awash in sun, our destination Abakh Hoja Tomb, a few miles northeast of town. At times she consulted her pocket translator, and the commonplace English words it gave her she pronounced with a quirky mellifluous flair: "hair" became "*khaiy*er"; "water," "*vattar*." Her accent was adorable, and I found I always wanted to hear her talk.

But at Abakh Hoja crowds of Chinese tourists turned our visit into a shoving and shouting match, and I could hardly make out her words. The green dome of the mausoleum, which looked altogether like any rather primitive mosque built of lime and clay bricks, sheltered a profusion of tombs. Signs in English posted here and there were cryptic yet minatory, and had nothing to do with the exhibits: DANEGROUS PLEASE DON'T DROPET and THE TILES WILL DROPPET ONTO HEAD.

"So who was Abakh Hoja?" I asked.

"Grandfaadder to Ikparkhan. Who was leading revolt against . . . against . . ."

"Against?"

"I do not know the history. Wait . . ." She called over an official Uygur guide, a doughy-faced young woman with a 1950s hairdo, who supposedly spoke English.

"Xiang Fei"—the guide said flatly, using Ikparkhan's Chinese name, which means "fragrant concubine"—"is buried here." She pointed to a tomb.

"What is she famous for?" I asked.

"She was married to Qing Emperor."

I had read the story: Ikparkhan had led a rebellion against Beijing, but she had failed and the emperor took her as a booty wife.

"This was before the Chinese called your land Xinjiang, I assume."

Both flashed me surprised looks.

The guide stiffened. "Our land is always called Xinjiang."

"That's the Chinese name, I know. But how could Uygurs call their own land 'New Dominions,' and why would they use Chinese?"

"It is Xinjiang," both said robotically.

"Right. But that's not the *Uygur* name."

Silence. Their eyes darted around in their sockets. The guide said a stiff goodbye and attached herself to a passing pair of Chinese tourists.

"The Uygur name for your land is . . . ," I said. "Turkestan" hung on the tip of my tongue, but something stopped me from uttering it.

"That part of our history is . . . unknown," Güzel whispered. "The history here, it is, *oooh*, it is false."

"How so?"

"I am 'fraid. I can't say or I break Chinese law. I can talk no more about it."

Her eyes fell.

"Okay, okay."

Our truncated excursion into history had shaken her. Saying nothing, we walked over to the nearby Jama Mosque, where she wanted to make a wish by an ancient tree in the courtyard.

"You walk around the tree and wish silently and the wish will come true," she said.

She took up position by the tree and looked skyward and paused, as if contemplating the heavens. She partly closed her eyes and started circumambulating. But a Chinese couple pushed past me and, blabbering loudly, their speech all *sh*'s and *ch*'s and retroflex *r*'s, fell in behind her. They were middle-aged and pear-shaped, the man dressed in cowboy boots and a cowboy hat emblazoned with the word MORLBARO. Güzel clenched her teeth and abandoned her wish, stepping away.

I felt terrible for her. I tried to imagine what it would be like to be overwhelmed in my own land by people who spoke a different language, bossed me around, and took all the jobs.

"Would you like to go to a Uygur restaurant, the best there is here, and eat pilaf?" I asked, hoping to cheer her up.

"Oh, yes! Pilaf we call *qamaklarna padishahi*—the King of Foods! I know *good* place."

We caught a taxi back into town.

KASHGAR'S PREMIER Uygur restaurant, the Orda, also happened to draw masses of—what else?—hungry Chinese tourists eager to eat local. We were, in fact, the only non-Han customers. The Orda was none-theless impressive, a high-ceilinged stained-wood temple of sorts. In the middle of its cavernous main hall cooks in brocaded blouses and embroidered shalwar trousers labored over a cluster of stoves and ov-ens. Nearby was a waist-high fence enclosing a trio of Uygur musicians who sat on cushions cross-legged and unsmiling, strumming a *ghijak* (lyre), pounding a *dap* (snakeskin tambourine), and blowing into a *dutka* (flute). This ensemble produced something close to a *türkü*, but higher pitched and whinier. Around the fence crowded Chinese pa-trons, who extended their digital cameras into the musicians' faces and squinted into the viewfinders, as if examining zoo animals, and flicked and flashed away.

The waitress, a harried Uygur, served table after table of Chinese be-fore she thought to hand us the gold-embossed leather menu. Foods were listed in Chinese and English, along with their alleged "prop-erties." "Mutton—providing nourishment." "Safflower oil—diarretik." "Garlic—building up people's health, regulates menstrual cycle, func-tion germisidal antiphogistic acesodyne and bacteriostatic."

"Tasty-sounding," I said. "Especially the garlic."

"It is!" said Güzel. "Best of food is here!"

After many pleading requests for service, the waitress brought our pilaf, nonchalantly excusing the delay by telling us, "What do you ex-pect? The Chinese eat more and pay more and there are many of them. So we serve them first." But the King of Foods did not disappoint; it was richer and more flavorful than anything I had tasted since crossing the border into Kazakhstan.

I looked around as we ate. I considered it a good sign that so many Chinese were interested in their country's minority peoples and were flexible enough to eat in a Uygur restaurant. I asked Güzel if she ad-mired anything about the Chinese.

"Yes. They are smart. They work very hard. Uygurs are smart but they don't want to work."

"I see. Are you going to stay and look for a job in Kashgar?"

"I would love to go to a developed city."

"Like Beijing?" I said, immediately regretting my words.

"*What?*" She looked away, and then back at me again. "I mean New York! Or Paris! Oooh, I will *never* go to Beijing."

"I understand. Sorry."

"My parents are peasants. They work on their land and earn ten yuan a day"—about $1.35. "I have never been anywhere but Kashgar. Here I can never sit in a café alone or go to a nightclub because of Islamic rules. I want life, life like in Paris." She paused. "But, oooh, I am in *China.*"

We looked down at our pilaf, and the musicians wailed away.

THE KASHGAR SILK ROAD MUSEUM seemed like it might be a good place to learn about the city. But it was decrepit and almost empty, with the air of a vandalized tomb, and many vacant stands and cracked glass display cases. Often only inscriptions remained (interspersed with BE QUITE! signs), and they all conspired to promulgate the same partial truth: the Han established a military governorship here in 60 B.C., and from then on the "Western Regions" (Xinjiang) were Chinese. In fact, only during the Han and Song dynasties did Beijing station troops in Xinjiang. At other times warlords ruled and invaders plundered.

I finished with the museum in short order and stopped at a café to buy a Coke. The sun was strong on the dusty streets, on the Chinese-language billboards and shop signs that far outnumbered those in Uygur. The man at a table next to me, a Uygur, was in his midfifties, lively and thin, with sparkling eyes. He spoke to me in Uygur, asking if I was Turkish. That prompted me to respond in Turkish, and I discovered that by speaking Turkish and dipping into Chinese for words he couldn't understand, we could hold a conversation. He told me that he had just spent ten years working as a mason in Urumqi, and so had acquired more Chinese than most Uygurs.

"Where do you live?" he asked. "New York?"

I told him.

"Ah, Russia!" he said admiringly. "Now *there's* a decent people. The men use their brains and the women are beautiful."

"You've been there?"

"Yes! To Moscow. Say, if you're from America, you know that there're a lot of Uygurs in the U.S. I bet they can find work there, unlike here in China." (Uygurs generally lack the Mandarin necessary to do anything besides manual labor; and Chinese bosses are disinclined to hire them anyway.) "Look around. The Chinese get jobs and drive fancy cars, and Uygurs have no work and ride donkey carts! My son, who finished medical school, spent six years, six whole years, looking for a doctor's job in Urumqi. The Chinese wouldn't take him because he's Uygur. How fair is that? Our political leaders they force to flee abroad. Is that just? *Everything* here is unjust." His eyes conveyed a benevolence that contrasted with his angry words, which skirted the seditious and could land him in jail if overheard by the wrong people. But his tone was rising still. "I wish all these *damned* Chinese would go back to Beijing and Shanghai and their villages and just leave us alone! I hate them. I *hate* them! They take everything for themselves here and leave *nothing* for us, and this is *our* land, not theirs! Please go back to the U.S. and tell the Americans one thing: Uygurs would be your best allies."

"Well—"

"Liberate us!"

"Liberate? How so?"

"Liberate us, just like you liberated Iraq! Do it!"

"I don't—"

"Bomb the Chinese! Bomb them! We have oil and coal and timber and all this land! We'd give it all to your companies, if you'd just liberate us the way you liberated Iraq!"

"That's probably the last thing any American administration would—"

"Why should the Kyrgyz, who are five million, have a state, but we, who are eight million, not? Or just let all the Uygurs immigrate to America—there's another answer! You helped the Iraqis, so help us!"

I tried to explain why the United States would not soon be starting a war with China over Xinjiang. The Xinjiang innings of the Great Game had ended at the Sino-Soviet split, and no rematch was scheduled. Finally, as I was preparing to leave, he grabbed my arm.

"Please, tell no one what I've said. Or they could throw me in prison."

I promised to keep mum.

THE NEXT AFTERNOON I boarded the express train, a modern train much roomier than the Talgo (and evidence of the Develop the West program; no rail line existed when I was here in 1998), for the twenty-two-hour ride west to Urumqi. I stretched out on my bunk by the window as we shot down smooth rails. The Tian Shan, lunar gray, pockmarked with craters and chasms, blocked the view to the north. To the south spread the Taklamakan Desert (which translates from the Turkic as "You go in and don't come out"), a blinding dead tableau of barrens and pebble-strewn loess (silty soil deposited by the wind) that occasionally rose into eolian dunes before flattening out again into more dead, glare-suffused waste. Absent were the camels and nomads one might expect to see. The extremely sparse vegetation has never supported the grazing of livestock; and the parched earth, even in the Taklamakan's few more fertile pockets, has resisted all attempts at cultivation. The Uygurs and Hui inhabiting the Tarim basin have always stuck to the oases around the edges.

During my first traversal of this desert, the gales of spring dust storms (*borans* in Uygur) wracked the land as they did every year, driving clouds of loess thirteen thousand feet into the sky and blanketing much of northern China for days on end, prompting millions to don surgical masks. Now all was still—a panorama of blazing desolation ruled by a despotic sun. At the few stops during the night hardly anyone got on or off. But the next morning the tracks veered away from the Taklamakan and we cut through the Tian Shan, roaring through tunnel after tunnel. The chipper Chinese conductor on the loudspeaker addressed us as *pengyoumen* (friends, not *tongzhimen*, comrades, as she might have in years past), informing us of the meals on offer in the dining car, the connecting flights from Urumqi (which she called by the Mandarin name, Wulumuchi). My Chinese compartment mates, two well-coifed men in Izods and chinos, read books most of the time, and went out into the corridor to talk. In every way, the ease of this ride contrasted with the misery of the overcrowded buses I had taken across China before.

Just after noon the next day, Urumqi reared up out of the wastes, all skyscrapers and smog, giant red and blue Chinese characters on blue-green glass buildings, beneath which swarmed crowds of Western-dressed Chinese, with a few gloomy Uygur faces among them.

This part of Xinjiang had fallen under Chinese control in the seventh century, but in the 750s the Tang dynasty withdrew its troops, and for a thousand years Uygur khans ruled. When Beijing established the province of Xinjiang in 1884, they made Urumqi its capital.

I felt a rush of excitement. Urumqi was big, brash, and vital, more so than anything I had seen since Moscow.

21

At 1,250 miles from the nearest sea, Urumqi is, of all things, one of China's most bustling ports. Located in the foothills of the Tian Shan along one of the later, northern deviations of the Silk Road, and commanding a pass leading from the pre-Siberian steppes of Dzungaria in the north to the deserts of central China in the south, Urumqi functions as the hub of trade with countries of the former Soviet Union. (The Chinese authorities encouraged this by granting it, in 1992, reduced-tax port status.) Since then, commerce, as well as abundant nearby gas and oil reserves (China's largest), has powered Urumqi's conversion from a frontier town set in a barbarian limbo five hundred miles beyond the Great Wall into a metropolis studded with skyscrapers rising mightily against a stark backdrop of dun-colored crags and loess-mantled steppe.

In 1998 I found the city under construction and chaotic, all skyscrapers going up and cement dust coming down, a kinetic cyclorama of grimy bulldozers and rotating cranes, and sidewalk vendors and peasant migrants jostling and rushing and hawking and spitting, searching for work and lodgings, pursuing dreams of prosperity mandated by Deng Xiaoping and his free-market reforms. Like Chicago in the nineteenth century, Urumqi was a "City of the Big Shoulders," China's "Player with Railroads and the Nation's Freight Handler; Stormy, husky, brawling." Carl Sandburg would have found it inspiringly familiar.

This time, as I rode in a taxi from the train station to my hotel, I saw that a good deal of the construction had been completed, and that, most strikingly, Uygurs had suffered a demographic rout in their own province's capital. Urumqi is now overwhelmingly a Han city; four out of five residents are Chinese. On the streets Uygurs ambled along, few and sullen and Islamically garbed, resembling hardscrabble dwellers of Parisian *banlieues* exiled among jaunty Chinese holiday makers for whom the Mao jacket is a relic from a distant past and Versace and Prada (or, more likely, facsimiles thereof) are the new sartorial desiderata. In many places the only evidence left of a Uygur presence is street signs painted in Arabic, or, in pockets in the suburbs of new high-rises for the Han, mud-hovel slums and pilaf joints.

But I was thrilled to arrive. Since leaving Moscow I had seen no city more vibrant or exciting. I put up at the gleaming, glassy Xinjiang Grand and gazed out over the town from my room on the eleventh floor.

Here I would pamper myself. I needed a haircut, so I took the elevator down to the lobby and asked for the barber shop. "Try the business center," I was told. There I addressed the smiling receptionist. Her smile oddly vanished on hearing my request, and she stiffened. She stood up and called out a female name and pointed at the next room. Puzzled, wondering if somehow I had made a faux pas in my Chinese, I thanked her and crossed the hall.

The salon—just a big chair and a mirror—was empty of customers. But a side door opened and a heavily made-up girl of twenty or so stepped out, wiping the sleep from her eyes, a messy unmade bed behind her.

"I'd like a haircut," I said.

"Room number?" she said, her breath acrid from her snooze.

I told her. She turned and examined her tight-bloused torso in the mirror, preening, pressing her breasts together and throwing back her hair. She then faced me and smiled, cocking her head.

"Well?" I asked. "Do you start by washing my hair?"

Her come-hither pose rendered my question suddenly ridiculous.

"Oh." She frowned. "Oh," she said again.

She slipped into the side room and grabbed a pair of scissors, thick ones more suitable for cutting paper than hair. She stared, puzzled, at them and approached me, as if about to trim my bangs with me still standing. She was, of course, no hairdresser.

"I've changed my mind," I said. "I'm sorry."

She scrunched up her face in a pouty grimace of disappointment, and I walked out.

I returned to my room. As I was unpacking there came a timid knock on my door. I opened it. In scampered a pigtailed Han of twenty or so, with butter skin and apple breasts.

"*Massagee! Massagee?*"

Grabbing at my crotch, she licked her lips and jiggled her head, like a debauched Minnie Mouse. She squealed, "Six hundred yuan!" (about eighty dollars).

Nonplussed by the abrupt walk-in (arranged by the hairdresser?), I balked and moved to reopen the door. She dropped to her knees and threw her arms around my waist, and, clutching me, hee-hee-heed and tittered like a tot, imploring me in rapid Mandarin to let her stay, rubbing her head against my crotch. Then the door swung open and another girl walked in, wobbling slightly on stiletto heels. She raised her T-shirt to show me her breasts.

In Chinese she told me she was eighteen and I could have her friend and her for the discount price of $150.

"Look, I'm sorry, but I think you'll have to leave."

"*Massaggee! Massaggee!* Please!"

I pulled free of the first girl and, checking to make sure my wallet was still in my pocket, reopened the door and motioned for them to leave. But Minnie and her friend kicked off their heels and tossed themselves on my bed, tittering and chattering away in Chinese I couldn't understand.

Whatever I said in response, they found utterly hilarious. Only by dialing the front desk did I prompt them to clear out.

I WAS EAGER TO MEET young people—regular young people, that is—and find out how they saw their future in this youthful city, which had changed almost beyond recognition since my last trip. I decided to explore the club scene, believing that there I would catch Xinjiang's young at their least guarded (and least surveilled)—when they're having fun. So, that night, after asking around and learning which club was hot, I slipped out of the marbled gilt lobby through revolving doors into an evening redolent of lamb kebab roasting somewhere unseen. A shiny green taxi swerved off Xinhua Bei Road and pulled up in front of me. I leaned through the window and shouted, "*Wo yao qu Chu Dong!*"

"Chu Dong? Ah, *Chu Dong!*" The cabbie almost expectorated my destination's name, and, nodding, swung open the door for me. *Chu Dong* (translation: Touch Club), I learned, had to be barked out breathlessly, each syllable accelerated and pitched downward in Mandarin's descending fourth tone. (In Chinese, each syllable carries its own tone; tones convey almost as much meaning as vowels and consonants.) To say Chu Dong otherwise—improperly inflected, that is—would provoke puzzled stares and get me nowhere.

We lurched along with the traffic, heavy despite the relatively late hour, progressing through a grid of streets lined with glitzy storefronts, and eventually reached a hectic roundabout. Beneath Chu Dong's marquee—a razzmatazz potpourri of Chinese characters glowing in red, yellow, and blue neon—we halted by the curb. Chu Dong occupied the ground floor of a twenty-seven-story building—no longer all that high for buildings in the center. Before hopping out, I paid the driver the six yuan shown on his meter, surprised that there was in fact a meter, given how rudimentary Urumqi had been before.

I walked through Chu Dong's spotless glass and steel doors, passed under the arches of a beeping metal detector, suffered a pat-down by apologetic bouncers in trim jackets and narrow ties, and boarded the escalator leading down into the black-walled, electric blue subterranean environs of the club. At the bottom, a maitre d' in a dark suit grinned, and, tilting forward, gave my hand a brief but vigorous shake. An immaculate white-tiled corridor led left, past a bar, to a cavernous chamber whirling with a silver confetti of light reflected from a disco globe hanging somewhere out of sight, but to the right a smaller room appealed more to me. There, stylized red Chinese lanterns glowed like giant bulbous embers dangling from the ceiling; set against the far white wall, which also served as a video screen, was a stage with a polished steel pole; high tables flanked by cushioned stools surrounded a dance floor and a DJ station; and a sort of mezzanine ran along the walls, its cozy recesses furnished with deep black sofas.

In the West or in Moscow, Chu Dong's interior would hardly stand out. But this was Urumqi!

The maitre d' informed me that the cover charge for the chamber down the hall was two hundred yuan (thirty dollars), but half that in the small room I had chosen. He didn't ask me to pay, however. I ordered a glass of red wine. After telling me that Touch sells wine only in bottles, he nevertheless brought me a glass. I eventually discovered that rules and prices varied depending on the waiter, and that it was best to buy drinks straight from the bar (set up to serve only staff)—a privilege accorded to me alone among customers, probably because of my exalted status as a foreigner.

It was ten o'clock—still early, especially for a Sunday night—and only a few tables were occupied. I chose one near the back. As soon as I settled in, a fellow dressed in black, with gelled cropped hair and an un-Chinese angularity to his face, strode across the dance floor and shook my hand.

"*Zdravstvuy!* Are you Russian?" he asked, addressing me with the familiar *ty*.

"I'm American," I answered in Russian.

"I invite you to play with us."

"Play?"

He wiggled his eyebrows. "Come on!"

He grabbed my wrist and led me across the room, introducing himself as Musa. Musa was from Kazakhstan, twenty-one, and studying at Urumqi University to be an interpreter. He claimed to have learned Mandarin in six months, which I disbelieved, until he added that he was a Dungan and spoke a dialect of Chinese at home. His roughshod Russian wasn't unusual here, given all the trade with the former Soviet Union.

Still, Musa's demeanor seemed suspiciously enthusiastic.

"You can play with Maya!" he said, his voice overly buoyant, as he offered me a seat at his table. Maya, also Kazakh, was chunky and amiable, dressed in black jeans and a fluffy chartreuse sweater. She smiled and raised her glass. In front of us stood a bottle of Jack Daniels and a wicker bowl of popcorn, plus a plate of green grapes and sliced melon. I raised my wine, which provoked consternation from Musa. "But she doesn't drink wine!"

"*Za znakomstvo!*" (To our acquaintanceship!) I said, not knowing what to make of his declaration. Was I supposed to order her a drink?

I glanced around at the other tables. Young women predominated. Many smiled at me, and one mouthed, "Hello." I smiled back, but something sank in my gut: *Why the friendliness to me, a stranger? Are they hookers? Is Maya some sort of B-girl? And Musa's congeniality . . . is he her pimp?* I had sowed my wildest oats in Russian clubs during the 1990s, where so much was for sale, and suspicion and cagey reserve never went amiss. There I knew the scene. But here in China I did not, as my run-in with the hookers earlier in the day had shown me.

"You're just a student," I asked him, hoping to tactfully dispel my apprehensions, "but you can afford to come here and drink bottles of whiskey?" He showed me a club card, which gave him 33 percent off. I relaxed somewhat.

"Everything here in China is promising," he said. "I hope to start a business and open a shop. But I like to *play* too, you know." A Russian rap song came on. He leaned away from me and started dancing in place, as did others. Then it occurred to me: by *igrat'* ("to play," in Russian) he must have meant "to dance." The two words are the same in Turkish, so I reasoned they would be so in Kazakh, from which he was doubtlessly mistranslating into Russian.

He put his arm around my shoulder and leaned in to me. "You know, I was spending so much time on Russian grammar, which is so *hard*. But my friends told me not to waste my youth on it. So I just talk to people and learn that way."

He should have wasted a little more youth, for his cheery banter was at times unintelligible. But soon my suspicion abated: he and Maya were having fun just talking to me, and former Soviet rules did not apply.

The video screen flickered on and they urged me to watch. Scenes from bars during spring break in Fort Lauderdale flashed above the gathering crowd, and all turned their heads. To Rod Stewart's "Do Ya Think I'm Sexy?" totally drunk American-looking college girls performed stripteases for the camera, squeezing their breasts, stroking their crotches, whooping and giving the thumbs-up, and now and then guzzling from pitchers of beer, all with their mascara-smeared eyes fixed on the lens. Musa and Maya checked my reaction. Cool, right?

As Chu Dong filled up, bodies closed around me, and the lyrics and raunchy video kept the crowd hopping. A burly Chinese fellow showed up at our table.

"Su Ling!" shouted Musa, hugging him hard, whacking him on the back. "Meet Su Ling from my school!"

After introductions we raised our glasses. *"Gan Bei!"* (Cheers!)

"Gan Bei!"

With all the alcohol and the toasting, I loosened up. At evening's end, Musa and I exchanged phone numbers and said goodbye. Maya was, after all, really just his friend, and drinking just a way of being companionable. My years in Russia had made me a cynic, and I resolved to be less wary here.

THE NEXT NIGHT I crossed Chu Dong's glittering threshold with Andy, also known as Ai Bin. He had chosen an English name for himself, both for its trendy Western cachet and to make dealing with foreigners easier. A spiky-haired, spindly bellhop of twenty-two from my hotel, Andy had told me of Chu Dong, his favorite hangout. For our outing he had switched his brown-trimmed mustard yellow work suit and white gloves for a modishly wrinkled tawny sports jacket and straight-legged black trousers. He spoke some English, and with my Chinese we found we could communicate well enough. He had picked me up in a taxi, accompanied by a beautiful Uygur girl sitting in the front seat, but when we got out at Touch she stayed aboard and gave us a shy wave goodbye.

"My girlfriend," he said. "She must go home to study. She's Muslim, so she doesn't go to clubs."

Once downstairs, Andy led me to the two-hundred-yuan room. It was huge, with star-spangled black walls and a high ceiling, its own music, a stage/runway, and a giant electronic billboard near the entrance that flashed the ceaseless gyrations of a virtual hip-hop dancing girl.

It was still early. At the few busy tables around us, people rolled dice in red plastic cups, which they slammed down, shouting, *Xiao!* (low) or *Da!* (high), before checking to see who had won. Sometimes losers had to drink a penalty shot, but for the most part, the jarring racket seemed to be an end in itself, suiting the Chinese love of noise.

Touch energized Andy. Glancing about and straightening his collar, pushing back his bangs, he ordered us wine from a waiter dressed in a checkered shirt that looked cut from a picnic tablecloth. The waiter returned with a bottle of Suntime red, plus popcorn and a plate arrayed with melon chunks, lime slices, clusters of grapes, and peeled bananas. With aplomb he uncorked the bottle and emptied it into a pitcher. He then popped open two cans of Sprite and poured them in too. The fizzy tipple that resulted was, to me at least, revoltingly sweet; the popcorn, it turned out, was sugarcoated.

"We like sweet drinks here," Andy said.

We got to talking. Andy was one of the numberless economic migrants from dustbowl Gansu province to the southeast. Urumqi was his City of Dreams. "There's no work where I'm from, but here there's a lot. You can make good money here!" His employer paid for his apartment, and he was able to save for the future. Education didn't figure in his plans, at least for the time being. All he wanted to do was make money and have fun.

"How are you called in Chinese?" he asked.

"Jie Fu," I replied, giving him the name a Beijing college student had contrived for me in 1998. The phonemes making up Chinese names have meanings that vary in accordance with tone. "Jie Fu" happens to mean "excellent husband." My family name she rendered as "Tai Le"—or "peaceful barbarian." Both seemed silly to me, but at my request she had striven to stick close to the sounds of my English name. (President Kennedy fared far worse: his name could, depending on tones, be sinicized as "gnaw mud person" or "willing Buddhist nun enlighten.")

Andy frowned and took my notepad and began scribbling in Chinese.

"Jie Fu . . . no, it sounds bad. In Chinese we have no such name."

"Well, then can I just be Jeff?"

"No. We don't have this name."

"In English so many foreign names have been introduced, we can't keep track. Why can't I keep my name in Chinese?"

"We don't accept foreign names in Chinese. You must have a *Chinese* name."

I stood my ground. Nothing is more personal than a name, so at the very least I wanted a Chinese moniker sounding like Jeff.

"Okay, okay," Andy said. He scribbled out a few characters. "How about Wang?"

"*Wang?*"

"Or Li?"

"Ah, I think—"

"There's nothing close that sounds okay. How about a minority people's name? Say, Anivar?"

"If I have to have a Chinese name, I'd really like to keep Jie Fu."

"No, please. Here." He indited a triumvirate of elaborate characters. "You can be this name: Wang Shao Wen!"

"That sounds nothing at all like my name."

"It's better than Jie Fu."

"Look, why can't you accept a non-Chinese name? Your girlfriend is Uygur. You don't try to rename her, do you?"

"Of course not." (I later learned that Uygur names have accepted sinicized renditions.) "It's her choice to be Muslim, to avoid pork and not come to the clubs. I could become a Muslim too, but I like my own religion"—Buddhism—"too much. I'm not against Islam. Maybe she could accept Buddhism too. I really don't know."

The room was filling up, with young women in groups of three or four taking seats and ordering spreads of alcohol and fruit.

I told Ai Bin that I would learn written Chinese just to read *Tao Te Ching* in the original.

He frowned. "Oh, that book is in ancient Chinese. It's too hard for me. Say, ah, you like a beauty?"

Looking around impatiently, he pulled out his cell and punched in a number. After shouting "*Wei! Wei!*" into the mouthpiece, he spoke in newly animated tones, his hand over his free ear. Half an hour later two young women showed up. Yang Yang (whom he introduced as Sami, her foreign, in this case Muslim, name) was plump, with a shag cut and easygoing smile; Xiujie, who went by Amanda, had an aquiline nose, a high but pimply forehead, and a sport-sculpted body. Yang Yang clasped hands with Andy and the two never parted, touching each other and horsing around. (His Uygur girlfriend was, he later told me, "like a wife"—but he wouldn't marry for "a *long* time," until he was twenty-four or twenty-five.)

Amanda spoke excellent English. She had migrated to Urumqi from the western town of Aksu (a Uygur name she pronounced Chinese-style, *A Ki Su*), studied hotel management in Beijing, and then found work here as a hotel receptionist. I learned little more about her: she came to dance, not talk. As the DJ turned up the music, she slipped into a trance. She lowered her head, raised her petite hands, and began shaking them in front of her face, as if flecking off water drops, while closing her eyes and mincing in place—moves straight from MTV.

"Dance! Dance!" she shouted to me.

So I danced.

An hour later I slipped off to the restroom at the room's far end. On my way through the vestibule I passed a sofa on which three or four girls in black bikinis lounged, chatting and smoking. They were statuesque and lithe, glabrous-skinned, glossy-haired, their torsos unmarred

by a single fold of fat, their legs tapering into black stiletto boots—
Touch's professional dancers. The bathroom turned out to be unisex.
By the mirror over the sinks, other dancers were pursing their lips and
fluffing their hair, powdering their cheeks and mewling in high-pitched
Mandarin. All the toilets were squat-style, set in mirrored seven-foot-
high booths open at the top. The dancers scurried in and out of them,
slamming doors and laughing, and gabbed away, unashamed of their
plops and squirts.

One of the dancers followed me out and climbed onto the runway;
another stepped off to cheers from a crowd now facing the stage and
swaying to an ever-more-oppressive techno beat. A similarly glabrous,
gel-haired male dancer joined her on stage, dressed in black briefs
cinched with a silver belt, and sporting a spike-studded collar around
his neck. They thrust their hips and flailed their arms artfully, executing choreographed techno moves conceived never to clash. Both wore
paper numbers on their hips.

The clubbers kept their eyes on them and sped up their own gyrations. The female dancer dropped to her knees at the male's crotch,
clutched his buttocks, and mimed deep-throat fellatio. He threw his
head back in mock ecstasy, adeptly pulled her to her feet, and grabbed
her waist. With acrobatic legerdemain he flipped her upside down and
plunged his face between her legs, licking the air between them. At the
number's end, Virtual Girl disappeared from the wall screen and Chinese characters flashed on a red ticker, followed by the numeral 5 and
an exclamation point.

Amanda jumped up and down. "Dancer five won! She won! What do
you think?" she asked me.

Andy and Xiujie smiled and shouted commentary across the table,
but the music drowned out their words.

I looked at Amanda and shrugged.

EACH DAWN since my arrival in China a couple of weeks earlier, the
sun had released a torrent of pitiless blue enamel light over Xinjiang's
fulvous wastes, the light of desert skies, a light now, however, heralding,
with its sharpening autumnal clarity, months of subzero winter cold to
come. But Tuesday broke humanely cloudy and cool.

That night, as I left my hotel for the club, a gentle rain pattered down,
transforming Urumqi's usually brilliant panoply of neon and halogen
into an impressionistic tableau of pastels, and offering relief from dusty

winds battering in from the loess wilderness outside town. Traffic was as herky-jerky as ever, but drivers negotiated it without the street-fight rage and apoplectic horn-banging so often a part of Moscow's grid-locks.

Still logy from the previous evening, I couldn't help marveling at how China (and outback China, no less) differs from Russia. Broadly speaking, China's growth derives from exporting manufactured goods; Russia's, from pumping hydrocarbons abroad. Hence there is no equivalent of Urumqi in Russia; Russia produces few goods anyone abroad wants to buy. But differences are farther-reaching than that. No drunks stumble about Chinese public squares; the Chinese labor long hours in apparent good spirits; and conversations don't revolve around conspiracy theories about how the cold war had been won or lost, or which politician or businessman should be jailed or shot for "robbing the people," but were about bettering one's life through study and work. Hundreds of thousands of Chinese study abroad; the Russian government does not even recognize foreign educational credentials. No one in China so far had pined aloud to me after Mao, as so many Russians now yearn volubly for a new Stalin or an Iron Fist. The West, now so unpopular in Russia, still evokes longing and enthusiasm in China. Which makes sense: the Chinese adopted Western market reforms (and pop culture) of their own accord; the Russians feel victimized by the West, deceived into enacting market reforms that impoverished most of them. The mood on Urumqi's streets was, thus, understandably up-beat in a way unheard of in Russia. My grim impressions of the city from 1998 were no longer valid.

And the mood was upbeat at Chu Dong. *Ni hao! Ni hao!* The guards and doorman shouted hello, smiling broadly and shaking my hand as I walked in. For the first time they spared me the concealed-weapons search. In the hundred-yuan room, I ordered my usual wine and savored my luck at being in Urumqi. The Chinese are now living better than they ever have, and it was uplifting to be with them.

The waiter appeared with a bottle of Suntime. Beaming at me, he uncorked it and poured a dollop of its syrupy red contents into a pitcher. I had only asked for a glass, but no matter, I would find someone to share it with.

But then he snapped the tab off a Sprite and poured that in as well.

"Oh, please, not Sprite again! Why?"

Wine and Sprite are "*hen hao he!*" (great to drink), he said, taken aback.

"Can I help you?" asked a voice in English. "Is there a problem?"

A tall Chinese fellow in a loose-hanging cream-colored sport jacket and tattered designer jeans was peering at me over the waiter's shoulder. His hair was longish and cut ragged; his unshaven face was lean, with a prominent nose and jutting jaw. All in all, he was stylishly unkempt in a way that wouldn't have stood out in Paris or Rome but did in Urumqi, where primping was the rule, and priggish dress announced one's liberation from the now shameful fetters of poverty.

"Oh, I just don't like Sprite in my wine," I said. "But no problem."

The waiter apologized and moved on. My accoster sidled up and asked where I was from. I told him and invited him to drink wine with me.

"I'm Villain," he said, accepting a glass. "That's right, Villain. Because I'm bad."

"You're bad?"

"I mean, I'm not handsome and I'm not rich. I lost my girlfriend to a rich man. She lied to me and went off and slept with him because he's rich. I'm angry. Hey, you know Slim City?"

I didn't. But, detecting a buoyant expectancy in his eyes, I lacked the heart to say so.

"Sort of."

"So you know their lyrics?"

"Well—"

"Which song do you like best? Do you love them? I *love* them. You seen the Slim City film? I get *strength* from their lyrics. Do you? Can you teach me their lyrics? My parents would kick me out if they understood the words!"

"You're really into music."

"Yes. It's my job. I'm a singer, at another bar. But what do you think about Slim City?"

I dodged further questions. His enthusiasm for music made me feel old. He asked me about Michael Jordan (had I met him?) and other American luminaries, whose names alone I recognized. That I'd spent the last thirteen years in Moscow was no excuse; he had never been to America but knew all about its celebrities.

"Your English is great," I said. "How did you learn it?"

"I study it hard because I want to move to Australia."

"Why?"

"To go to school. I want to study business in a university. People are good in Australia. Not like here in China. Chinese are hungry. Always wanting money, money, always they want money."

"I don't think that's a specifically Chinese failing."

"And also, here we can't have good hip-hop, because the government doesn't allow cursing in songs. I think you can say 'fuck' all the time in the U.S. because there's freedom. But you can't here."

He asked me to join him in the two-hundred-yuan chamber because he'd come to pick up girls. So we moved there. Along the way he kept up his banter. "Do you think I have a chance, to find a girl tonight?"

"Why not?"

"No, I mean *really*, can I find one *tonight?* Hey, you like Mike Iverson?"

"Who?"

"The basketball star! He has tattoos all over. I want a tattoo too. What do you think of my earring, by the way? Are you angry about it?"

"Of course not. Relax."

We set our drinks down by two of his friends, paunchy types who kept their eyes on the girls turning up all around us. A few were quite pretty Uygurs, with a sultry poise that made them look more mature than their chipper Chinese counterparts.

"They're so exotic," Villain remarked. "I want a Uygur girl! But do you think girls should be allowed to smoke? I don't." He shifted on his stool and started downing his wine at a faster pace.

"Liquid courage?" I asked.

"I'm not handsome, so talking to girls is hard for me. What should I do? Will I get a girl?"

Slumped on his stool, hagridden by libido, he reminded me of myself at his age.

"Just relax and be yourself."

"I want to talk to that one, over there." He pointed to three girls across the hall. "But I have no confidence."

"Why don't I go with you?"

"*Really?*"

We grabbed our glasses and walked over to them. They had dressed in knits and tweeds, like sisters from a geek sorority. In my halting Chinese I made introductions. The stout-browed object of Villain's affections smiled wanly, told me her name was Zhi Yuan, and asked us to join them. But soon they were looking bored and staring off into Touch's glittering cosmos. Villain exchanged a few words with Yuan, and finally nodded at me to follow him back to our table.

"She's coming over. I try not to press them. Some girls get angry if you ask for their phone numbers, you know, like all you want to do is sleep with them. But she'll come over."

"Where would you take her, anyway?"

"To a cheap hotel. I couldn't sneak her into my parents' apartment."

It was no surprise to me that they never joined us. But it made Villain antsy, and he began telling me he wanted to leave China and find his fate elsewhere. He then pointed to a row of canopied tables against the far wall, set apart on a raised area—the section for rich people. At one table a brash Chinese fellow all in black was pouring a Uygur woman a glass of whiskey.

"I want to fight him," Villain declared. "For his girl."

"That you can do without me."

"Meeting girls is so hard. How can it be easy?"

"Look," I said. "What about this club where you sing? Why don't you try your luck there, on your own turf?"

"Ah, oh, that's not a club to visit. It's . . . it's a gay club. Oh, no, hey, no! Hey, I'm not gay!" He threw up his hands.

"Who says you are?"

"I'm not. I just work there. There is no good for women."

Our talk turned to other things. He was certain of the duplicity of the Chinese, the honesty of Westerners. As insecure as he was, his interest in the world beyond Urumqi suggested ambition and some degree of sophistication. I told him that I bet he'd go far in life.

A bikini-clad dancer drifted by, smiling and eyeing us, taking a languorous drag on her cigarette.

"She's a beauty, correct?" he asked. "You want her? I can go talk to her. Dancers here dance, but most of all they sell themselves. You don't want?"

"I don't want. Here, let's drink to your success! Cheers!"

"Cheers!"

AFTER FOUR OR FIVE HOURS of fitful sleep, sunrise returned me to a murky semblance of wakefulness, my senses dulled and my tongue purpled, still tart with the grape. Gazing through my window onto already surging traffic and dawn-gilt skyscrapers, I felt befuddled wonder and a contemplative, winy listlessness that weren't entirely disagreeable. My nightly clubbing was wearing me out. Gradually, though, I was finding something reassuring in it: each evening I had somewhere to go, something to do, people to talk to. And always, so far, people who, to my surprise, accepted me outright, with a civility that I could only ascribe to China's Confucian traditions, which enjoined respect for elders. No one asked my profession or wondered at my age—a good twenty years higher than the club's average. Their acceptance seemed so spontaneous that I was almost inclined to forget the age differ-ence—something that in a Russian nightclub I couldn't manage.

"What nationality are you?" was always the first question put to me, followed by inquiries about my wife and family. Not surprisingly, no one broached politics or inveighed against Bush or the ruling Commu-nist Party. Still, it didn't seem they feared expressing themselves about these subjects (as one might suspect they would, since China is a police state), but that at their age, with their hormones and proclivities for having fun, they just didn't care. Even my speaking Chinese hardly im-pressed; so many foreigners in China do these days. I was steadily being drawn into a lazy rhythm of days without consequences, the rhythm of youth, in which carpe diem is all that matters and the yearning for a blowout escape through music and booze, plus the desire for a quick coupling, keeps heads turning, eyes alert.

That I was relaxing this way in China, the homeland of Mao and the Gang of Four, where people perished by the millions in civil war, fam-ine, and campaigns of violence, and in Urumqi, no less, a longtime re-doubt of warlords and Great Game spies, all made it wondrous that Touch existed and that I could go there to do something as pleasantly ordinary as drink and make merry. Theoretically at least, I might just have been able to settle down here, and drift on and on, creating a new life for myself. I was even more flummoxed by how much manners toward foreigners had improved since 1998. The city in which chil-dren on the street eight years earlier had taunted me with cries of *bai ren* (white person) and *gao bizi* (high-nosed one) I could now—al-most—call home. The All-Under-Heaven had room for me.

IN THE THINLY POPULATED hundred-yuan room a video was playing on the wall screen. A blond American stripper dressed only in a thong and black boots swung around a pole with perfunctory grace, thrust her rear at the camera, and bent over and spread her legs, massaging her buttocks with spangled nails. Smiling blandly, she erected herself and whirled about the pole again. The clubbers observed her on the screen with dull eyes and drifted back to their drinks. I paid the waiter for my wine with bills displaying Mao's full-cheeked portrait. So much for the revolution.

A short, chubby girl with a gold-streaked brown shag cut hurried toward me across the dance floor.

"Hello, hey, can I talk to you? Who are you?" she asked in English.

Her name was Rose (or Liu Fei). Rose's pancake-flat face twinkled with piercings; her puffy silvered lids half occluded childlike eyes. Baby fat spilled over the belt beneath her black blouse, and on her tiny feet were untied sneakers. With her was a darker-complexioned girl, also twinkle-faced with metal, whose nose and lower jaw protruded in an erotically vulpine way; she lacked the nervous tittering smile of so many girls in Touch. She wore a flaming red shiny jacket, and her midriff was taut and bare between hip-hugging jeans and a cut-off T-shirt. Rose introduced her as Bao Bao. Bao Bao had no English name because she only spoke Chinese.

"Please over come to talk with us," said Rose. With the stripper video playing behind them, I took a seat by their table, which was set with Uzual Metal whiskey, bottles of mineral water, and fruit. Across from me sat a friend of theirs who giggled into her cell phone and never looked my way. She was in a navy blue pleated skirt and a white button-down shirt with a diamond-shaped blue tie, and her hair hung in bangs across the forehead, with pigtails in back. She had dressed to look fifteen, but she was surely twenty. She reminded me of Japanese schoolgirl porn, with its legal-aged actresses done up like pubescent teens.

In sharp tones Bao Bao asked me my age.

Forty-five, I said. Rose told me she was nineteen.

"How old am I?" asked Bao Bao, hitting my forearm. "Guess!"

"Oh, I'm terrible at that."

"Guess!"

"I'd say twenty."

She grabbed her drink and scurried off, without looking back.

"Why did you say that?" asked Rose.

"Why? Say what?"

"You called her *old!*"

"No, I didn't. Is twenty so old?"

"Twenty is so so old, *too* old! She's *nineteen*." The Japanese schoolgirl giggled hee-hee-hee, louder and louder, into her phone. "At nineteen a girl can't smoke but at twenty she *can*. No one wants an *old* girl."

"Well, who wants an *old* man?"

"Why you say this? Forty-five is not old for man! All girls want older man. But no man here wants the older girls. Twenty is *too* old!"

Did men in China prefer Pippi Longstockings to Pamela Andersons? I remembered the Minnie Mouse hookers at the hotel. Maybe girls who looked mature, or even legal, didn't catch the lusting eye here. But I felt terrible about hurting Bao Bao, and I wanted to apologize. Moreover, I was drawn to her, to her brusque demeanor, her confidence, and her appraising eyes—the very attributes that made her look older. But Rose told me not to worry: Bao Bao would cool off and come back.

After asking me my name, disapproving of it, suggesting I become Wang or Huang, or even Zhang (pronounced with a robotic-sounding flat "first" tone), and finally accepting that I'd prefer to remain Jeff or Jie Fu, Rose told me that she worked as a waitress and studied English because it was cool. She didn't earn much, but it was enough to come here every night with Bao Bao.

"Do you have a boyfriend?" I asked.

"In the past, I did."

"When was that?"

"Last month. But I broke up with him. I'm too young for boy-friends."

"Urumqi has changed a lot since I was here in 'ninety-eight. It's really developed."

"Oh, I don't like this city at all! I want to go to a *developed* city, where there's *developed* life, like Beijing or Shanghai. But Urumqi? No."

The DJ dimmed the lights and amped up the music. The video screen darkened, and a bikini-clad dancer, one of the cat-eyed mewlers I had seen near the toilets my second time here, mounted the stage, ignoring the pole. To a techno tune she executed her moves flawlessly. With her makeup and ripped build, her pursed lips and haughty poise, she looked *sophisticated*—a novelty in Touch. Soon the collared male dancer in briefs joined her, with his own retinue of kicks and jabs.

Most around us watched the show, but not Rose. She danced in place and kept her eyes on me.

"You're not watching the dancer?" I said.

"Why should I! I'm dancer too!" She grabbed my hand and her face brightened. "Dance, dance, you too!"

So, I danced.

THE NEXT EVENING, on a Thursday, I dismounted the escalator at Chu Dong and walked into a startling, barked-out chorus of *Huanying! Huanying!* (Welcome! Welcome!) from waiters aligned in the bluish haze like recruits awaiting reveille—a sign things were picking up with the weekend approaching. In the hundred-yuan room, Rose skipped over to me and pulled me to her table, at which Bao Bao and the Japanese schoolgirl were sipping King Horse Tennessee whiskey and munching on sugared popcorn.

Bao Bao looked at me and raised her glass. *"Gan bei!"* (Cheers!)

"Gan bei! Gan bei!"

Her toast absolved me, and I was relieved.

Rose had streaked her eyelids with forked flourishes of black mascara, which gave her face a Catwomanish cast and made her seem older—a thought, of course, that I kept to myself. But I did tell her, in English and out of earshot of the Japanese schoolgirl, that in Russia dressing like a teenybopper would not be cool in a club like Chu Dong. Why did it enjoy such a vogue here?

She raised her eyebrows and announced, in a didactic tone, "All Chinese girls must try to look as young as possible always. Every man likes girls who are fourteen or fifteen."

"Fourteen or fifteen?"

"Yes. Girls like the older men. A twenty-year-old cannot have a good job or money. So girls must sleep with the older man." Must? "Must," she said. "They must, to keep him."

As in Russia, so here, a sort of demographic determinism deriving from rural poverty and urban promise obtains. A relentless influx of peasant migrants heightens competition for work in the cities. To get by, young men search for jobs in the labor sector, as do women, but the latter have another option: marriage to an already-well-off male. A woman's natural inclination, for her own sake and the sake of her future family, would be, here as in Russia, to seek out an older, "established" guy rather than tie her fate to an unproven youngster of dubious net worth.

Rose stood close to me and minced, as if preparing to bare her soul. "Can I ask you a question?"

"Of course."

"Which . . . which do you prefer, Coke or Pepsi? No, please answer me: I'm serious. Coke or Pepsi? I think Coke is too sweet. Really."

Bao Bao made a run to the bar for a fresh bottle of King Horse. I found myself watching her.

The music blared and set the clubbers afoot. Having poured herself a shot, Bao Bao came over and, giving me an inscrutably adamantine look, squeezed my hand, then slipped away. Her gesture set my blood racing. I glanced around at the other tables, and another young woman winked at me and smiled—not a seductive smile, but a *huanying!* grin welcoming me to Chu Dong.

Was I really so popular? What was going on?

Then it occurred to me. Here I was more than my middle-aged self, showing up rather pathetically (in my judgment) night after night to hang out with teens. As an American, I was presumably wealthy, an acting ambassador of the West, a representative of the clubbers' adopted culture—the culture promoted by the Communist Party following Mao's death in 1976 to transform China into a major economic power.

As a prelude to market reforms, in 1978 Deng Xiaoping (Mao's successor) had ordered Chinese television to run programs displaying the prosperity of American life, so that his people would recognize their own economic backwardness and strive to enrich themselves, and announced, "One must learn from those who are most advanced before one can catch up with and surpass them." As a result, in few non-Western countries are the appurtenances of American consumerism as ubiquitous, and as wholeheartedly accepted, as they are in China. There really is no other choice; Mao's killing fields and "social experiments" swept away much traditional culture, which was already suffering convulsions and rejection before the Communists came to power. Looking back over centuries of insularity and hardship, who today could deny China's youth the chance to dress cool and have fun, to lunge after instant gratification, to eclectically tinker with their identities by assuming Western names? Whatever the demerits of Western pop, it offers its fans the quickest way to boogie down and get off.

Rose was distraught. "The music tonight, oh, it's terrible!" she said, stomping her foot. "The DJ—he just doesn't know what he's doing."

She shook her head and went on complaining. Tonight's music mattered because she wanted to have fun *now*.

I finished my wine and slipped off to the restroom.

The two-hundred-yuan room was packed and wild. Virtual Girl, black-suited, apache-cut, and masked, flared on screen, performing the manic techno fandango also enacted by the dancers on stage. Red lasers strafed the crowd mimicking her thrusts and kicks. This was a rave, mindless and frenetic; and it held absolutely nothing for me. Walking into the restroom, I skidded in a splatter of vomit. Splatters led right up to the stalls.

When I emerged, Virtual Girl was a skeleton doing gangsta moves; the dancers were gone; and a musician clad in a white suit was grappling with a saxophone, blowing red-faced into the mouthpiece, his ponytail flailing as he wrestled his instrument about the stage.

I found Rose and Bao Bao standing by the bar with two Uygur guys, recognizable by their curly hair, prominent noses, and square cheekbones.

"Meet Hu Shan!" Rose said to me, referring to the lanky one dressed in a tweed jacket. That and his horn-rimmed glasses lent him a brainy hauteur. But his goateed stubble and block-toed loafers showed attentiveness to fashion.

"You with these girls?" Hu Shan asked in fluent English. He pulled me aside. "My real name is Hussein. But the Chinese make me change it to Hu Shan. I bet they tried to force a Chinese name on you too, didn't they? Incredible, aren't they?"

"I've been having a good time with them."

"The Chinese don't care about any people besides themselves. It's just the way they are—they can't change." He lowered his voice. "I want to talk to you. Can we leave? You can come with us? Come with us to another bar for a drink?"

"Why not?"

He and his friend turned out to be medical students. Out on the street, away from the racket, Hussein breathed freely. "We have our own culture, and it's totally different from the Chinese. Our language has grammar, unlike Chinese. Chinese is baby talk. I speak it so *easily* and so can you. Please." He held open the passenger-side door of his compact blue car, and I jumped in.

We peeled out. His speech was erratic and unfocused. I wondered if he was drunk, but I smelled no liquor. He recited a litany of common Uygur grievances against the Chinese. The Han are pompous aliens who flood into their land and threaten their survival as a people, speak a cacophonous tongue, discriminate against them, and treat them as second-class citizens. Unlike Uygurs I had met in 1998, however, he didn't call them *kupar* (infidels), and neither did he mention East Turkistan.

"I can't get a job in this fucking country," he said, leaning in to the steering wheel. "All the jobs go to Chinese; they just hire each other." He swerved down lanes puddled with light from street lamps, but mostly empty of cars. "Can I be your friend? Say, you *are* American, right? The American embassy wouldn't give me a visa. They see my Chinese passport—no visa! They think all Muslims are bin Ladens. We're Muslims but we don't believe the same as bin Laden. Can you help me? Can I be your best friend?"

We lurched onto a main avenue and veered around the few cars on it.

"Where're we going?" I asked, growing worried.

"To have a drink."

"But where?"

I heard the flick-flick of a lighter from the back seat, and soon I smelled the heady reek of hash. His buddy was puffing a joint. Hash surely accounted for Hussein's rambling loquaciousness. Soon cloudlets of pungent smoke were wafting around the cabin. A proffering hand reached over my shoulder and nudged me. I declined, but I became anxious: would the police stop us for Hussein's crazy driving and discover the drugs? In some countries, just being in the same car as a smoker could be incriminating. And where were we going?

"Xinjiang is *our* country," he said. "*Uygur* country, but look at all these Chinese *everywhere*. The Chinese are afraid to let us express ourselves, because, *wow!* Think of what would happen!"

We trundled onto a road leading into the dark wastes outside town.

"Look, tell me where we're going."

"We're going for a cup of *kumys*. So, what can I do to get a U.S. visa? Are you an original American, or do you come from somewhere else?"

"You know, it's late. I don't think I'm up to drinking *kumys* tonight. I'd rather head back to my hotel."

"Ah, okay, okay."

We reversed course. Ten minutes later we bumped against the curb by the Xinjiang Grand and I jumped out, relieved, and promised to catch them the next night at Touch.

THE AUTHORITIES DISPLAY the party line concerning ethnicity in Urumqi's Xinjiang Museum. A trilingual (Chinese, Uygur, English) placard near the entrance informed me that the museum had been designed "to show the contributions of peoples of all nationalities in Xinjiang have made for safeguarding the reunification of the Motherland and to make the masses of the audiences receive the education in patriotism." Exhibited were well-lit maps, samples of folk costumes, crude wooden utensils, mockups of traditional "minority-people" life (yurts and stuffed camels and sheepdogs and mannequins colorfully dressed as natives), and a placard with a narrative lacking any reference to Uygur separatism. One got the impression that, quoting the narrative, "Xinjiang is an inalienable part of the territory of China" where "peoples of all [forty-seven] nationalities . . . have worked in unity and helped one another . . . [and] where civilizations of the world assembled and syncretized." The Uygurs came off as exotic bumpkins whose lifestyle could be relegated to the reliquaries of museum exhibits.

As in Tibet, the growing Han presence in Xinjiang has brought modernity: running water, paved roads, electricity, a sleek railway—development, in a word. In Urumqi, I saw—aside from dual-language street signs, the occasional pilaf and kebab stand, and the odd Turkic face drifting among the Chinese crowds—that there was no longer much that was overtly Uygur at all, and certainly little that was Uygur and *modern.* Nevertheless, inside Touch, the remaining Uygurs (young ones, at least) socialized with their usurpers, and shared in the consumer-culture boom that has, finally, reached their capital. Any notions of establishing "East Turkestan" here were absurd. The Uygurs had lost the fight.

ON SATURDAY EVENING (my last in town) I arrived later than usual to find Touch almost empty. Disappointed, I wandered into the hundred-yuan room. A tiny fist hit me between the shoulder blades. Bao Bao. She grabbed my forearm and pulled me to her table.

There Rose was sipping whiskey with a low-browed truck driver she introduced as He Wu. After a nod in my direction and a throaty *gan bei!*, Wu dropped his hand to Rose's thigh and kept it there—she was his. He spoke no English, which I assumed accounted for his taciturnity in my presence. But I ventured into Chinese and discovered I was wrong.

"I'm twenty-two," he said, arching his eyebrows in a world-weary, if already inebriated, way. "I've seen all the good clubs around. I've seen it all. *Gan bei!*"

After a *gan bei* of sympathy, I said to Rose, "It's good that you have Uygur friends. Have you known Hussein long?"

"*Hu Shan?* He's nice. But I can't say I like Muslims in general. We're all Chinese in this country. We're a multiethnic region, with no difference between Muslim and Chinese. What difference could there be if we all speak Chinese?"

"Not all Uygurs speak Chinese or like Beijing here."

"We're all citizens of a multiethnic country and we're all Chinese."

"I don't like Uygurs," harrumphed Wu.

People drifted in, some taking clumsy steps and knocking into tables. Villain showed up, rakishly coifed and dressed in a natty black jacket, and came straight over to me. "Please, say hello to my friend. It's his nineteenth birthday." I took my leave of Rose and Wu and squeezed through the crowd, following him. "I'm feeling lucky tonight," he said. "A guy who *always* gets girls is with us."

At their table near the DJ's, the corpulent birthday boy slumped sweating and drunk on his stool, toasting with a handsome guy in black, whose feathered hair glistened and bounced as he shook it; he might as well have been auditioning for a shampoo ad.

Villain cast me a proud look as beauties stopped by to greet his friend. "We've got four girls coming to meet us tonight," Villain told me, putting down his glass. "We're going to drink with them and then go someplace private. We want to play cards with them."

"Cards?"

"We don't know them well enough to play strip poker, but we do think we can get them drunk and kiss them and feel them, you know. What do you think? Can we do it?"

"Well . . ."

He frowned. "I like this one girl here tonight, but she doesn't like me. I feel numb when I think about her. N-U-M-B."

A hand grabbed my shoulder. Hussein and his friend were teetering, bleary-eyed, behind me.

"I'm sorry," Hussein said, in lieu of a greeting. "I can't drink with you now. I—" He shot Villain and company a displeased look. "These Chinese are your friends?"

"Yes. What's going on?"

"We've got to fight these guys. Right outside the club."

"Chinese, I assume."

"No, Uygurs. One insulted me."

"Is fighting the answer? You want to be a doctor, for God's sake."

"I have to fight him, that's all."

He pulled his friend away and made for the escalator. Villain shook his head. "Oh, Uygurs. They anger so quickly. And they have knives. They fight always over nothing. Don't go outside to watch or their enemies will think you're on their side."

Bao Bao had left and He Wu was pounding down shot after shot, his hand still on Rose's thigh. People kept staggering in. Eyes in the crowd were reddening, voices loudening, feet missing their marks. At a change of songs, the birthday boy pulled me out onto the narrow dance floor. He shimmied up close to me, breathed whiskey in my face, and grabbed my other hand. I pulled away and slipped back through a crevasse in the bodies, almost knocking over a drunken girl. Her male friends held her to their table, and, when she lolled her head back, they poured a shot of whiskey down her throat. They guffawed, and she retched, her knees buckling.

I felt, all at once, like retching myself: I could stand no more clubbing. Being forty-five and done with it was a blessing.

Two Russian speakers I had met earlier, Kun Lei and He Bin, pulled me out of the crowd and up into the mezzanine.

"Come sit with us."

We ensconced ourselves in a sofa in the dark. Kun Lei's girlfriend, shapely and with hair flowing down to her kidneys, got up and danced, imitating the American stripper of the video screen, moving her hands over her curves, swaying her rear in our faces, proud to show me how American raunchy-girl culture had made it to Urumqi. Kun Lei, grinning and proud of her antics, told me he worked in Kazakhstan, but the music prevented me from hearing more. The drunk girl at the foot of the stairs sank onto the steps and dropped her head between her knees.

I got up, ready to flee. But Bin grabbed my hand and pulled me back onto the sofa. "Make a fist," he shouted in Chinese.

Reluctantly I did. He probed my hand, opening my fist and tracing the lifeline on my palm, closing my fingers and crushing them with one hand, feeling my thumb's ball with his other, and probing more painfully into the flesh between my knuckles. This irritated me and I tried to yank free, but he held on.

"I'm going to tell your fortune," he said. "To see if you have *hu qi*" —tiger energy, vigor. "Oh, *bu hao!*" (not good), he declared. "*Bu hao!*"

That did it. I pulled my hand free, stood up, and walked off. Side-stepping a puddle of alcohol and vomit near the steps, I broke free of the crowd and headed for the exit.

"Hey, you call me!" shouted Villain, near the escalator.

"Sure," I answered.

Up by the metal detector I ran into Bao Bao. I stopped.

"You're leaving?" she asked. "So early?"

"Yes. In fact, well . . ."

"You'll be back again tomorrow, right?"

I kissed her hand and walked out, knowing I would not return.

The next afternoon, I boarded the train for Jiayuguan—my first stop in "Chinese" China.

22

Unfolding in ever-more-dismal vistas of saltwort scrubs and gypsum flats, of saline marshes and rock shard plateaus, the Gobi Desert inherits the lifeless desolation of the Taklamakan that begins at the Pamirs and ends south of Urumqi, and carries it on toward Beijing, to cover a total of some 500,000 square miles. As the sun lowered, my train rolled east, transporting me deeper and deeper into its wastes, halting in rare flyblown hamlets, one-well Uygur and Hui villages of stone and cement dwellings where goats and gaunt cattle pastured in refuse heaps, where battered tractors trundled down cratered roads, raising trails of dust that blew back and shadowed their drivers, turning them into shade-figures of an apocalypse now. I had come almost halfway across northern China, and always through desert—a stark reminder of the country's dilemma of population versus sustenance. With almost four times as many people as the United States, China has roughly the same land-mass, but only 10 percent of it is arable.

As we neared the death-skull crags of the Bei Shan, the sun finally expired, leaving the sky aglow, the land darkening. Outside my window tamarisks drifted by, dendriform specters gnarled and charred, putting me in mind of Marco Polo's description of this desert, which he wrote of crossing more than seven hundred years ago while traveling to Beijing: "At [some] halting-places the water is salt and bitter. . . . In this tract neither beasts nor birds are met with, because there is no kind of food for them. . . . This desert is the abode of many evil spirits, which amuse travellers to their destruction with many extraordinary illusions." Always the spirits preyed on men they found alone during the month-long traversal, appearing in the guise of their companions, imitating their voices and calling out to lure them from the road, or impersonating attacking armies that prompted them to flee and lose the way, or assailing them with disorienting "sounds of all kinds of musical instruments, and also of drums and the clash of arms."

No sooner, it seemed, had I fallen asleep than the sky paled above the black mountain ridges. It was five-thirty in the morning. We were in Gansu province and entering the Hexi Corridor, the ten-mile-wide passage between the Bei Shan and the Qilian Shan by which the Silk Road exited ethnically Han Chinese China to wend its way west. Ahead, far from the tracks, pinpoints of golden light appeared. They closed in on us, and, as the sky luminesced with dawn, we drew into the boxy cement warrens of Jiayuguan, abandoned-looking, rifled over by a gritty wind.

I disembarked alone on the cold station platform, and the train creaked away. The air here was dry and biting. A few minutes later a taxi was whisking me down straight empty lanes, stirring trash into eddies, beneath wind-lashed red and white political banners, past blocky modern apartment buildings standing stark on gravel lots, almost unreal in the auroral half-light, the sfumato of a dream.

A FEW HOURS LATER, from atop the last watchtower of the Overhanging Wall, in the tawny wilderness just beyond town, I surveyed the Great Wall's crumbling final segment, a ten-foot-high pile of eroded bricks that marks the limits of the traditional Chinese heartland and stretches more than three thousand miles to the east, growing stately and magnificent where it nears Beijing, and ending near the Yellow Sea. The Han emperor Wudi began work on this part of the wall in the second century B.C. Nomads who had accepted Chinese suzerainty helped him construct it, for they too would benefit from the protection it offered from raiding brethren of the grasslands to the north. The Ming general Fengsheng arrived in the mid-1400s to defeat the last warriors of the Yuan (Mongol) dynasty and erect the fortress, Cheng Lou, that still stands to the west of Jiayuguan. From this spot at the edge of the Gobi, where the Bei Da River provided fresh water, the Chinese could defend the Hexi Corridor at its narrowest (between Mount Mazong of the Bei Shan in the north and the Qilian in the south). Nevertheless, shifting confederations of Xiongnu (mounted nomadic warriors of Chinese blood) periodically attacked the wall from the north, and caravaneers venturing through the pass onto the Silk Road found themselves at their scant mercy.

The Great Wall, manned by one million soldiers by the time of the Ming dynasty (1368–1644), has been derided as a costly and colossal failure, since, after all, the enemy often bribed the guards to open the gates, or simply circumvented it. But the wall (really a network of bulwarks) served as an elevated highway over rugged terrain, facilitating the movement of troops and couriers across northern China. Its very existence and maintenance spurred development in the Chinese military. Officers started keeping records detailing their troops' training and progress, and worked out elaborate means of post-to-post signaling, using smoke and flags by day; by night they burned wood and grass, adding sulfur to increase the blaze's brightness; messages could thus be relayed three hundred miles in two hours. Pulverized dung was kept on hand; under the right conditions, soldiers could toss it into the wind and blind attackers. Rotating shifts came into being to assure the wall was manned around the clock. A pre-perimeter of smoothed sand was established so that any intruder's footprints might alert guards and so defecting soldiers would give themselves away. Broadly speaking, the wall was an institution that prefigured the complex (and lethal) defenses that China and Soviet Bloc countries would devise around their borders to deter defectors.

Most of the wall's soldiers were garrisoned in Cheng Lou, the "Impregnable Defile under Heaven," which I visited after the wall. There 2,300 feet of moated ramparts with walkways wide enough for the passage of half a dozen horses abreast enclose the three-story pagodas of Guanghuamen and Rouyuanmen guard towers and a complex of barracks, abodes for senior officials, and courtyards. Engineers built the sixty-foot-high towers (miraculously high, for the time) from the top down, by first piling up earth and then assembling the frames around it. Ox-drawn carts brought bricks from kilns forty miles away. The entrance's massive stone foundation plates (ten feet long and a yard thick) were hewn out of the mountains and slid down iced-over roads in winter. In a way, I thought, by passing through the gates of Cheng Lou now, I was stepping into the All-Under-Heaven in a more tangible historical sense than I had when I crossed the Kyrgyzstan border eleven hundred miles back.

I spent the morning at Cheng Lou, staring out over the Gobi and noting the wall's watchtowers on mountain peaks, trying to fathom time scales and distances of the wall, and China. Four thousand years of recorded history, 12,400 miles of land borders, 8,700 miles of coast-line, 1.3 billion people—all this was too immense to grasp. The sun was bright but the air cool, and I could revel in the empty landscape, people it with Xiongnu and Han soldiers, imagine imperial epochs come and gone long before my own country existed, before even Europe north of the Mediterranean was anything more than a dark realm of forest and bearskin-clad tribes.

My driver was a young woman named Duan whose taxi I had hired outside my hotel. I finished my tour and found her waiting for me out-side the fort. Bespectacled, pear-hipped, with too-short arms, Duan grinned irrepressibly as she gripped the wheel of her cab and, looking resolutely ahead, moved out into traffic, pounding on the wheel to pro-duce a plethora of warning honks. Once rolling she cruised steadily at a good ten miles an hour beneath the thirty-mile limit. Suspecting I knew the answer, I asked her if she had been driving long.

"Twenty days. How am I doing? *Hao ma?*" (Okay?)

"*Hao! Hao!*" I replied, not wanting to distract her.

We cut our way through traffic, mostly bikes traveling at a leisurely pace, but still coming close to collision at times because, no matter what, Duan would not apply the brakes for fear that she would bungle the changing of gears.

"What's your name?" she asked.

"Jeff. I haven't really settled on a Chinese name."

"Jeff is fine. Why do you want a Chinese name?"

"Why? Well . . . well, I thought I had to have one here. I'm glad you like my name."

Now I felt comfortable with her. And here in ethnically Han China, there would be no calls for America to bomb Beijing, no faith-based animosity.

A column of cars was stopped ahead for a light. We proceeded steadily toward the last vehicle, in the hope that the light would change and everyone would start moving in time. But it didn't. So, just before we hit the fender, she jerked the wheel and we passed on the left, cut-ting into the opposite lane. The light flashed to green as we entered the crosswalk.

I gripped my seat as oncoming traffic swerved and honked, and Duan took her time to return to our lane.

"Would you like to get lunch somewhere?" I asked a few seconds later. "What's the best place in town?"

"There's a big new hotel now with good food. Let's go there. But it's back that way."

She made a sharp U-turn, bringing to a wobbly halt a dozen slow-poke cyclists, and we set off down another long, straight boulevard.

We were almost the only customers in the Western-style dining room, which had a panoramic picture-window view of Jiayuguan and the desert beyond, all now drained of color by the noontime sun. Duan ordered for us a pork dish, chicken spiced with Sichuanese chili, green peppers, and chili-sprinkled beef cold cuts.

"Oh, there are so many tourists now!" she said, noting the one Western couple eating at a corner table. "These last few years so many Westerners come. Jiayuguan is developing."

"Are you from here?"

"Yes. In fact, Jiayuguan is the only city I've ever seen. I'm married and have a child. My husband really loves the child, and I'm happy about that." Though I had to ask her to repeat herself at times, I found her Chinese intelligible. I relaxed even more, and felt thoroughly wonderful about being in *Chinese* China, high on the rush of novelty and a new friendship. "But I have no time to go anywhere anyway. Got to drive the taxi and make money."

The waiter brought us our meal. Before I could do anything, Duan took care of me, loading chunks of chicken onto my rice and helping me position the chopsticks between my fingers. I was touched. She rightly assumed that I, a denizen from beyond the wall, would not excel in the ancient but simple use of chopsticks.

"What does your husband do?" I asked.

"He drives a truck, taking most of the western routes, from here to Urumqi and on. There's not much work in Jiayuguan, so driving of one kind or another is about all we can do here."

My mouth burned deliciously with the chili.

"What's there to do for fun in Jiayuguan?"

"Buy DVDs and watch them. But we don't even have the money for them. So I listen to music on the radio. Mostly, we raise our child, and that's fun enough."

She added more food to my bowl, calling me nonchalantly by my name and telling me about her toddler.

I had not expected to feel so comfortable in China. As in Urumqi, I sensed that, were the circumstances right, I could find a life here. I based my conclusion on superficial impressions, to be sure, but my gut feeling now contrasted so sharply with the alienation and stress I had known during my 1998 trip that I wanted to believe it justified. What had really changed? China had developed, to be sure, but maybe I had also mellowed with the years. China had also opened up to the world in a way still unimaginable in Russia; this openness I could now feel *personally*.

"I want to show you the Wei and Jin dynasty tombs," she said, with bright eyes. "After lunch, *hao ma*?"

"*Hao.*"

Archeological sites usually leave me cold, but I had no objection to the additional jaunt, which would let me pay her more and enjoy her company awhile longer.

After lunch, on the way back to the cab, we stopped to say hello to her husband, who was out strolling with their son. I had imagined a grimy brute trucker, but he was trim and clean, dressed in an ironed white shirt with a collar, and shook my hand with a smile.

We drove east out of town and back onto the Gobi's table—flat barrens, which were drenched with coppery light from the slanting sun. A half-hour's ride landed us by a small concrete museum, built over a few of the eighteen tombs that have been excavated.

I woke the guard snoozing on a cot by the entrance, and he led me through a doorway and down into a narrow stone staircase, through stone portals. He flicked on the lights. In their sepulchral glimmer I examined the walls, made of bricks painted with miniature scenes from life during the third-century Wei and Jin kingdoms following the collapse of the Han Empire, at the beginning of the turbulent Age of Division. Against a creamy background, the artists had applied their brushes frugally but expressively, leaving thin strokes, mostly black, to outline forms, with fill-in daubs of color for people and animals. Depicted were charging cavalrymen and spear-wielding soldiers and courtiers, as one might expect in a time of war, but also shown were ordinary folk: peasants trudging along behind ox-drawn plows; baggy-trousered hunters aiming their bows and arrows at skittering fowl; musicians playing the flute and strumming away on lyres. The style was abbreviated in an el-

egant way that recalled the bamboo and silk handscroll landscape mas-
terpieces of the Ming and Song dynasties, and that in fact resembled
New Yorker covers from decades past.

In the taxi again, I thanked Duan warmly for her suggestion, and,
smiling, she pulled out onto the highway, slowly as ever, for the nonstop one-gear ride back to town.

23

A **spiffy late-afternoon** train carried me out of Jiayuguan, across Xining province and toward the city of Baotou, on the northernmost bend of the Yellow River, deep in Inner Mongolia. Near Baotou I hoped to visit a Tibetan-Mongolian Buddhist monastery and, of course, on the sweeping grasslands of the Ordos Plateau, Genghis Khan's mausoleum. Strictly speaking, I was once again leaving the All-Under-Heaven and venturing out into the "uncivilized" realms beyond the Great Wall, but judging by the fashionably garbed ethnic Mongolian passengers in my car, there were no barbarians aboard, at least in soft class.

Established by Chinese Communists to demonstrate their concern for minority peoples' rights, Inner Mongolia, or, officially, the Inner Mongolia Autonomous Region, is a crescent of grassland and green hills stretching 1,700 miles around the rump of the republic of Mongolia. The region has historical roots as a border zone in the millennia-old conflict between Han farmers and the warriors of the steppes to the north, including the Han's ethnic brethren, the mounted Xiongnu (and later, of course, the Mongols).

The Han struggle with the steppe dwellers was the "war on terror" of its day, a battle between peoples of widely differing, and irreconcilable, worldviews. Starting in the fifth century B.C., the nomadic Xiongnu harried the Chinese agriculturalists, whose wealth they coveted and whom they disdained as weaklings leading a plush settled life. Han emperors tried to co-opt the attackers, hiring them to police the wall, but this only partly succeeded in stemming their raids; long-term alliances, diplomacy, and judiciously arranged marriages between the ruling elites eventually won the day. Nevertheless, even after the Xiongnu disappeared from history in the fifth century A.D. and the Tang dynasty (618–907) garrisoned troops on the grasslands, the Mongols were to reoccupy the area and, eventually, invade and achieve dominion over the All-Under-Heaven. In 1271 Kublai Khan, Genghis Khan's grandson, founded the Yuan dynasty that Marco Polo would describe in his *Travels*. Only when the Qing dynasty (1644–1911) reasserted Chinese control would Baotou develop into a town of note, a trade emporium famously exporting abroad (through Beijing and Tianjin) the wool, felt, and animal hides produced by the steppe peoples.

A reddish dusk came on as we glided down shiny rails through dry farmland and canyons of chiseled granite. The mood aboard was festive. In their various compartments passengers read and chatted and stretched out. Cheerful conductors, women in starched powder blue blouses, white nurse bonnets, and white gloves, made the rounds, checking tickets. Men tapped at the screens of their cell phones with polished steel toothpicks, occasioning a delicate chorus of beeps and bings; women with bud lips leafed through Chinese-language glossy mags.

But these soft-class folk were clearly the elite riding through a *terra damnata*. Outside, sunburnt peasants and shepherds, their faces covered in rags against the gritty wind, lugged sacks on their backs and grazed dirty sheep. In trash-strewn villages of concrete and mud hovels, families bounced about on rusty tractors. As the sun fell, dust clouds arose and obscured the ever-starker poverty of the scene; and then all was lost to the dark. China's 140-million-strong "floating population" of migrant workers comes from just such desiccated environs.

At sunrise I awoke to find we were approaching Baotou, a million-plus city of burgeoning industrial ugliness where metallurgy, coal-coking plants, and steel manufacturers conspire to shroud residents in perpetual smog. Smokestacks spewed ember-leavened scoria into a purgatorial ashen sky; nuclear reactors hunkered monstrous and menacing in the suburbs; and along the beat-up roads to the center lumbered grime-coated trucks, their ill-secured loads high and wavering, as precarious as the lives of their hollow-cheeked drivers.

THE MONGOLS CONQUERED TIBET in the thirteenth century, but the Tibetans in turn vanquished them, in a way, by converting them to

Buddhism (of the Mahayana school), which became Mongolia's national religion. Tibetan-Mongolian Buddhist temples thus dot Inner
Mongolia's countryside. The largest of these is Wudang Monastery,
about an hour and a half by car northeast of Baotou. I rode there
through the Yin Shan, rumpled grassy hills cut with red-earth ravines. I
might just as well have been in Mongolia proper. On the verdant slopes
grazed fat sheep tended by Mongolian shepherds, whose adolescent
faces had already been reddened by subzero winds. In roadside villages,
where cows mooed and donkeys brayed, corpulent Mongol men and
women sat on stools in front of whitewashed stone houses adorned
with banners that were streaked with sayings in Mongolian script, inky
curlicues that resembled vertically written Arabic.

A scattering of two- and three-story whitewashed buildings, Wudang
sits atop a low rise, framed by willow groves, on a plot of land covering
some fifty acres. Its style is that of the Potala in Lhasa, but on a very
modest scale.

I bought a ticket at the entrance booth and crossed through the
painted gates, finding myself amid broad-shouldered lamas, shaven-
headed, draped in robes of red and saffron, shod in scuffed-up sandals.
The signs in Mongolian and Chinese stymied me, so I returned to the
office and hired a Mongol guide, a woman named Tuya. In her early
twenties, Tuya was petite and dressed in pink jeans and a pink T-shirt;
even her sneakers were pink. She had drawn her long black hair into a
ponytail, which emphasized her sculpted cheeks and wide black eyes,
her full pink lips. She spoke only Mongolian and Chinese, but this
would not bother me; I had been reading up on Buddhism in pinyin
and felt that discussing the Enlightened One was one thing I could do
with relative confidence in Mandarin.

We set off strolling toward the main shrine. "Are you Buddhist?" I
asked her.

"Oh, yes. I come here and pray when I'm not working."

"I suppose that's no problem now, right? I mean, it's not like in Mao's
time, when the state repressed religion."

"I was very young then. Then, the masses couldn't pray here, but the
lamas were allowed to. But now they let in everyone, even Americans!"
She laughed. Before the Communists came to power, she said, twelve
hundred monks had lived here. She didn't know how many monks were
left; maybe a few dozen.

We stopped by Dong Kuo Er Palace. It had a rustic exterior, with chipped white walls and a sagging wooden balcony, but its crimson columns and gold filigree were gorgeous and grand, and its roof sported bronze Tibetan-style conical ornaments. The interior was a gloomy chamber supported by a profusion of purple beams and hung with red-framed portraits of past lamas and, of course, the Buddha.

Lamas were busy lighting incense and droning prayers. Tuya stood beside them and began cheerfully (and loudly) describing the monastery, which dated from 1727, in the Qing era, and was the third-holiest in Tibetan-Mongolian Buddhism, after the Potala and the Ta Er Temple, in Qinghai province. When she finished I asked her quietly if we might be disturbing the lamas.

"Oh, no. All the lamas know me. So it's okay."

They sure did know her. A young lama came up and chatted with her in Mongolian, wiggling his eyebrows and hee-heeing, and let loose a joke of some sort that made her blush. I wondered if my Western notions about solemn comportment in places of worship might not apply here.

I studied the intricate Mongolian texts hanging on the walls. "You can read this script?" I asked.

"Yes. It says *om mani padme hum*"—the main Sanskrit Buddhist mantram, meaning "hail the jewel in the lotus."

Tuya's lama suitor laughed and said something to her, pointing at me.

She smiled. "He says you're so serious about learning about us. He thinks it's funny."

He grinned and so did I. The spirit here was ludic, certainly more appealing than the edgy air of Xinjiang's mosques. Two Han Chinese men soon walked in and felt no qualms about answering their cell phones and yakking away and laughing loudly, and no one took offense.

We wandered back outside and among the buildings farther up the hill, stopping by the various shrines. The multitude of colorful murals, copper Buddhas, lamps with quivering flames, prayer wheels, and clouds of incense and hanging banners dazzled my eyes in a way that inspired peace and reflection.

By the lamas' sleeping quarters—chilly white cells strewn with metal-mesh cots—another lama wiggled his eyebrows at Tuya. She laughed dismissively.

"They can't sleep with women," she said, shrugging, taking his apparently ribald remark in stride. "So they joke."

Near the tour's end, back by the front gates, she paused by a wooden coffer. "Would you like to make a donation?" she said. I dropped in a bill. "Thank you. What do you think of Buddhism?"

"Oh, I'm very interested in it. In fact, I'm more a Buddhist than anything else."

"Really? How can this be?"

"Well, I'm reading various texts and like what I'm learning. I can't say I believe in reincarnation, but you don't have to be Mongolian or Tibetan, you know, to see the truth in much of what the Buddha said."

"Really?" she said.

She smiled and uttered what I took to be an abrupt goodbye. Puzzled, I returned to the lot to find a ride back to Baotou.

In fact, her skepticism made sense. All we had seen at Wudang—the effigies, the incense, the gaudy portraits and filigreed balconies and the praying lamas—I found interesting, but foreign, bearing little on the sense of what I had been reading in various sutras and the *Dhammapada,* texts that explained the Buddha's teachings but did not enjoin worship of him or specific rituals. For worship I had no use; ritual seemed a matter of culture and upbringing that I could regard as "exotic" but find little meaning in. I was studying the Buddha's words as postulations to be questioned and appreciated on their merits—no more.

THE NEXT DAY in Baotou broke cool and cloudy—or at least I thought it was cloudy.

"This is a floating dust day," announced the hotel receptionist cheerfully when I handed in my room key. A wind was blowing loess in from the deserts to the west, mixing with the smog. "You have no surgical mask?"

"No."

She gave me a pitying smile.

Outside, under a loess-tinted sky that reached down to haze over the roofs of Baotou's buildings, I bartered with a taxi driver for the 115-mile ride south to Genghis Khan's mausoleum, on the Ordos Plateau. No one knows whether the khan's bones really lie there, but it's doubtful. He is believed to have died in 1227, somewhere on the grasslands beyond the Great Wall during a campaign against China, probably after falling off his horse, owing to the advancing feebleness of old age, but legend also has it that a captured princess castrated him to prevent him from raping her, and he never recovered. In any case, most likely the Mongols carried his corpse back to the mountains around Ulaanbaatar, the capital of present-day Mongolia, near the Onon River where he was born, and interred him there in strictest secrecy, killing all who might know the location of his grave. However, the Darhut, the tribe entrusted with guarding his remains, did settle on the Ordos Plateau in Ming days, and Mongols in both China and Mongolia revere the mausoleum as the eternal resting place and sanctum sanctorum of the greatest son their nation has ever produced.

Situated on a gentle yet commanding rise, the mausoleum's three giant domes, umber cupolas encircled by pagoda-style tiled eaves of royal blue, loom in awesome majesty over rolling empty steppe, fully befitting the memory of the ruler of the largest empire of all time. A sort of Mongol Arc de Triomphe marks the beginning of the esplanade ascending from the parking area a hundred yards to the shrine. As I passed beneath the arc, blue banners flapped in a ripping wind over surging crowds of rowdy mausoleum-bound Mongolians, many carrying bottles of *bai jiu* (fifty-proof Chinese firewater). One of the most ruthless and prolific shedders of blood of all time retains a following of millions; and many drink *bai jiu* to honor him as Father of the Mongol Nation. Menace, vague but palpable, hung in the air, and the grandeur of his mortuary seemed to shout "ALL HAIL THE MIGHTY KHAN!"

I approached the mausoleum with a guide who was anything but menacing, however. Her name was Gerile, and I had hired her at the ticket office by the entrance. She might have been a china doll, her features were so petite and finely sculpted, her hands and feet so tiny and perfectly formed. She was dressed in a traditional Mongolian pantsuit of blue and white silk. She told me that she was half Mongolian, her father having been Han, and had attended university in Xi'an. She enhanced her cuteness by asking me, in precise English, to call her by her English name, Apple.

"Come to see our khan," she said, and gestured toward the esplanade. We strolled up the walkway. "No one knows exactly where Genghis Khan's bones are, though possibly they are in Ningxia province, since that's where he died."

"They had no records in those days," I volunteered. The Mongols then were illiterate, and employed scribes from subject nations to write for them.

"No, that's not why. We always have disposed of our dead in secret.

Back then, we just tied the body to a horse and whipped the horse, and he ran off, and wherever the body fell off, there it lay, until vultures and wolves ate it. So, in this way, we come from nature and return to nature. We never killed others to be buried with our dead leaders, as the ancient Chinese did. Even now, we dig the grave and secretly put the body in, with no tombstone. When the grass grows over, no one will ever know a burial took place. My parents did this with their grandparents."

"So why is the mausoleum here then, and not in Ningxia?"

"Because he was once passing by here and he dropped his whip. This is a bad omen. But he saw there was water and grass for horses, so it was the best spot. Oh, oh, look!"

Five white horses were emerging from shrubbery and nosing about on the grass off the walkway. As we approached, they clattered onto the esplanade, occasioning gasps from the crowd, which stopped and stared.

"The reincarnation horses!" said Apple. "They are *sacred* horses! They roam all over the three square miles of our complex, but we rarely see them. I've only seen them *once*. Seeing them brings such good luck!"

We entered the main dome—that of the mausoleum proper—which shelters the satin-draped biers supposedly enclosing the remains of Genghis Khan and his wives. The dome also shelters three yurts. By the central one a robed shaman (the Mongols in Genghis Khan's day were shamanist, though he himself took a fancy to Buddhism and Taoism as he aged) was selling bottles of *bai jiu*. I thought to ask Apple why Mongols drank in his honor, but Apple clasped her hands girlishly and exclaimed, gazing up at a wall-size map of Eurasia showing the Yuan (and thus Mongol) Empire's astonishing boundaries, "Look at his empire! Genghis Khan conquered four-fifths of the known world! I'm so very proud! He was such a great man!"

I couldn't help frowning at her last words. "Great? Well—"

"Why not great?" she asked, startled. "He expanded Mongolia from here to Europe! He did this all in the thirteenth century, so the number thirteen is the Mongol lucky number. He fought all the time for his homeland, always winning territory for his four sons. Fifteen *million* square miles, he conquered! Is it not *wonderful?*"

Her enthusiasm took me aback. Somehow I had expected more modesty, given the millions of innocents his troops murdered. Yet she wasn't the only one to admire the killer. Marco Polo had eulogized "Chingis-khan, one of approved integrity, great wisdom, commanding eloquence, and eminent for his valour," who "began his reign with so much justice and moderation, that he was beloved and revered as their deity."

"What's wrong?" she asked, frowning.

"Oh, nothing. I just . . . Let's see what else there is here."

In a side room, glass cases displayed items supposedly belonging to the deceased khan, among them an ancient-looking goblet, engraved and silvery, and a huge bow made of rhino tusk.

"It takes eighty kilos of strength to bend this bow," Apple said. "So he had to be very strong. From its length we know he was one point nine meters tall" — 6.2 feet.

This may be true. A contemporary Chinese chronicler described Genghis Khan as "a man of tall stature, of vigorous build, robust in body, the hair on his face scanty and turned white, with cat's eyes, possessed of dedicated energy, discernment, genius, and understanding, awe-striking, a butcher, just, resolute, an overthrower of enemies, intrepid, sanguinary, and cruel."

Apple continued. "But he was not only a warrior. He was a poet too. He wanted people to treat each other kindly. He was most of all against rudeness."

"What? Genghis Khan? Against *rudeness?*"

"Yes. And he *developed* the regions he conquered."

"*Developed?*"

Nonplussed, I followed Apple into another side room, where silver-plated passports from his day lay glinting under glass. She cited these as evidence that the Mongols were ahead of their time. Certainly they established a rudimentary postal system across Eurasia; enforced a code of laws that applied to all, from peasants to princes; and tolerated the diverse religions of their subjects. All of this, in a way, made them progressive for their time. But development was not the forte of a people who dwelled in yurts and lived for battle.

I refrained from arguing with her. Instead, I asked what being a Mongol meant to her.

"Mongol life was all about killing a sheep and eating meat. We cannot live without meat. So a Mongol eats meat, rides horses, drinks milk tea, and must be free. And he drinks *bai jiu*."

"You love meat and *bai jiu?*"

"Of course. I'm a Mongolian, so I can drink half a bottle and still walk."

"But surely the Chinese government doesn't let you live that freely now."

"Freedom? Now it is illegal to roam. We must have registered permanent addresses by law. Anyway, we know now that roaming, roaming . . ." Here she pulled out her pocket computer translator and punched in letters and furrowed her tiny brow at the English words popping up. She read them aloud. "Roaming 'and grazing turns pasture into desert and pollutes the land' with horse manure. We must not roam, to save the environment."

That was nonsense to be sure. The Soviets also forced nomads to settle for reasons that had nothing to do with ecology.

Murals in other adjoining rooms told the story of Genghis Khan's life. His father had stolen his mother as a bride from the Tatars. The Tatars then poisoned his father. When a Tatar tribe stole his own wife, young Genghis, already invested as khan at age twenty-seven, turned to another chieftain for help in recovering her and exacting revenge on her captors. From there, his conquests began—with a punitive expedition in 1202 against the Tatars and their subjugation. The paintings showed scenes from these events, minus the gore.

"Genghis was so kindhearted," Apple said, her eyes fixed on a mural depicting a bearded barbarian standing tall over captured Tatars whom his aides were about to put to the sword. More of Marco Polo's words came to mind. "Wherever [Genghis Khan] went, he found the people disposed to submit to him, and to esteem themselves happy when admitted to his protection and favor." But the historical record left no doubt as to the murderous reality of his conquests.

"Apple, I'm sorry, but how can you see kindheartedness in that picture? It's terrifying."

"No. Genghis was kind. He had only those men taller than a cart wheel killed, those who could have poisoned his father. He spared the women and children. He did everything to unify the country, for his sons, everything for the Mongols."

We walked on.

A Chinese chronicler had written of the Mongols: "They respect only the bravest; old age and feebleness are held in contempt."

"I've read," I said, "that the Mongols in his time worshiped strength and despised the weak and the old, and let them die or enslaved them."

"We did use the weak as slaves. It was natural then. Now we revere our parents and we care for them till they die."

"What about all the killing he did abroad?"

"What killing?"

"The killing, you know, of a third of the inhabitants of Kiev, for example. Of the entire populations of towns that refused to submit."

"As far as I know, he only killed his military enemies."

"But everyone apart from the Mongols was his enemy when he took over other countries. There were no 'civilians' back then. He didn't conquer half the known world by being against rudeness, did he?"

"Hmm. Well, every coin has two sides, as you say in English. But he killed only in wartime. I am so proud that he expanded Mongolia!"

Back in the main hall, a red felt carpet led to an altar where a Darhut priest was tending hunks of lamb roasting on coals—sacrificial offerings. The odor was delicious. Those who adored Genghis Khan were clearly given to sating their appetites.

We walked over to the priest and said hello. Apple lit three incense sticks and placed them in a thurible. The priest turned to us and poured two goblets of *bai jiu*.

"Come here," said Apple. She pulled me along until we stood just before two felt ottomans by the central yurt. "Now, to your knees, please!"

"What? Why?"

"Worship!"

"Worship what?"

"Genghis Khan!"

"Are you—I mean, no, I can't. I won't."

"Down, please!"

She dropped to her knees and tugged at my wrist. The priest stared at me, his eyes narrowing. He said something hoarse in Mongolian and nodded that I should do as Apple did.

"Worship his spirit!" she said.

"I'm sorry, Apple, I just can't. I won't."

She looked hard at me, her eyes revealing more hurt than offense. She said something in Mongolian to the priest, who grunted. I was dearly glad that Genghis's drunken followers had already left the mausoleum and we were alone.

I tried to think of a polite way of excusing myself. "I mean, I'm sorry, Apple—I don't believe in God, so I don't worship."

Apple said, "Oh, okay," and bent down and gracefully touched her forehead to the felt four times.

She arose and smoothed her trousers. The priest handed us cups of *bai jiu.* "Please," she said, "at least drink to his soul, to its peace."

That I would do. We downed the *bai jiu.* It was actually tasty. We thanked the priest and walked toward the door.

"Why won't you worship Genghis Khan?" she asked in a hurt voice.

"Apple, he and his sons killed millions of people. His troops killed off entire towns in Russia. They murdered millions from here to Hungary. And for what? For his sons' territory? What about the rest of humanity? His murdering sent Russia back to the dark ages. And anyway, I would never worship anything or anybody, let alone a murderer." She winced at my last word. I tried to personalize it. "I don't think my Russian wife would forgive me if I prayed to Genghis Khan."

She cocked her head. "Genghis Khan is not popular in Russia?"

"No, Apple. He's regarded pretty much all over the world as the very exemplar of a barbarian."

"Oh. Well, I'll have to check my history books about that. Maybe he did kill, but it's not what we learned in school."

This I took as a significant concession. I had read that the Chinese held the khan and his successors in high esteem for effectively extending China's Yuan dynasty borders all the way to Europe. High-ranking Chinese government and party officials still visit his mausoleum, to demonstrate solidarity with the Mongols, a minority people with a large autonomous region; in fact, there are more Mongols in Inner Mongolia than in the republic of Mongolia. Any other approach to Genghis Khan might disrupt an already fragile sense of national identity. As a result, as Apple's remarks suggested, Chinese schools teach Genghis Khan Lite, the hero without the gore.

"Well," I said, "I suppose the Chinese government has to teach you good things about the most famous Mongolian. And the Yuan dynasty was magnificent."

She beamed on hearing these words.

We walked outside and strolled for a while. The sky had turned creamy, the air warmed. The reincarnation horses wandered past us again, and she remonstrated in sharp tones with a man who presumed to shoo them back onto the grass.

But my refusal to worship still troubled her. Finally, as we were about to part in the parking lot, she said, "Anyway, as far as *I* know, Genghis Khan did all he could to unify Mongolians. He conquered China in 1211, and Kublai Khan united China with Tibet and Xinjiang. My family is mixed, but we feel comfortable being both Chinese and Mongolian."

The wind was still blowing, and the blue pennants strung along the mausoleum grounds were flapping hard. As long as people worship those who murder in the name of a cause, be it the greatness of a nation, the expansion of empire, or even democracy and liberation, there can never be peace. The offended, or their ancestors, will seek revenge, and repay blood for blood.

Maybe my protest planted a seed of doubt in Apple's heart; possibly she will read up more thoroughly on her hero. I don't know.

24

On October first—National Day, the anniversary of the founding of the People's Republic, in 1949—I found myself in Inner Mongolia's capital, Hohhot, poised to complete the final 265-mile stretch of my journey to Beijing. The week around National Day is the worst of the year for traveling in China: the entire country goes on the move then, vacationing and visiting relatives, and tickets for public transport not arranged far in advance are tough to come by.

After fruitlessly spending two days searching for space aboard a bus, I gave up and decided to hire a taxi to Beijing. I got an early start. My bag slung over my shoulder, I slipped through the revolving doors of my hotel and out into the steel-and-glass canyons of office buildings and shopping centers along Zhongshan Xi Street, Hohhot's main drag. The air was cool; the sun, filtering down through the floating loess, was pleasantly warm. The jubilant chaos of the crowds and street-peddler commerce and squawking loudspeaker adverts from gaudily decorated department stores buoyed my already elevated spirits. I was exhilarated about ending my trip, and the people about shared my mood—the only mood possible amid all the color and tinny music and playful mayhem of China on holiday.

Green taxis tooted and trundled by, just beyond the bike lane, careful not to disturb the cyclists—men, women, and children pedaling along, at times several to a bike, with some tots standing on the handlebars as their fathers cruised. Soccer balls bounced into the stream of vehicles, and children ran out chasing them, but the slow pace of traffic allowed everyone the chance to brake, and no one suffered.

I hailed a passing cab. It slowed, and the driver, checking for cyclists, pulled over to me.

"I want to go to Beijing," I said, jumping in.

"What?" said the smiling, handsome woman in her forties at the wheel. She laughed. "Beijing? You know how far it is?"

"I do. But there're no bus or train tickets available, with the holiday."

"Well, I'm sorry—I don't even know how much to charge you. It might be as much as twelve or thirteen hundred yuan"—$150 to $160, just what the hotel concierge had told me would be fair. "And I don't know my way around Beijing. I've never even been there."

She grabbed up her cell phone and started punching in numbers and asking prices. She had shoulder-length wavy hair and a Rubenesque figure. Her cab was clean and smelled of freshener, with every surface polished—an achievement in this part of the country, with all the desert winds. I liked her forthrightness and cheer. She was the one, I felt, who should take me on my ride of triumph into Beijing.

She put down her phone and told me, almost wincingly, that the fare would be fifteen hundred yuan. I agreed straightaway.

"Well, *hao!*" she replied, somewhat amazed.

We picked up her boyfriend, a skin-and-bones fellow with big eyes and a shock of prickly hair; he would help her drive, if she got tired. We then drove out to the road for Beijing. Ahead rose rugged sandy mountains—how close the desert wilds always are, in China's northern outback!

BY MIDAFTERNOON the dust had cleared. A hundred and twenty-five miles were left, but we were still rolling across Inner Mongolia. It was easy to see why Kublai Khan had chosen the garrison town of Beijing for his capital; it was so close to his homeland. But gone was the desert; the road now ran through villages and hayfields. Mountains were greening, blanketed with shrubs; trees had been planted along the highway and were flourishing. As the tarmac improved, traffic sped up, with trucks rushing by and fancy foreign-made passenger cars overtaking us, honking cacophonously. It seemed everyone was, like me, in a huge hurry to get to Beijing.

Toward evening we slowed for a tollbooth at the start of an expressway, the Badaling. The Badaling was divided, with sleek railings and freshly painted lane markers—the first Western-style thoroughfare I had seen in seven thousand miles. Then, forty miles from Beijing, meandering from ridge to pass, stretching from the northeastern to the southwestern horizons, twenty feet thick and marked with medieval guard towers, all splendidly gilt by the late sun's glow, was the Great Wall!

My driver and her boyfriend leaned forward, their eyes widening. *"Changchen! Changchen!"* (The Long Wall!) They were as thrilled as I was, and we exchanged excited glances. I had never seen more than the dilapidated last segments near Jiayuguan.

Speeding traffic soon whirled with us down the expressway into Beijing. For centuries giant walls had ringed the city, but the Communists tore them down in the 1950s, and now, from the Badaling on, hectic jumbled conurbations of steel and concrete and glass stretched as far as one could see. On and on we drove, having no directions to my hotel, which I at least knew to be in the central quarter of Qianmen, but then Qianmen itself was huge. We roared through tunnel after tunnel; we swerved around lines of cars stopped in traffic jams to bounce along the shoulder, using it as our own express lane. My driver pounded the horn when she saw any car ahead pulling out to do the same.

Finally we made it downtown. Double-decker buses emblazoned with ads, nattily attired crowds surging over pedestrian bridges, unpainted matchbox apartment blocks, and chasms of blue-green skyscrapers all closed in on us as darkness fell, with red and yellow neon Chinese characters radiant above thoroughfares broad and straight and streaming with headlights.

We quickly got lost. We stopped repeatedly to ask directions, but the driver and her boyfriend couldn't follow them; for small-town folk, Beijing was too obstreperous, flashy, and confusing. They eventually asked me, with pained politesse, if I wouldn't mind taking a Beijing cab to my hotel. Of course not, I told them. I paid, we said the warmest goodbyes, and I jumped out.

Twenty minutes later I walked incredulously into my hotel in Qianmen, feeling as I always do at an expedition's end, as thrilled as relieved, happy to have finished yet sad with the demise of an adventure. My life on the road was over. At least for now.

TIANANMEN SQUARE was overflowing with thousands of Chinese visiting from the provinces for the festive week following National Day.

Under a smogged-out morning sky and yet still hot sun they thronged, carrying tiny Chinese flags, aiming digital cameras or posing for them. Everyone was laughing and shouting and talking. Blue-uniformed police hectored us through loudspeakers: "Don't stand there! No leaning on the railings! Keep to the right on entering the underpass!" Soldiers in khaki were as numerous as tourists, or perhaps were tourists. Dongchang'an Jie's twenty traffic-clogged lanes separated Tiananmen from the brick ramparts of the Forbidden City, where Mao Zedong's portrait commanded the main entranceway. Beside the square, atop the Great Hall of the People and the Museum of the Revolution, red banners writhed in an erratic breeze.

A quarter of its size when first cleared in 1651, expanded (with the demolition of much of old Beijing) to its present dimensions in 1958, Tiananmen is the largest square on earth, a hundred acres of concrete that overwhelm and intimidate in a way Red Square does not. One might think it fitting that the capital of a country of 1.3 billion should have such a square, but Tiananmen is more than just a huge empty space. It represents the indomitable might of the state as conceived by Mao and the Communists, and so, essentially, harks back to Lenin and Stalin and their crushing totalitarianism.

After weeks of pro-democracy protests, hundreds or even thousands of students had been felled here by the Chinese military's tanks and machine guns at dawn on June 4, 1989, yet not a hint remained, save perhaps for the numbers of security forces on patrol, wary of new demonstrations. Did the crowds of mostly young holiday-makers around me know that political reform had died here on that bloody day, now so long ago? Did they care? I could not know. Heeding the badgering calls of the police to move along, I walked until I reached, in the center of the square, the end of a dense queue, a mile-long, seven-person-deep mass of bobbing black heads snaking between ropes and yellow lines painted on the pavement. Their destination was Mao's mausoleum, the Chairman Mao Memorial Hall, a soaring columned sanctuary that makes Lenin's tomb on Red Square look like a matchbox. Once in line I found myself jostling too, stepping to the pace set by garbled commands from loudspeakers and maintained by stern men in black and white whose white-gloved hands prodded our elbows to keep us moving.

Considering it "tantamount to paying tribute to Hitler," as a Russian dissident friend of mine had put it, I had never, in all my years in Moscow, visited Lenin's mausoleum. But Mao's seemed remoter from me, and I yielded to curiosity. Like Lenin, Mao superbly utilized the turmoil of his time to lead the Communists to power. But in contrast to Lenin, the masses loved him, at least initially.

Born into a well-off peasant family on the twenty-sixth of December, 1893, in the southern province of Hunan, Mao attended a teachers' college in Changsha and then left for the capital to work in Beijing University's library. Slender, handsome, and charismatic, he took part in Marxist study groups and attended the Communist Party's first national conference, convened in Shanghai in 1921. China at the time was divided, modernizing, and aboil with ideas for reform. Its two-thousand-year-old monarchical tradition had ended in 1911 with the fall of the Qing dynasty to (non-Communist) revolutionaries, and power across much of the country had devolved to warlords. Xinjiang and Tibet had broken away. The Russians, British, Japanese, French, and Germans occupied entire provinces and were busy exploiting their resources; and foreign ideologies, including democracy and Marxism, were popular among the intelligentsia, which wanted to resurrect China as a modern power worthy of its uniquely rich past. In 1928 the warlords formed a central government, led by the Nationalists, but they ruled precariously in the cities, leaving large swaths of the countryside in anarchy, prey to local tyrants and roving armies of bandits. As had happened after the tsar's abdication in Russia, political power lay in the streets. But who would grab it?

The Communists might have perished in various campaigns of Nationalist repression had not the Soviets succored them with financial aid and advisers. The Russians also, paradoxically, helped the Nationalists, hoping to strengthen China against rising imperialist Japan, their most feared adversary in the Far East, and aiming to spark the bourgeois revolution that was supposed to proceed to a proletarian uprising. They concentrated on the cities. But Mao, soon driven into the countryside, focused the Communists' efforts on working with the peasants—the overwhelming majority of Chinese. In the expanding Communist enclaves and elsewhere, his party won their plaudits by helping them with their harvests, redistributing land equitably, teaching literacy, and, most important, battling Japanese occupiers. Outright civil war between the Nationalists and the Communists broke out in 1947, but the former never had a chance. In 1949 the Nationalist leader

Chiang Kai-shek fled with his troops to Taiwan, and Mao, with the backing of the peasant masses, took over in Beijing.

"The people have stood up," said Mao, declaring the victory of his revolution. Soon he would retake Tibet and Xinjiang, and China, for the first time in centuries, would be united within its maximal historical boundaries.

With capitalism now so long entrenched in China, I had thought Mao might be passé (as Lenin certainly is in Russia), but how mistaken I was. Around me people in line talked excitedly. A dozen yards from the steps leading up into the mausoleum, a cherubic woman shouted, *"San kuai qian! San kuai qian!"* (Three yuan apiece!), over waist-high piles of plastic-wrapped yellow roses. Queuers minced over to her, paid three yuan, and minced back, roses in hand.

We began ascending the steps into the hall. "Two by two! Two by two!" was the next order, barked at us by an official in a dark suit at the head of a doorway wide enough to admit only two people at a time. His assistants, their white gloves flashing, manhandled crowd members who failed to array themselves correctly. The queue fell silent and snaked through the door and split so all could singly pass by a glass booth, flanked by soldiers standing at attention. In it Mao lay luminously in state beneath a shroud of white silk, his face orange and drawn. All were quiet, and there was only the shuffling of shoes.

Once in power Mao launched Soviet-style "reforms" that led to Soviet-style death and misery but on a Chinese scale—the collectivization of agriculture, the Great Leap Forward, the Cultural Revolution . . . Millions died in purges and famines before his death in 1976. Outdoing Stalin, he became the greatest mass murderer of the twentieth century. Yet his admirers—and even judging solely by this crowd, there are legions—laud him for ousting foreign occupiers, unifying China, and, for the first time in centuries, putting their country on a par with other world powers. That crowds throng to his embalmed body even now tells us that the future of this country probably does not belong to liberal reformers, that not all people march when freedom calls, that atrocities can be suffered and forgotten, and that justice is a malleable concept.

In Russia Lenin's mausoleum stands deserted, his ideology discredited, but a new Slavic nationalism is replacing it; if the country, as the Soviet Union, lost half its resources with the secession of its republics, it has gained something close to a majority ethnic unity. From Red Square through the Caucasus, across Central Asia and into China, I had met people prosperous enough to accept the (for now minimal) restrictions imposed by their authoritarian governments as the price of stability. If markets are not free and elections unfair, conditions (at least outside the mountain fastnesses of Dagestan and Chechnya) are nowhere bad enough to spark revolt and sufficiently tolerable to inspire an obedient conservatism.

The West (and in particular, the United States) should now accept the inevitable: Eurasia will stand on its own, outside entangling alliances, comprising not one but several powers sufficiently rich in natural resources for independence, powers autocratic and capitalist, possessing (unfairly, from the West's point of view) a unity of state-controlled media and companies, monopolies, military might, and financial clout. Ten or fifteen years ago no one expected such authoritarian capitalism would arise, but it is now strengthening by the day, carried forth on the shoulders of a compliant citizenry. Russia and China are working toward a rapprochement. Whether they succeed remains to be seen, but one thing is clear: the new Great Game that began with the collapse of the Soviet Union has ended, and victory has gone to the home teams. The West is out.

All at once we exited into a high-ceilinged hall where salesmen stood over glass cases full of Mao pendants, Mao busts, Mao rings, Mao badges, Mao tie clips, Mao portraits, Mao watches and table clocks and pens. The queuers dispersed, rushing to the counters to dicker over the souvenirs they wanted. Mao was selling, and selling well.

Acknowledgments

I would like to thank Anna Bachurina, Yulia Konstantinova, Dmitri Mironov, and Oksana Kirzhanova from Gazenergoset' in Moscow for putting me in touch with so many helpful people along the way. My gratitude goes to senior diplomat Andy Passen for his good cheer, contacts, and advice, which he has offered since we met in 2003, while he was U.S. consul in Dakar. As always, I would like to thank my agent and friend, Sonia Land, for her faith in me and her vigor in promoting my work. Special thanks go to Valery and Nina Shchukin. Finally, my wife, Tatyana, saw me off from Red Square and welcomed me home from Tiananmen Square, enduring yet another of my lengthy absences, and helped me research some of the former Soviet Union's most obscure places. Her presence in my life makes all my sacrifices worthwhile, and to her I owe my greatest debt of gratitude.

AND MAY THE BUDDHA rest the soul of Murat, of Makhachkala, who helped me so much during my stay in his home city, and who died of a heart attack before this book could be published.